TIME
The Civil War
An Illustrated History

A TATTERED UNION *A soldier from a Northern color guard unit, most likely the 37th Pennsylvania Regiment, 8th Reserves, displays a torn flag in 1861*

TIME

MANAGING EDITOR Richard Stengel
ART DIRECTOR D.W. Pine

The Civil War
An Illustrated History

EDITOR Kelly Knauer
DESIGNER Ellen Fanning
PICTURE EDITOR Patricia Cadley
MAPS Jackson Dykman
RESEARCH Tresa McBee
COPY EDITOR Bruce Christopher Carr

TIME HOME ENTERTAINMENT
PUBLISHER Richard Fraiman
GENERAL MANAGER Steven Sandonato
EXECUTIVE DIRECTOR, MARKETING SERVICES Carol Pittard
DIRECTOR, RETAIL & SPECIAL SALES Tom Mifsud
DIRECTOR, NEW PRODUCT DEVELOPMENT Peter Harper
DIRECTOR, BOOKAZINE DEVELOPMENT & MARKETING Laura Adam
PUBLISHING DIRECTOR Joy Butts
ASSISTANT GENERAL COUNSEL Helen Wan
BOOK PRODUCTION MANAGER Suzanne Janso
DESIGN & PREPRESS MANAGER Anne-Michelle Gallero
BRAND MANAGER Michela Wilde
ASSOCIATE PREPRESS MANAGER Alex Voznesenskiy

SPECIAL THANKS TO:
Christine Austin, Jeremy Biloon, Glenn Buonocore, Jim Childs, Susan Chodakiewicz,
Rose Cirrincione, Brian Fellows, Jacqueline Fitzgerald, Christine Font, Carrie Frazier,
Lauren Hall, Mona Li, Robert Marasco, Kimberly Marshall, Amy Migliaccio, Nina Mistry,
Dave Rozzelle, Ilene Schreider, Adriana Tierno, Jonathan White, Vanessa Wu, TIME Imaging

Copyright © 2011 Time Home Entertainment Inc.
Published by TIME Books, an imprint of Time Home Entertainment Inc.
135 West 50th Street, New York, NY 10020

ISBN 10: 1-60320-171-8; ISBN 13: 978-1-60320-171-1
Library of Congress Control Number: 2010941155

We welcome your comments and suggestions about TIME Books. Please write to us at:
TIME Books, Attention: Book Editors, PO Box 11016, Des Moines, IA 50336-1016

If you would like to order any of our hardcover Collector's Edition books,
please call us at 1-800-327-6388, Monday–Friday, 7 a.m.–8 p.m., or Saturday, 7 a.m.–
6 p.m., Central Time.

FRONT COVER: Library of Congress Prints and Photographs Division (4).
BACK COVER: Union Cavalryman (left) Dr. Thomas P. Sweeney—Time Picture Collection; Confederate
Cavalryman (right) Peter Newark Military Pictures—The Bridgeman Art Library International
ENDPAPERS: Library of Congress Prints and Photographs Division

---

PANORAMA OF WAR *Union soldiers take in the vista of the Army of the Potomac's
encampment at Cumberland Landing, Va., in the Peninsula Campaign of May 1862*

LIBRARY OF CONGRESS PRINTS AND PHOTOGRAPHS DIVISION

Contents

The Soldier

He may have signed up for glory, but too often he felt despair.
The novelist walks a mile in the shoes of an unknown warrior

By Jeff Shaara

I T HAD RAINED FOR TWO DAYS, THE ROADS a river of thick sludge, soaking through what was left of his shoes, stripping away the skin on his heels, bloody sores he tried not to feel. Around him, the others did as he did, plodding with a mindless rhythm, a column of men who kept their suffering to themselves. The stinging in his feet was pushed away by the sharp aching in his gut, a hunger that had weakened him, numbing his mind, slowing his march even more. In his dirty hand rested the butt of his musket, dead weight that had dug a slicing soreness into his shoulder. Beside him, the sergeant seemed not to notice or to care. The man was older, a hot temper that kept his men in line, that kept them moving forward, no matter the mud or the rain or whatever ailments they endured. Some of the torment came from inside their weakening bodies, but some came from beyond, attacks by unseen vermin, lice or fleas, rising up from the soggy ground, swarming though what might remain of a ragged uniform. The mosquitoes came as well, flickering and dancing close to his face and ears with a soft whine, silent only when they lit down on the tender places.

He barely noticed the others, all of them making the same automatic motions, slow steady footsteps. With each step through soft muck, his free hand slapped at the plague of insects, scratched at raw skin. In the other, he shifted the weight of the musket, tried to jostle the backpack and the wet blanket that grew heavier every hour. He stared down, nothing to see, the countryside bathed in a soft fog, distant trees and open fields, nameless places. It was not his job to know where they were, where they were going, or why. Even the sergeant didn't know, never seemed to care, just performed his single task, keeping the men in line, pouring out vicious wrath on any man who fell out of line or simply collapsed in the mud. But this time, the men had kept pace, and the soldier blinked through the wet in his eyes, the torment of the mosquitoes, heard no other sound but the soft hiss of the rain, the slurping of feet in deepening mud.

After long hours on the march, the smells close to him had gone unnoticed, the intense stink that rose mostly from his own clothing and the unwashed bodies of the men around him. At their last bivouac there had been no creek, no place for anyone to cleanse away the sweat and the filth, and so, in the camps the smells were always there, surrounding them, inescapable. On the march, the rain swept that one misery away, but now, something grabbed his brain, a new smell, fresh and sharp. It flowed over them all with a thick sweetness, and then, much worse, a powerful stench that pushed into every part of him.

He glanced to the side, saw an open field littered with wreckage, shattered tools of war, crushed wagons, cannons perched at odd angles, only the steel barrels whole. There were burial crews now, half a hundred men with shovels and pickaxes, hardworking men who did not look up. The pace was slowing, too many men absorbing the scene, and the sergeant responded, a sharp call: "Keep moving! Nobody stops!"

The march resumed, but he could not look away, watched the men with shovels tossing the muddy earth into piles. Some of them were down in the fresh trenches, knee deep. Behind each trench, there were rows of bodies, thick bundles, bloated and frozen, some with limbs reaching upward, filthy curled hands, crooked fingers. He had seen this before, did not want to see it again, but it was the hands that held his stare, as though a dying man had been grabbing at something, trying to claw his way back to life, or reaching for some place where there might be peace, warmth, comfort. In so many of the fights, the desperately wounded had called out for their mothers, a strange and different horror none of the survivors joked about. But the bodies he saw now were a day or more gone, cut down in a fight he knew nothing about.

It was the same in every fight: once the hand of death had squeezed out the last breath, it took barely a day for a man to become something else, the blood and filth changing to a

EARLY DAYS *Confederate soldiers pose for a photograph in Richmond, Va., in 1861, not long before the South won the war's initial large-scale engagement, the First Battle of Bull Run, also known as First Manassas*

bloated stink, the body twisted and grotesque, the faces not faces at all. Then the burial crews would come, offering the only relief they could, putting a man into the ground, hiding the smells and the horror away from those who would return to the march.

He turned away from the field, stared again at the mud, his own feet heavy with the thick goo. In every fight, he had done all he could to avoid the faces. The soldier had moved away from the dead, any dead, as quickly as he could. He was not proud of that, had tried to convince himself to listen to the chaplain, that God had taken command, the dead man in a better place. But the body always remained, and the soldier had seen too many of broken pieces of men. He had never been assigned to the burial squads, was grateful for that, could not stomach the sweet odor of death, could not stomach it now. He felt the sickness rising up through the empty pain of his hunger, fought it, stared ahead, shifted the musket again. He had waged the violent argument in his own brain, that he would not do this anymore, would not obey the order to fight. But if he ran away, there was really nowhere to go, and he would certainly be caught.

It was a different fear, the horror of the firing squad, something they had all seen before. The officers had done that on purpose, of course: an example, executing deserters in the presence of the entire regiment. No, you cannot run, he thought. You can never run. He glanced again at the field, more wreckage, dead horses, a different horror, the smells much worse. He wanted to pick up the pace, but the men in front did not give way, and so he closed his eyes for a brief second, fought the smells, resumed the march.

In front of him, someone shouted, and he glanced up, saw the soggy flag, a simple scrap of color that was meant to inspire, giving meaning to whatever they were supposed to endure. The horseman who carried it moved out to the side of the road, surrounded now by other horsemen, who did not suffer the mud. A bugle sounded, the column ordered to halt, and he obeyed, grateful, felt the weakness in his legs, overwhelming, looked for some place to sit. But the sergeant kept his place beside him, as though reading his thoughts, a glare on the man's face that kept the soldier where he stood.

And now, a new sound came, hard rumbles out in front of them, and the soldier felt the sharp thunder deep in his chest. He stared out past the horsemen, saw another approaching, riding hard, the uniform of a messenger, the man speaking to one of the officers, pointing away. The man wheeled the horse about, was gone quickly, his job complete. The rest of the officers were spreading out, one man riding back toward the troops, his horse kicking up slop on the men as he passed.

The soldier kept his stare to the front, but there was nothing else to see, the flag, the column of men, one of the horsemen familiar, the captain, pointing his sword. The rain had grown softer, the sounds of the artillery louder now. The column stayed motionless, every man waiting for the next command. Some of the men around him beginning to fidget, shoulders hunched, reflex from those who knew what the thunder meant, what the artillery fire would bring, what the men would be ordered to do. The soldier knew it as well, his eyes fixed on the captain, the man who knew.

The bugle sounded again, loud and manic, the order to continue the march. He waited for the men in front to move, then followed, but the pace was slow and deliberate, no one rushing forward, no one eager to join what he knew would be one more fight. He knew, as they all did, that there would be a time for running. Sometimes the bugles had ordered retreat, no one slow to understand that something had gone wrong, that the enemy might be far too many, that some officer far behind them had made a disastrous decision. But there were other times, the very good times, the bugle and the officers screaming out with raw excitement, driving them forward, infectious fury, pursuing panicked and beaten men.

For now, he kept his deliberate pace, the stirring inside of him, the fear, what might soon be terror. His hand gripped the butt of the musket, and he stared ahead, saw only the backs of the soldiers, the flag, the captain, his mind filling with the silent image of what might be out there. He tried to find the hate for those men they called the enemy, a reason why they should die, but it was never really there. He thought of that often, had wanted to talk to one of them, to find out if the man hated him. But hate or not, he knew that across the way, on whatever field they would find, he had to believe there was a man just like him, who had suffered the misery of the march, who endured the weight of his musket and blanket, his canteen and cartridge box, who slapped at the vermin and fought the hunger and the holes in his shoes, who never escaped the agonizing fear that this time, when the killing began, the burial parties might come for him. ■

Jeff Shaara is the author of two best-selling novels of the Civil War, Gods and Generals *and* The Last Full Measure. *After writing several books about other U.S. conflicts, in 2011 Shaara will revisit the Civil War in a new series of novels*

BROTHERS IN ARMS *A Union soldier tends to a wounded Zouave colleague in this May, 1863, photograph taken in Falmouth, Va., near Fredericksburg*

1850s

"'A house divided against itself cannot stand.' I believe this government cannot endure permanently half slave and half free. I do not expect the Union to be dissolved—I do not expect the house to fall—but I do expect it will cease to be divided. It will become all one thing or all the other."

—ABRAHAM LINCOLN, JUNE 16, 1858

WORK IN PROGRESS *This photograph, taken in 1859, shows the U.S. Capitol under construction as its old dome, designed by Charles Bulfinch, was being replaced by a new, larger structure. Like its seat of government, the Union itself was in flux during the years before war broke out in 1861*

CANADA

Washington Territory
Organized 1853

Portland

OREGON
*Became a state
in 1859*

LINCOLN

*Snake
River*

Nebraska Territory
Organized 1854

Fort Pierre

*Unorganized
territory*

MINNESOTA

St. Paul

WISCONSIN

LINCO

Sacramento

Carson City

Salt Lake City

*Continental
Divide*

Residents of territories
could not vote in
presidential elections

IOWA

Chicago

San Francisco

Utah Territory
Organized 1850

ILLINOIS

CALIFORNIA
*Became a
state in 1850*

*Colorado
River*

Kansas Territory
Organized 1854

DOUGLAS

St. Louis

MISSOURI

Los Angeles

New Mexico Territory
Organized 1850

*Unorganized
territory*

ARKANSAS

Little
Rock

MISS.

TEXAS

Jackson

BRECKINRIDGE

LOUISIANA

Austin

Houston

New
Orleans

Pacific Ocean

MEXICO

Gulf of Mexico

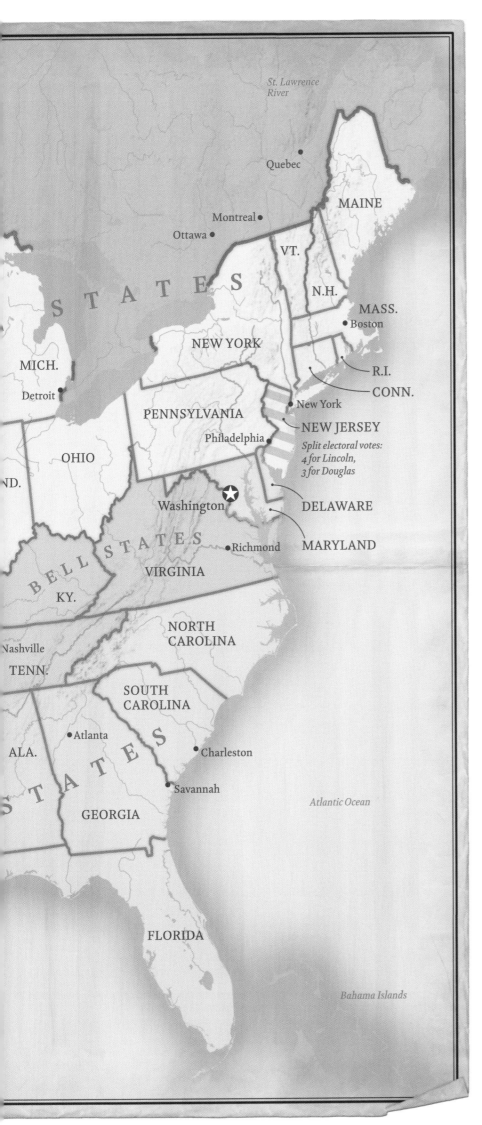

The 1860 Election

After the Democrats split apart along regional lines, Lincoln won election handily. Most states that voted for Breckinridge and Bell would join the Confederacy in the coming months.

Abraham Lincoln

The Republican candidate won most of the populous Northern states and the two young states in the far West, California and Oregon. Lincoln's real coup was to beat William H. Seward to capture the party's nomination.

POPULAR VOTE	ELECTORAL VOTE
1,865,908	180
40%	**59%**

Stephen A. Douglas

The Northern Democrat could not hold his party together: at the National Convention in Charleston, S.C., in April and May, Democrats split in two, almost ensuring victory for the Republican candidate.

1,380,202	12
29%	**4%**

John Bell

Further fracturing the pro-slavery vote was Bell, the candidate of the new Constitutional Union Party, which attracted moderate antisecessionist voters who formerly considered themselves Whigs and followed Henry Clay.

590,901	39
13%	**13%**

John C. Breckinridge

James Buchanan's Vice President, a pro-South Kentuckian, was the candidate of the Southern Democrats and swept the pro-slavery vote. He later served in the Confederate Army, leading a valiant charge at Stones River.

848,019	72
18%	**24%**

A Tale of Three Nations

The North

"KEEP YOUR SPLENDID SILENT SUN,/ KEEP YOUR, woods O Nature," wrote Walt Whitman, a rare poet who preferred the bustling city to the hushed forest. "Give me faces and streets ... Give me interminable eyes ... Give me Broadway." Whitman's words captured the delight with urban life that in the first decades of the 19th century helped transform the Northern states of the Union from a colonial backwater into a commercial and industrial power-house that boasted dense cities, advanced technologies and steam-driven factories. The region's accelerated new pace of life was also driving social change: young unmarried women left their homes on farms and in small towns to work in the extensive textile factories of Massachusetts, or in the office buildings of Philadelphia and Manhattan. Most Northern cities were home to communities of free blacks, some of whom operated prosperous businesses and enjoyed

most of the rights of white citizens, although racism was widespread and interracial marriage was against the law in most Northern states.

The dynamic cities of the North were far removed from the proudly agrarian society of the South, where life was strictly ordered by race and class, and social life hewed to traditional, conservative norms. Human bondage was the wedge issue that strongly divided the Union along geographical and sociological lines. As the 19th century advanced, more and more Northerners began to reject the practice of slavery, in line with a worldwide abolition movement; after a long crusade, slavery was abolished across the British Empire in 1833. But in addition to North and South, there was a third face to U.S. society: the expanding Western frontier, rapidly being settled as new states joined the Union. The emergence of this powerful new force would upset the uneasy balance of power between North and South over slavery and spark the Civil War.

TRADE WEALTH *Ships crowd the piers of lower Manhattan in 1859, after New York City had become a maritime metropolis. "Give me the shores and wharves heavy-fringed with black ships!" wrote Whitman*

INDUSTRIAL MIGHT *A woman works the huge looms in a textile mill in Lawrence, Mass. In contrast, Southern planters rejected factories and shipped their raw cotton to England or the North to be spun into textiles*

CHINA, GLASS —AND— CROCKERY WARE. 190

J. COLLAMORE JR, & CO.

URBAN DENSITY
In 1859 carriage traffic was clogging Boston's Washington Street. The cradle of the Revolution was no longer a quaint colonial city but the busy capital of New England and a center of the abolition movement

BIG MUDDY *Steamboats crowd a dock on a New Orleans levee in 1862. The Mississippi River was the vital waterway of the West, and the Union and Confederacy vied to control it through the first years of the war*

A LEG UP *At left, a slave at the Legree Plantation on Capers Island, S.C., holds a horse for his master. Slave society was highly hierarchical, with "house slaves" outranking "field slaves"*

KING COTTON *On facing page, blacks bear bales of cotton back from the South Carolina fields in a photo taken by George N. Barnard, one of the corps of Northern photographers directed by Mathew Brady*

The South

IF THE NORTHERN STATES MOVED TO THE NEW pulse of railroad timetables, steam engines and telegraph tickers in the first half of the 19th century, the states of the South were more attuned to age-old agrarian rhythms: the planting, tending and harvesting of crops, the daily chores of raising livestock. Major Southern landholders presided over vast plantations, worked by black slaves, where a single crop, King Cotton, dominated agriculture. Life in the South bore little resemblance to life in the North; it was closer in spirit to the plantation culture of the Caribbean islands, where British and French planters also ran large operations reliant on cheap labor and devoted to exporting crops to Europe.

The world of the antebellum South has now been subjected to some 150 years of relentless romanticizing, and it's difficult for us to imagine that vanished era without resorting to the Technicolor dreamscapes of *Gone With the Wind*. But not all Southerners were wealthy planters. Some were hardscrabble landholders, whose fore-

bears were Scots-Irish immigrants from Europe and who minded their small farms without slave labor. Nor was the South devoid of cities: each Southern state had at least one large, bustling port, along whose crowded wharves cotton was shipped to Europe and the North and slaves were shipped to other states. In 1840, New Orleans was the third-largest city in the U.S., a cosmopolitan hub alive with the languages and fashions of a multitude of cultures.

But such big port cities were an exception to the stately pace of life in the South, which its citizens struggled to defend in the war—and which, in the end, guaranteed its destruction. When war came, the South, while wealthy, was no match for the North in important ways. The population of the northern states in 1860 was more than 18 million; the population of the South, excluding black slaves, was 8 million. The North had twice the density of railroad lines as the South and made 97% of the nation's firearms. The military odds in the Civil War were never even; the South was outmanned and outgunned from the first salvo to the last.

The West

THE FUTURE OF AMERICA'S THIRD FACE—ITS GROWing Western frontier—was the smoldering fuse that finally exploded in full-scale Civil War. Had the U.S. persisted as the 13 original colonies that joined to fight Britain in the Revolution, North and South might have maintained an uneasy truce, their individual states content to pursue separate futures within a common, loose Union. Early on, a rough balance of power between new free and slave states was maintained, sometimes by careful legislative maneuvering, as when the Missouri Compromise of 1820 allowed Missouri to join the Union as a slave state while Maine entered as a free state.

By the 1840s, however, Western expansion was rapidly transforming the Union, as pioneers began swarming into Kansas, Nebraska, Iowa and other states of today's upper Midwest. Two major technical advances—the railroad and the telegraph—tamed distance itself: trains brought the vast spaces of the West within reach of anyone who could afford a ticket. In 1845 the nation's sweeping new spirit found a rallying cry in the term "Manifest Destiny," coined by journalist John O'Sullivan to describe what he saw as the U.S.'s inexorable future: to become a continental power stretching from the Atlantic Ocean to the Pacific. Exuberant expansionists rallied behind President James K. Polk when he pursued an aggressive war with Mexico that ended with that nation ceding great expanses of Western land, including all or part of seven future states, to the U.S. In the Pacific Northwest, Polk pursued a tough policy with Britain that would bring the land now inhabited by the states of Washington, Oregon and Idaho under U.S. control.

When gold was discovered in California in 1848, the Gold Rush that ensued changed Manifest Destiny from a distant ideal to a present reality. But now the burning question arose: Would the new states and territories of the West welcome slavery? "No!" cried voices in the North. "Yes!" insisted the people of the South. Throughout the 1850s, the struggle to control the future of the West—and the Union—was joined. In the 1860s, it would erupt into a full-scale war. ∎

BUILDING TOWNS *In 1857, St. Paul, Minn., was taking shape; a year later, it became the capital of Minnesota when the state was admitted to the Union. At the center is the dome of the Central Presbyterian Church, built in 1854 and no longer standing*

MOVING WEST *At left, a group of homesteaders in Custer County, Neb., prepare to bust the sod of the Great Plains. Although most of the Western territories were not conducive to slave-based plantation agriculture, advocates of slavery fought to extend the practice of human bondage into the new states of the Union*

SETTLING IN *Atchison, Kans., once no more than a prairie settlement, became a small town with sturdy buildings lining its main street in the early 1860s, left. In the 1850s, "Bleeding Kansas" had become a flashpoint between pro- and anti-slavery forces*

UNITING SETTLERS *Though Chicago was a burgeoning metropolis in 1860, and the site of the Republican Convention that nominated Abraham Lincoln for President, much of the state was still frontier territory. At left, a steam locomotive, the dynamo of Western settlement, makes a stop in Peru, Ill., in 1866*

A Less Than Perfect Union

The issue of human bondage bedevils the United States, bitterly dividing the nation

WE HAVE THE WOLF BY THE EAR, and we can neither hold him, nor safely let him go," Thomas Jefferson wrote to his friend John Holmes on April 22, 1820. "Justice is in one scale, and self-preservation in the other." The wolf Jefferson referred to was human bondage: slavery. And as of 1820, the "peculiar institution" of slavery was threatening to sunder the bonds that linked the former English colonies in North America that had come together to fight a common enemy, imperial Britain, and had gone on to link their destinies under the U.S. Constitution.

As Jefferson wrote, the Union was being threatened as Americans debated the future of a territory across the Mississippi that had made up part of his Louisiana Purchase, the great land acquisition that had foreseen a continental destiny for the former 13 colonies clustered near the Atlantic Ocean. Now an incendiary question troubled the land: Should this potential new state enter the Union as one in which slavery was legal, as it was in all Southern states and a few in the North? Or should Missouri enter as a free state, in which slavery was outlawed?

Jefferson, more than any other Founder, must have felt the enormous irony of the question. For it was he, a slave owner, who had written what historian Joseph Ellis calls the "magic words" of U.S. history, in the Declaration of Independence of 1776: "We hold these truths to be self-evident: that all men are created equal, that they are endowed by their Creator with certain unalienable Rights, that among these are Life, Liberty, and the Pursuit of Happiness." But if all men were created equal and endowed with an unalienable right to liberty—then how could slavery be legal in the United States? Jefferson wrote to Holmes: "This momentous question [Missouri's

fate], like a fire bell in the night, awakened me and filled me with terror." The future of Missouri, Jefferson knew, would decide the future of the Union. And for how long could the wolf of slavery be restrained from destroying that Union? Today we know the answer: through various compromises, politicians managed to hold the Union together for exactly 41 more years before Americans went to war with each other to decide the future of the Republic.

How did these states, so happily united in 1776 and then bound together under the U.S. Constitution in 1789, become so disunited? The first slaves arrived on American soil a year before the Pilgrims landed at Plymouth

AMERICAN IDYLL *In the bucolic illustration above, Virginia plantation owner George Washington inspects his fields, tended by slaves.*

The man at right, Renty, a Congo-born slave, was living on a South Carolina plantation when his portrait was taken in 1850

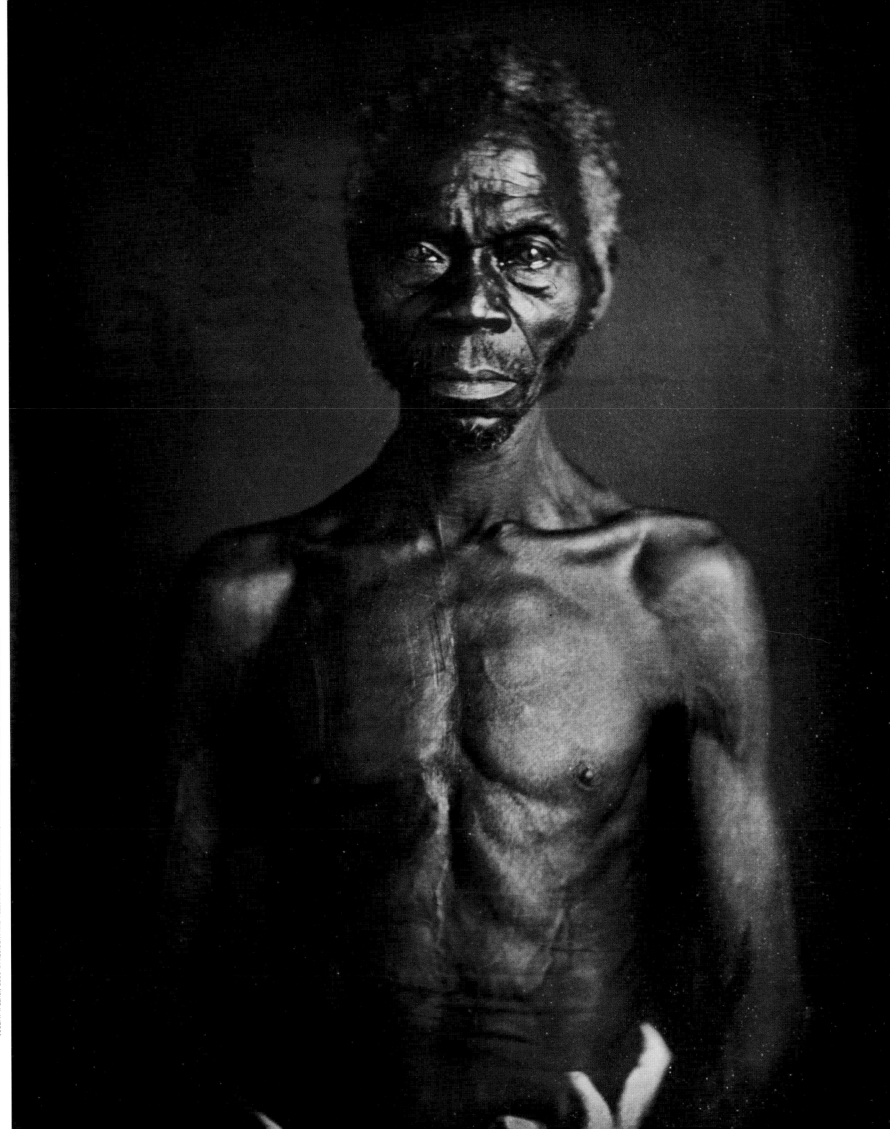

Rock, when a Dutch ship carrying 19 slaves accidentally made landfall at the British colony in Jamestown, Va. The slaves were put to work, and as a plantation economy developed in the South, slave labor became an integral factor in the economic equation that made its cotton fields one of the planet's richest creators of wealth.

CONSTITUTIONAL COMPROMISE When the most brilliant political thinkers in the U.S. gathered in Philadelphia in 1787 to hammer out a new Constitution to replace the inadequate Articles of Confederation, the future of slavery was the most divisive issue on the agenda, for the former colonies were clearly divided along regional lines over its legality. Opponents of the practice won one victory when the Northwest Ordinance was adopted, forbidding slavery in the Northwest Territories, the future states of Ohio, Indiana, Wisconsin, Michigan and Illinois. But Southerners insisted slavery must remain legal in their states.

The stated goal of the Constitution was laid out in the preamble to the document: "We, the people of the United States, in order to form a more perfect Union ..." But the truth was, the Union that was created under the Constitution was less than perfect, for in aiming to reach a consensus, the document glossed over the issue of slavery, never

mentioning that some 17% of those residing in the new nation were slaves who did not enjoy the same rights and privileges as other Americans. Indeed, the only reference to slaves in the Constitution was for purposes of enumeration and representation: the document states that one slave represented three-fifths of a free white man.

By 1804 all the states in the North had outlawed slavery. And in 1807 those who were eager to abolish slavery everywhere, the abolitionists, won a great victory when Congress outlawed the importing of slaves into the U.S. But that measure didn't stop the growth of the slave population in America: between 1619 and 1860, the number of slaves in the U.S. grew from 19 individuals to 4 million.

The "fire bell in the night" that so troubled Jefferson—the future of slavery in Missouri—was resolved through the Compromise of 1820, in which Missouri was allowed to enter the Union as a slave state at the same time Maine entered as a free state. In the years that followed, careful attempts were made to keep the number of slave and free states relatively equal.

In the early 1830s, the state of South Carolina threatened to secede from the Union and its legislature passed the Ordinance of Nullification, declaring that states had the power to nullify federal laws if they so desired. The

"So you're the little woman who wrote the book that started this great war."

—ABRAHAM LINCOLN, TO HARRIET BEECHER STOWE. THE REMARK IS MOST LIKELY APOCRYPHAL

Before the War

Clay

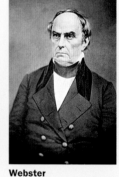

Webster

Calhoun

1850
A Compromise Holds the Union Together

With sectional divisions increasing as the 1850s began, three giants of the U.S. Senate tried to craft a compromise to save the Union. But Henry Clay of Kentucky, Daniel Webster of Massachusetts and John Calhoun of South Carolina, along with President Zachary Taylor, could not persuade a majority in Congress to sign on. When Taylor died, Stephen A. Douglas of Illinois, working with new President Millard Fillmore, managed to pass a compromise that temporarily held the Union together: California entered as a free state, but a new Fugitive Slave Act held that citizens in the North must assist Southern slave-holders in recovering fugitive slaves. The new law provoked further outrage against slavery in the North.

1852
Uncle Tom's Cabin

No work of art has so strongly influenced the course of U.S. history as Harriet Beecher Stowe's sensational novel of slavery, *Uncle Tom's Cabin*. Originally appearing in monthly serial form in an abolitionist newspaper, the novel was published in full in the spring of 1852 and became a sensation. Its tale of slave life in the South, and of the runaway slave Eliza's crossing of the ice-clogged Ohio River at Cincinnati, converted readers by the tens of thousands to the antislavery cause.

Though to modern readers the novel's plot is creaky and its racial stereotypes simplistic, there is no denying its power as a piece of propaganda: it sold 500,000 copies in its first year of publication, a remarkable figure for the time. The writer, a daughter of noted abolitionist minister Lyman Beecher, and her husband Calvin Ellis Stowe had sheltered runaway slaves while living in Ohio and Maine. Stowe wrote the strongly Christian book, she said, as a direct response to the Fugitive Slave Act and modeled in it part on the autobiography of Josiah Henson, a black man who fled slavery in Maryland to live in Canada.

135,000 SETS, 270,000 VOLUMES SOLD.

UNCLE TOM'S CABIN

FOR SALE HERE.

AN EDITION FOR THE MILLION, COMPLETE IN 1 Vol., PRICE 37 1-2 CENTS.
IN GERMAN, IN 1 Vol. PRICE 50 CENTS.
IN 2 Vols. CLOTH, 6 PLATES, PRICE $1.50.
SUPERB ILLUSTRATED EDITION, IN 1 Vol. WITH 153 ENGRAVINGS,
PRICES FROM $2.50 TO $5.00.

The Greatest Book of the Age.

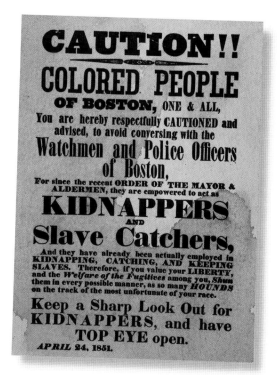

SLAVERY HEADS NORTH
The poster at right, printed in 1851, warns free blacks in Boston to beware of slave-hunters, who were empowered to search for runaway slaves in Northern cities by the Fugitive Slave Act of 1850. Above is an iron neck collar used to subdue slaves

surrection by local slaves that ended with the death of more than 50 whites. The uprising was soon put down amid hideous cruelty, but Nat Turner's Rebellion threw white Southerners into a panic from which they would not soon recover. Across the South, slaves were treated more brutally than previously, and fears that Northern abolitionists would support further slave rebellions accelerated the Union's division along regional lines.

In 1833 abolitionists around the world rejoiced when slavery was outlawed across most of the British Empire. It was a humiliating moment for slavery's foes in the U.S.: the empire against whose tyranny Americans had revolted had now outlawed slavery, while in the U.S. it was still legal. But for much of the 1830s and '40s, the issue of slavery bubbled under the surface of U.S. society, which at that time was experiencing a growth spurt of unparalleled proportions. A host of political, social, technological and economic issues—the contentious presidency of Andrew Jackson, battles with Native Americans, the advent of the railroad and telegraph, the growth of cities, rancor over exploding immigration, the surging drive to settle the frontier, a war with Mexico—made America a pulsating and rambunctious Republic in this era but pushed the question of slavery off the national agenda.

U.S. Congress then passed the Force Act, authorizing the Government to use force to make the state comply with its laws. But the issue that spawned this crisis was not slavery: it was high U.S. tariffs that directly harmed South Carolina's economy, based on export trade with Europe.

Another, more frightening event reminded all Americans of the wolf they held by the ear: in 1831 a Virginia slave named Nat Turner broke out of bondage and led an in-

---

The 1850s
Voices for Abolition

In the late 18th and early 19th centuries, a potent image circulated across Europe and North America: a kneeling, manacled slave raised his head to the sky, above a caption reading "Am I not a man and a brother?" The work became an emblem of the growing antislavery movement around the world.

The image helped Britons opposed to human bondage, whose most famous champion was the politician William Wilberforce, achieve their goals: slavery was outlawed in Britain in 1807 and across most nations of the British Empire in 1833.

The movement to abolish slavery in the U.S. took root at the time of the Revolution, when its champions were often Quakers. The most eloquent black voice calling for abolition before the Civil War was that of Frederick Douglass, left, who was taught to read by his master's wife, then escaped from slavery and moved to the North, where he became a powerful speaker, orator and activist for abolition—and a living rebuke to those who argued that blacks lacked the intellect to succeed in U.S. society. Another

former slave, Sojourner Truth, was a similarly inspiring role model for U.S. blacks. Among the strong voices in the white press who converted thousands to the cause of abolition were the editors William Lloyd Garrison and Horace Greeley. Such abolitionists were deeply scorned in the South, and many in the North regarded them as extremists and meddlers.

Garrison   **Greeley**   **Truth**

17

GO WEST The legacy of the Louisiana Purchase and the new lands gained by the war with Mexico forced the issue of slavery back on the front burner of U.S. politics. When the Mexican War ended in 1848, many more territories west of the Mississippi now under U.S. control prepared for statehood. The issues that had created the Missouri Compromise of 1820 once again began tolling in the night: Would slavery be legal in these parts? After a long impasse, the great Compromise of 1850 attempted to settle the issue of slavery for the near future.

The Compromise was a complex package of five separate bills organized by Illinois Senator Stephen A. Douglas. Among other provisions, these measures placed the future of slavery in the territories of New Mexico and Utah in the hands of their residents, a concept called popular sovereignty. To win Southern votes, the compromise included a reform of the Fugitive Slave Act, as long demanded by the South. Under the new law, all citizens, including those in the North, were required to assist in the recovery of fugitive slaves. Moreover, the act declared that slaves had no legal recourse to prove their freedom.

As a result, the horrifying apparatus of human bondage—including slave-catchers roaming the streets and posting WANTED notices seeking runaways—began regularly appearing in Northern states. A spasm of revulsion ran through the North as citizens confronted the brutal facts of slavery. The ranks of abolitionists swelled, and the Underground Railroad that helped slaves escape to freedom in the North and Canada grew more extensive.

The Compromise of 1850 was designed to assuage the nation's growing differences over slavery, but it only aggravated them. The passage of the Fugitive Slave Act was only the first of a series of explosive events that would make the 1850s one of the most contentious and ugly periods in American history.

Not all these events were political. In a compelling example of how popular culture can help shape social views, the publication of Harriet Beecher Stowe's novel *Uncle Tom's Cabin* in 1852 turned millions of Americans into rabid opponents of slavery. Stowe's melodramatic narrative brought the lineaments of slavery to life for hundreds of thousands of readers who may never have seen a slave. With its compelling cast of heroic African Americans and demonic, slave-driving villains, the novel galvanized the battle over human bondage. It is probably a myth that President Abraham Lincoln, on meeting Stowe a decade after the novel was published, hailed her as "the little woman who wrote the book that started this great war."

SECOND BILLING *This 1840 poster from an unknown Southern town announces a raffle in which a 20-year-old slave, Sarah, takes second billing to a horse, Star*

Before the War

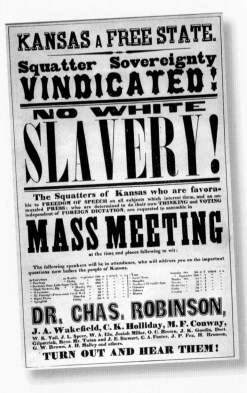

1854
The Kansas-Nebraska Act

In 1854 America's debate over slavery grew even more heated when the Kansas-Nebraska Act became law. It declared that the citizens of these two territories, rather than the U.S. Congress, should be allowed to decide by popular vote whether their regions would be slave or free.

Senator Stephen A. Douglas of Illinois and Southern supporters championed "popular sovereignty"— as did the white pro-slavery squatters in Kansas who published the broadsheet at left, claiming their property rights would be violated if slavery were outlawed. But slavery's foes denounced the act as a Southern plot to extend the practice across the nation. The law helped give birth to a new, quickly popular antislavery party in the North: the Republican Party.

1856
"Bleeding Kansas"

With popular sovereignty now the law in Kansas, the new territory became the epicenter of the debate over slavery. Pro-Southern sentiment ran high in neighboring Missouri, brought into the Union as a slave state under the Missouri Compromise of 1820. Even though slavery was not a vital aspect of Missouri's economy, locals detested what they considered the arrogant posturing of anti-slavery abolitionists. Armed bands of Missouri vigilantes began conducting raids into Kansas to torch the homes of abolitionist "free soil" settlers, and rowdy Missourians crossed the border to cast illegal votes for pro-slavery tickets in Kansas elections. In May 1856, a mob of some 800 pro-slavery men ran riot in the free-soil stronghold of Lawrence, Kans., burning buildings, beating local residents and plundering stores. A proxy civil war had broken out on the frontier.

TYPECAST This unidentified slave family is labeled on the original caption of this photograph, dating from the 1850s, as "Uncle Tom and family," indicating the extent to which the stereotyped characters from Uncle Tom's Cabin had entered American culture

But the anecdote was believed by so many Americans because it rang so true.

BLEEDING KANSAS In the mid-1850s the fires over slavery flared most brightly in Kansas, another territory ripe for statehood. Would it enter the Union as a slave or free state? Senator Douglas of Illinois again took the political reins: he shepherded the passage of the Kansas-Nebraska Act in 1854, guaranteeing that the future of these states would be decided by popular sovereignty. The act plunged Kansans and their neighbors into a political nightmare, as votes for and against slavery were bought and sold for the price of a drink, phony "Kansans" crossed the state border from Missouri to vote for slavery, and bands of "border ruffians" roamed the countryside, terrorizing those who disagreed with them.

By now it was clear: slavery was an infection, a cancer, a toxin in the American bloodstream that poisoned all it touched. The violence seen on the frontier spread back to Washington, where the floors of the House and Senate resembled armed camps, as legislators swore their hatred of one another and demonized their political opponents.

The battles over slavery reached a crescendo with the U.S. Supreme Court's decision in the case of *Dred Scott*

1856
A Beating in the Senate

As a bitterly divided nation edged toward civil war, Northerners and Southerners vilified and demonized each other. In May 1856 the hostility erupted into bloodshed on the floor of the U.S. Senate, when Preston Brooks, a Congressman from South Carolina, viciously beat radical abolitionist Senator Charles Sumner of Massachusetts with a metal-tipped wooden cane. Three days before, Sumner had attacked the character of Senator A.P. Butler of South Carolina; Brooks was Butler's cousin. Sumner was so severely injured that he was not able to resume his duties in the Senate for three years.

1856
The Buchanan Administration

James Buchanan, the President who preceded Lincoln, won election because he represented an attempt to bridge the nation's divisions. But as is often the case with would-be middlemen, rather than becoming an honest broker between the two polarized sides of the slavery debate, he ended up denounced by both. In office, he was considered a "doughface," the popular term for a Northerner with Southern sympathies. His term began amid furor, for he claimed the Supreme Court would soon solve the slavery problem. Instead, the *Dred Scott* decision, which he appeared to support, helped ignite the Civil War.

In his last message to Congress, in December 1860, Buchanan declared that secession by the states was illegal. But he went on to note that should states secede, the Federal Government could not stop them. A few weeks later, South Carolina seceded, while Buchanan, a very lame duck, looked on, helplessly.

Buchanan

v. Sandford in 1857. Once again, as it had in the Fugitive Slave Act and the Kansas-Nebraska Act, the Federal Government, this time in the form of the Supreme Court, took the side of the slave states. The judges decided, 7 to 2, that simply because Scott had moved from a slave state to a free state, that did not make him a free person.

Chief Justice Roger B. Taney's decision in this case is among the most infamous public documents in American history. Setting forth the history of slavery in America, Taney declared the writers of the Constitution regarded slaves as "beings of an inferior order ... so far inferior that they had no rights which the white man was bound to respect." The decision electrified slavery's foes, who charged that the gleaming ideals of the Declaration of Independence had been compromised by the squalid inequities of bondage.

The Scott decision led more and more Northerners to begin to agree with a former U.S. Congressman who had been drawn back into politics three years before by the issue of human bondage. "I hate [slavery] because of the monstrous injustice of slavery itself," Abraham Lincoln had declared in 1854. "I hate it because it deprives our republican example of its just influence in the world—enables the enemies of free institutions, with plausibility, to

taunt us as hypocrites—causes the real friends of freedom to doubt our sincerity, and especially because it forces so many really good men amongst ourselves into an open war with the very fundamental principles of civil liberty—criticizing the Declaration of Independence, and insisting that there is no right principle of action but self-interest."

These powerful words were, as always, balanced by the powerful realities of centuries of American slavery. By 1860 there were some 4 million slaves living in the U.S. Some 30% of the citizens in the South owned slaves, and in some Southern states the population of slaves outnumbered that of whites. The Southern economy was so firmly dependent on slave labor that no one could imagine how slaveholders could be compensated should the slaves be freed. And how could those slaves—most of them systematically excluded by state law from being taught to read or write—learn to survive and thrive in American society? Or should they perhaps be removed to Africa or other nations to begin life anew?

The questions seemed insoluble: Americans had the wolf by the ear and could not let it go. But ready or not, when Lincoln was elected President, the debate over slavery erupted into civil war, offering Americans a chance, at last, to start over and build a more perfect Union. ∎

> "I hate [slavery] because it deprives our republican example of its just influence in the world—enables the enemies of free institutions, with plausibility, to taunt us as hypocrites ..."
>
> —ABRAHAM LINCOLN, 1854

Before the War

1857

The *Dred Scott* Decision

The case of Dred Scott had been percolating in the judicial system for more than a decade before it was argued before the U.S. Supreme Court, and before the court's controversial decision rocked the nation.

Scott had been a slave in Virginia, Alabama and Missouri, which entered the Union as a slave state in 1820, balanced by the entry of Maine, a free state, under the Missouri Compromise. When Scott's first owner died, however, he was bought by a doctor who moved to Illinois and the Wisconsin Territory, taking Scott with him. Both Illinois and the Wisconsin Territory had been decreed forever free of slavery under the Northwest Ordinance of 1787. In Wisconsin, Scott married Harriet Robinson, and the couple had two children; eventually, Scott and his owner ended up back in Missouri.

Scott's suit argued that once he had been transported to a free state, the terms of his bondage no longer applied. The court's decision, as articulated by Chief Justice Roger B. Taney, a Marylander, not only dismissed Scott's claim but also found that even free blacks had no standing to bring a suit in federal courts because they were not American citizens—and never

could be. In other words, there was no such thing as an African American.

Attempting to read the minds of the Founding Fathers, Taney declared that they had regarded blacks as "beings of an inferior order, and altogether unfit to associate with the white race, either in social or political relations, and so far inferior that they had no rights which the white man was bound to respect." Taney and six fellow judges also ruled that, because the U.S. Constitution guarantees the right to personal property, and because slaves were a form of property, it was unconstitutional for the Federal Government to prohibit slavery in *any* U.S. territory. In other words, the Missouri Compromise itself was unconstitutional.

The decision ignited a firestorm of protest in the North, accelerating the sense that the "Slave Power," as the opponents of bondage called the slave states, was taking control of the levers of political power in the nation and would not rest until all the states were opened to slavery. The New York State legislature declared, "[This] will bring slavery within our borders, against our will, with all its unhallowed, demoralizing, and blighting influences."

A Raid in Virginia Offers a Preview of War to Come

Abolitionist John Brown takes the law into his own hands—and pays the price

THE EXTREMIST *At far left, Brown holds the flag of the Subterranean Pass Way, a group he founded in the 1840s to aid the Underground Railroad. At near left is the engine house at Harpers Ferry where he was captured.*

Brown remains a divisive figure. Lawrence, Kans., librarian Kerry Altenbernd declared in 2009, "To say he is a homicidal maniac misses the point. He is someone who could not live with 4 million people in bondage and had to do something about it"

American society in the first half of the 19th century was alive with currents of religion that bore the stamp of the Old Testament. It was an era of bearded patriarchs and enormous campground revivals, a time when strange new cults and fads bloomed and faded, an age when the Church of Jesus Christ of Latter-day Saints could arise, thrive, suffer persecution for its practices, then see its leaders embark on a great journey across the plains to found a new society in the desert. No one embodied the sense of stern Old Testament judgment, righteousness and vengeance more than one of the most vocal advocates of abolition, John Brown, who capped his unlikely career as a prophet of freedom by conducting a military-style raid on a U.S. government armory in hopes of starting a slave insurrection.

Brown was a specimen familiar to today's Americans: a fanatical zealot who fathered 20 children, he believed he had been singled out to enforce God's will on earth. And that will called for the elimination of human bondage in America. After years of preaching against slavery in Ohio and upstate New York, where he was a livestock breeder, Brown began actively agitating to fight the "Slave Power." He had sent five of his sons to Kansas to help keep it from becoming a slave state. When they sent word that their task demanded rifles, he took the weapons there himself. After Southerner sympathizers burned Lawrence in 1856, Brown took a bloody revenge. With a small party he went in the dead of night to his foes' cabins, took slavery advocates out of their beds and hacked five of them to death in cold blood. After this

Pottawatomie Massacre, he and a few followers became outlaws, hiding, fighting, running for their lives.

When government troops finally broke up Kansas' civil war, Brown's little army scattered. But now a larger, more dangerous idea began to consume him. On Oct. 16, 1859, the citizens of Harpers Ferry, Va., woke to sinister rumors. Brown and 21 followers had captured the town's Federal armory, cut the telegraph wires into it and proclaimed a slave insurrection. But to Brown's suprise, no slaves flocked to take up the 100,000 weapons stored inside. Virginia militiamen surrounded the engine house where Brown's tiny "army" made its last stand, holding the men captive until U.S. Marines under West Point graduate Robert E. Lee arrived and took Brown into custody. He was tried in Virginia, found guilty of treason and sentenced to death.

Brown's strange saga, ending in his hanging on Dec. 2, 1859, further polarized Americans along slavery's great divide. He was hailed as a martyr in the North, denounced as a fanatical madman in the South. Americans on both sides of the slavery issue were struck as never before by the width of the chasms that now divided them, and the episode served as an eerie reveille for the war ahead. Within two years, Union soldiers would be marching into battle singing the words "John Brown's body lies a mouldering in the grave/ His soul is marching on." The song's stirring tune, taken from an old camp meeting song, and its irresistible refrain ("Glory, glory, hallelujah") were later used by Julia Ward Howe for the great Union anthem *The Battle Hymn of the Republic.*

Lincoln's Election Sunders the Union

Americans vote one of slavery's most eloquent foes into the presidency, igniting the fuse of Southern secession

B Y 1859, WHEN JOHN BROWN MOUNTED his failed raid at Harpers Ferry, Va., his nation had become a mockery of its own name. The United States were no longer united: indeed, they were so deeply divided over the issue of slavery that the secession of the Southern states from the Union, once viewed as unthinkable, had become a real possibility. The rush of events in the 1850s had put the very concept of the Union in play, and the election to the presidency in 1860 of a relative newcomer on the political scene, Abraham Lincoln, was the tipping point that plunged the South into secession and the nation into war.

Lincoln was a man shaped by his times: by the frontier hardships of his youth; by his early encounters with slavery and the South; by a single, ineffective term in the U.S. House of Representatives; by his growing opposition to human bondage; and by his sense that the Union could not survive as what he so memorably called a house divided. In a period chockablock with extreme stances, passionate arguments and violent emotions, he stands out as a calm voice of reason, a shrewd observer who was able to penetrate the fog of rhetoric and passion surrounding the nation's plight. He identified America's malady, articulated its symptoms and prescribed remedies for its relief.

Born in Kentucky—about 100 miles from his contemporary, Jefferson Davis—Lincoln was raised in small frontier settlements in Indiana and Illinois. His mother died when he was only 9, and his stepmother Sarah encouraged his love of reading and learning, elocution and politics. He received little formal education but taught himself, while earning a living as a hired hand on local farms. He gained notice for his unusual stature—fully grown, he stood 6 ft. 4 in.—and for his love of oratory. As a teen, he

would entertain friends and townspeople by imitating political speakers and traveling evangelists.

Lincoln's world expanded when he labored as a hand on two flatboat trading trips down the Mississippi River to New Orleans, where he encountered firsthand the realities of slavery. In his early 20s, he became part-owner of a small general store in New Salem, Ill., which failed. He enlisted in the Black Hawk Indian War and served without distinction; upon his return, he worked as a surveyor and postmaster and had his first romance, with Ann Mayes Rutledge, daughter of one of the settlement's founders. The love affair ended in tragedy when Rutledge died, apparently of typhoid fever. Lincoln became so distraught that he contemplated suicide before recovering.

Alert, ambitious and a masterly storyteller, Lincoln was well liked by his neighbors, who in 1834 elected him to serve the first of four terms in the Illinois house of representatives. An adept politician, he eventually became a leader of its Whig faction. Led by Kentucky Senator

PARTNERS *Lincoln's running mate in the 1860 campaign, Hannibal Hamlin, was a Senator from Maine included on the ticket to attract New England voters. The two men remained distant during the election, and Hamlin played only a small role in the Lincoln Administration. At left, a portrait of Lincoln in 1860*

★

A Senate Campaign Puts Lincoln in the Spotlight

Acclaim for his losing 1858 race propels the Republican to the presidency

publican example of its just influence in the world—enables the enemies of free institutions, with plausibility, to taunt us as hypocrites."

Lincoln's remarks drew national attention, but four years later, another speech galvanized Americans even more strongly. In 1858, when Lincoln accepted his party's nomination to run for the U.S. Senate against Douglas, he depicted the U.S. as a "house divided" and predicted it would not endure half-slave and half-free. He had dared to assert what many believed but no one had expressed so forcefully: the argument over slavery had reached a pivotal moment; it must be resolved, one way or another, once and for all.

In the Senate campaign that followed, Lincoln and Douglas engaged in a series of debates across the state of Illinois in which each argued his case: Douglas for popular sovereignty and the extension of slavery in the territories; Lincoln for the limitation of slavery to the Southern states with an eye to its eventual abolition. Lincoln lost the election, but he gained a larger prize: he had become the most eloquent voice opposing slavery in the North, and his newfound popularity would carry him to the presidency in 1860.

After his single term as a Congressman, Abraham Lincoln lost interest in politics, he told friends. But he was appalled by the passage of the Fugitive Slave Act in 1850, part of the Compromise of 1850 that promised to allow the extension of slavery in the territories. And he was so angered by the passage of the Kansas-Nebraska Act in 1854—which explicitly allowed that practice and was spearheaded by his onetime romantic rival, Stephen A. Douglas—that he decided to return to politics to argue against the extension of slavery beyond the Southern states.

On Oct. 16, 1854, Lincoln faced off with Douglas to debate the Kansas-Nebraska Act in Peoria, Ill., and he delivered a savage indictment of slavery and its influence in America. "This declared indifference, but as I must think, covert real zeal for the spread of slavery, I cannot but hate," Lincoln declared. "I hate it because of the monstrous injustice of slavery itself. I hate it because it deprives our re-

LINCOLN'S FOE *A fireplug of a man, Douglas stood only 5 ft. 4 in., and the rangy Lincoln towered above him. At right is a poster from the 1858 campaign. At left, an illustration of a debate*

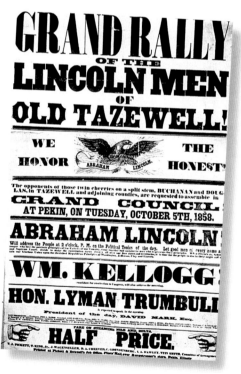

★

ON THE MARCH *"Wide Awake Clubs" were composed of radical Republicans who were among the strongest supporters of Lincoln in the 1860 presidential campaign. Strongly opposed to slavery and its extension, they staged large parades at night, singing and bearing lanterns. This marching band of Wide Awakes hailed from Mohawk, N.Y.*

Henry Clay, Whigs opposed the pro-slavery policies of Democratic President Andrew Jackson and advocated government investment to build canals, roads and railroads, "internal improvements" that they believed would shower prosperity on the nation's burgeoning frontier.

In 1837 Lincoln moved to Springfield, where he trained as a lawyer by "reading" the law and serving as an assistant to a mentor from the Black Hawk War, John Todd Stuart. He rose to become Stuart's partner in the law and capped off his ascent from rawboned frontier youth to citified attorney by marrying Stuart's cousin, Mary Todd, late in 1842. Along the way he bested a romantic rival, rising lawyer and future political foe Stephen A. Douglas.

The young couple began a family and Lincoln rode the circuit of local trials, traveling throughout Illinois for much of the year. Yet politics still beckoned, and in 1846, running as a Whig, Lincoln was elected to the U.S. House of Representatives. But he served only one term, for he strongly opposed Democratic President James K. Polk's war with Mexico, which he viewed as a trumped-up land grab. His constituents did not agree, and Lincoln chose not to stand for re-election. Returning home in 1849, he vowed he would never again seek office.

History had other plans. The passage of the Kansas-Nebraska Act in 1854, stage-managed by Lincoln's old rival, Douglas, now a U.S. Senator from Illinois, drew Lincoln back into political life. He began making the case against popular sovereignty in speeches and articles; a speech that year in Peoria, Ill., was circulated nationally as a compelling indictment of slavery and its advance.

As the Whig Party collapsed amid divisions over the slavery issue, Lincoln joined the new Republican Party, supporting its candidate for President, John C. Frémont, in the party's first national election in 1856. Frémont lost, but Lincoln became a key figure in Illinois Republican circles, and in 1858 he ran for election to the U.S. Senate, arguing against the incumbent Douglas in a series of debates that brought him further attention, if not victory.

The loss was bitter, but Lincoln relished his growing national profile. His "house divided" speech was widely reprinted, and his debates with Douglas, packaged into a book in 1860, became a best seller. Early that year, Lincoln traveled to the East, where he delivered a memorable speech at the Great Hall at Cooper Union in Manhattan. The gaunt figure with the high-pitched voice and the backwoods accent electrified his audience with a clarion call to oppose slavery. "Let us have faith that right makes might," he declared, "and in that faith, let us, to the end, dare to do our duty as we understand it." Slavery's foes rejoiced; they had found an articulate new advocate for their cause.

Even so, Lincoln's selection as the Republican nominee for the presidency was no coronation: it required the services of a close-knit band of Illinois allies, who won their first victory when they brought the party's convention to their home turf, Chicago. There, in a vast hall built for the occasion, they staged an upset, packing it with "Lincoln men" and snatching the nomination from the front runner, Senator William H. Seward of New York.

The election that followed revealed the fissures that were dividing the nation. Not two but four major candidates vied for votes. Lincoln, the Republican, appealed to anti-slavery voters in the North. The Democratic Party, like the Whig Party, some years earlier, split over the issue of slavery. Lincoln's 1858 Senate foe, Douglas, represented Northern Democrats, who favored slavery and sought to appease the South. Incumbent Vice President John C. Breckinridge of Kentucky represented the rabidly pro-slavery Southern Democrats. A moderate, Senator John Bell of Tennessee, ran as the candidate of the fledgling Constitutional Union Party, helping divide the votes.

On Nov. 6, 1860, Lincoln—who was so hated in the South that his name did not appear on most ballots there—carried the popular vote over Douglas and won victory in the Electoral College by a massive margin. A powerful voice against slavery would soon occupy the White House. The echo of Lincoln's victory quickly resounded across the land: within seven weeks, South Carolina became the first Southern state to secede from the Union. ■

FAMILY MATTERS *Two of the Lincoln children, Willie, left, and Tad, are shown with their mother circa 1860. The couple had four boys, but the eldest son, Robert, was the only one to live past 18. Second son Edward died, most likely due to tuberculosis, in 1850 a month shy of age 4; third son Willie died of a fever in 1862 at 11. Tad outlived his father but died, also probably of tuberculosis, in 1871 at age 18*

MAN OF THE HOUR *Supporters marching in an 1860 political rally in Springfield assembled for a photo at the candidate's home. Lincoln greeted his political allies; he can be seen here, without his familiar top hat, to the right of the front door*

1861

—————◆—————

"It is really, or rather was, a town of some note, but the ruin, absolute devastation now in its place is beyond anything I ever dreamed or saw or heard tell of."

—A UNION OFFICER OF THE 10TH MAINE VOLUNTEER INFANTRY REGIMENT, VIEWING THE AFTERMATH OF THE BATTLE TO CONTROL HARPERS FERRY, VA., IN 1861

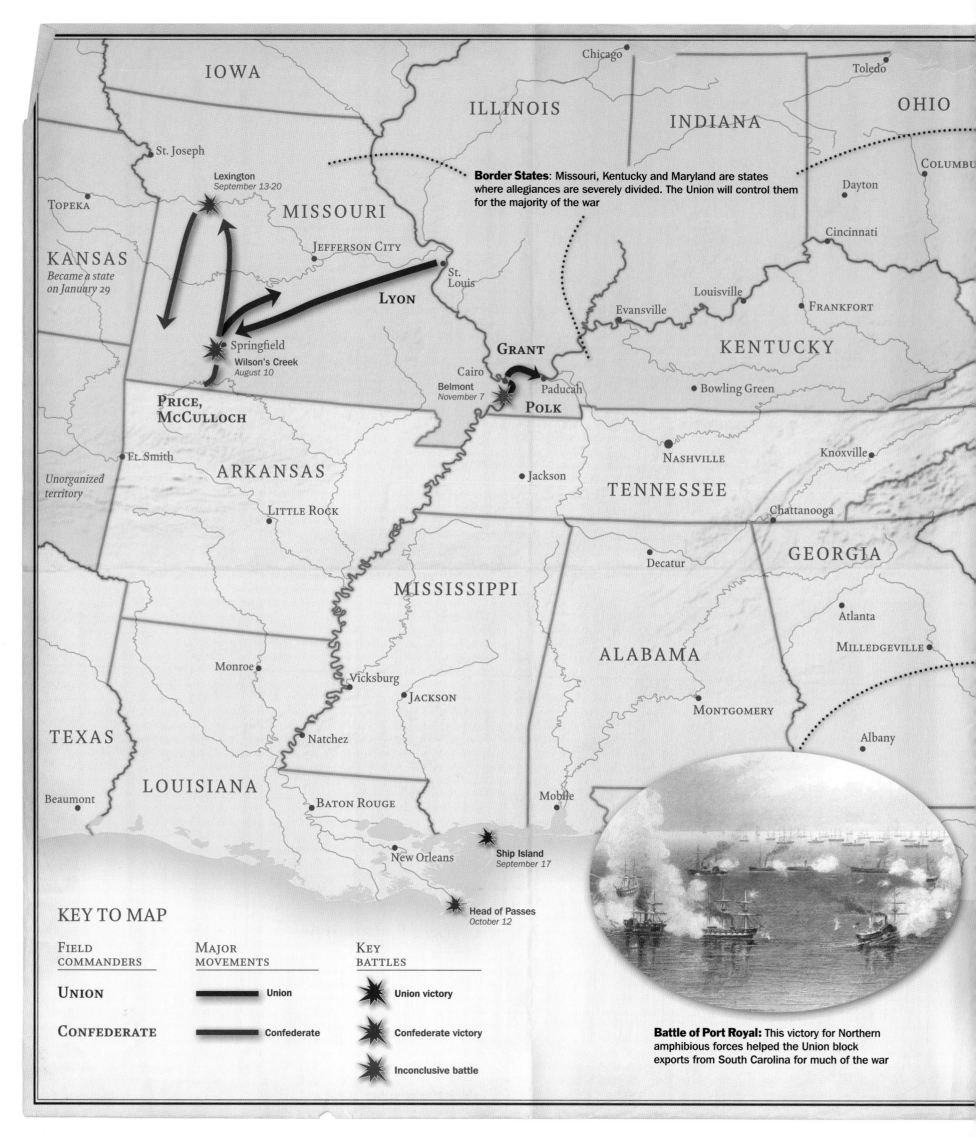

IOWA

ILLINOIS

INDIANA

OHIO

Chicago

Toledo

COLUMBU

St. Joseph

Lexington
September 13-20

MISSOURI

Dayton

TOPEKA

Cincinnati

KANSAS
*Became a state
on January 29*

JEFFERSON CITY

St.
Louis

Border States: Missouri, Kentucky and Maryland are states
where allegiances are severely divided. The Union will control them
for the majority of the war

Louisville

FRANKFORT

LYON

Evansville

GRANT

Springfield

Wilson's Creek
August 10

Cairo

Belmont
November 7

Paducah

KENTUCKY

Bowling Green

**PRICE,
McCULLOCH**

POLK

Ft. Smith

ARKANSAS

Jackson

NASHVILLE

Knoxville

TENNESSEE

*Unorganized
territory*

LITTLE ROCK

Chattanooga

GEORGIA

Decatur

MISSISSIPPI

Atlanta

ALABAMA

MILLEDGEVILLE

Monroe

Vicksburg

JACKSON

TEXAS

Natchez

MONTGOMERY

Albany

Beaumont

LOUISIANA

BATON ROUGE

Mobile

New Orleans

Ship Island
September 17

Head of Passes
October 12

KEY TO MAP

| FIELD
COMMANDERS | MAJOR
MOVEMENTS | KEY
BATTLES |
|---|---|---|
| **UNION** | ——— Union | ✶ Union victory |
| **CONFEDERATE** | ——— Confederate | ✶ Confederate victory |
| | | ✶ Inconclusive battle |

Battle of Port Royal: This victory for Northern
amphibious forces helped the Union block
exports from South Carolina for much of the war

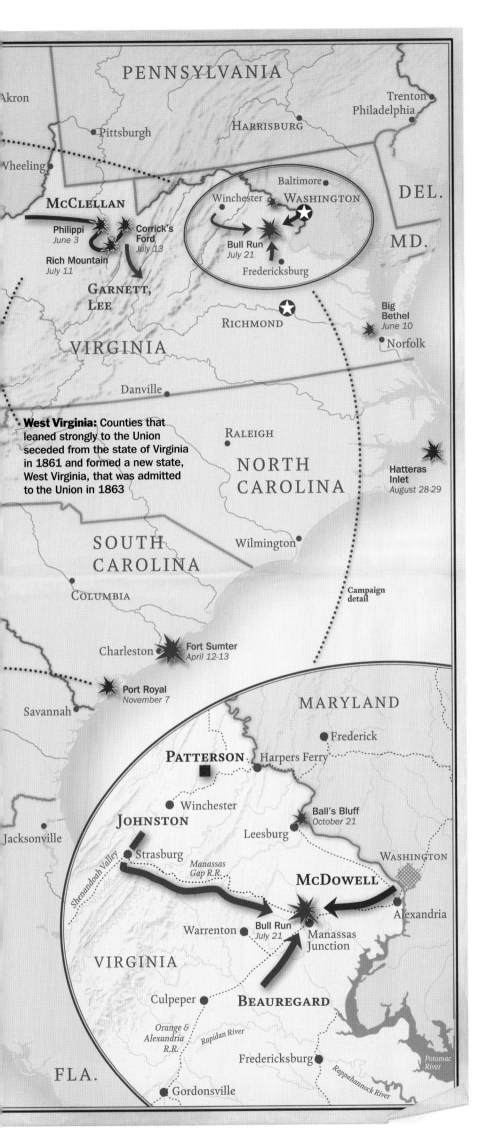

1861
Situation Report

The first year of the war is relatively quiet. When President Lincoln prods Union generals to action, Northern troops are routed at Bull Run. In the West, Confederates win a narrow victory in Missouri.

Jan. 9-Feb. 1 Mississippi, Florida, Alabama, Georgia, Louisiana and Texas follow South Carolina's late-1860 lead and secede from the Union.

Jan. 29 Kansas is admitted to the Union as a state with a constitution prohibiting slavery.

Feb. 4 The Confederate States of America (C.S.A.) is formed. Jefferson Davis, a former U.S. Senator from Mississippi, is inaugurated as President on Feb. 18.

March 4 Abraham Lincoln is sworn in as the 16th President of the U.S.

April 12-13 The war begins when Fort Sumter, a U.S. fortress in Charleston, S.C., is fired upon and surrenders to the C.S.A. Lincoln soon calls for 75,000 volunteer soldiers, and on April 19 he orders a blockade of all Southern ports.

April 17-May 20 Virginia, Arkansas, Tennessee and North Carolina secede from the Union, and the Confederacy takes its final shape, with 11 member states. The Union will soon consist of 21 member states.

May 24 Union troops cross the Potomac River from Washington and capture Alexandria, Va., and vicinity. On May 29, Richmond, Va., becomes the capital of the C.S.A..

July 21 Confederate forces win a major victory at the First Battle of Bull Run (Manassas), as Union troops under General Irvin McDowell retreat in disarray to Washington.

Aug. 10 In the first major battle in the Trans-Mississippi West, Confederates win a close victory over Union troops at Wilson's Creek in southwest Missouri.

Nov. 1 Lincoln appoints General George B. McClellan as general-in-chief of all Union forces after the resignation of the aged General Winfield Scott.

Nov. 7 Union troops beat Confederates at Port Royal Sound in South Carolina and move north to take Beaufort and control much of the state's coastline.

★

The South Secedes

Rejecting Lincoln's election, Southern states withdraw from the Union and form the Confederate States of America

LONG BEFORE ABRAHAM LINCOLN WAS elected President, many of the citizens of the slaveholding states had ceased to think of themselves primarily as Americans and had begun to think of themselves as Southerners first. The bonds of Union had already been severed emotionally; perhaps that is why they were so quickly dissolved politically. Within six weeks of the Nov. 4 election, the "Fire-eaters" of South Carolina—always the most rabid and vociferous enemies of the Northern states—led their state into secession. On Dec. 20, state legislators, assembled in a special convention, voted 169 to 0 to render "the Union now subsisting between South Carolina and other States" null and void.

This decision of the utmost gravity was reached in an atmosphere of levity. Two days after Lincoln's election, citizens of Savannah, Ga., had gathered in Johnson Square and held a gigantic torchlight procession, singing and cheering and unveiling a "Flag of Independence" that featured the coiled snake, symbolizing resistance to tyranny, familiar from the Revolution. Other cities had followed suit. Now South Carolina had channeled the cheers into political action. Across the South, the decision to shift allegiance from Union and nation to state and region was inspiring, exhilarating. Like the popping of a champagne cork, it released pressures that had been building for decades, and like champagne, the taste proved intoxicating. Following the proud tradition of their forefathers, Southerners told one another, they were declaring their independence and seizing liberty from the hands of tyrants who sought to limit their rights.

The secessionist impulse spread like wildfire: Alexander Stephens of Georgia, a moderate, declared that Southerners "are wild with passion and frenzy, doing they know not what." In the weeks after the holiday season, the states of the Deep South followed South Carolina's lead, vying for the honor of being among the earliest

to secede. Mississippi was second, on Jan. 9, 1861. Florida seceded a day later, Alabama on the 11th. By Feb. 1, Georgia, Louisiana and Texas had joined them.

The seceding states quickly began coming together to form a new union of their own, which they styled a Confederacy. Meeting in Montgomery, Ala., delegates from the rebel states pondered the choice of a man to lead them. Passing over some of the more radical of the secessionists, the delegates selected the widely respected Mexican War veteran and former Secretary of War, Mississippi Senator Jefferson Davis.

Davis, 53 in 1861, was a firm defender of Southern rights but a moderate: he had spoken eloquently against secession as recently as Jan. 21, when he resigned his Sen-

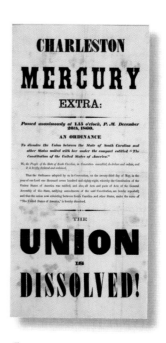

FORMING A GOVERNMENT
At left, a crowd at the statehouse in Montgomery, Ala., heralds the Inauguration of Jefferson Davis, above, as the first President of the Confederate States of America on Feb. 18, 1861. Almost two months had passed since a Charleston, S.C., newspaper handbill had trumpeted that state's withdrawal from the Union. When Virginia joined the Confederacy, Richmond became the rebellion's capital

33

ate seat after Mississippi seceded. His wife later recalled his reaction to the news that he had been selected President: "... when reading the telegram he looked so grieved that I feared some evil had befallen our family." Yet Davis accepted the offer and was sworn in at Montgomery as the first President of the Confederate States of America on Feb. 18. In his Inaugural Address, he declared, "I have been chosen with the hope that the beginning of our career as a Confederacy may not be obstructed by hostile opposition to our enjoyment of the separate existence and independence which we have asserted."

Even as the Southern states seized the initiative in the crisis by seceding, the Northern states were handicapped by the election process then used, which called for a lame-duck period of four months between the November presidential election and the March Inauguration. Outgoing President James Buchanan made feeble gestures toward compromise, but Northern Republicans loudly denounced them as overly sympathetic to the South. Kentucky Senator John J. Crittenden's compromise proposal also failed in the Senate, for it would have allowed the extension of slavery into some territories.

Lincoln could only watch the events unfold as an observer. The incoming President adopted a policy of "watchful waiting," refusing to declare how he would react to the acts of secession. On Feb. 11, he left Springfield, Ill., and began a long, winding train trip that took him to many major cities of the North, allowing his new constituents to get a view of this still unknown President-in-waiting. But his refusal to declare a firm policy toward the South led some Northerners to fear he lacked backbone.

Yet Lincoln had already reached one decision that would guide his policy until the end of the war: he would refuse to recognize the existence of the Confederate States of America as an independent entity. Instead, he would treat the secessionists as rebels, and he would urge foreign states to do the same. And he had a precedent for doing so: in the 1832-33 Nullification Crisis, President Andrew Jackson had threatened to use federal troops to quell a rebellion in which the South Carolina legislature declared that states had the right to "nullify" federal tariffs. The diplomatic battle over the potential recognition of the C.S.A. by Britain and France would be fought in the years to come as diligently as any battle on the ground.

Meanwhile, as Lincoln held his counsel, the situation on the ground was rapidly changing. Without bloodshed, U.S. forts in the South were rapidly being surrendered by Union forces and taken over by Southern rebels. When Lincoln was inaugurated, only four forts in the South—Sumter in South Carolina, Pickens and two minor forts in Florida—remained in hands loyal to the Union.

"We are not enemies, but friends. We must not be enemies. Though passion may have strained, it must not break our bonds of affection. The mystic chords of memory, stretching from every battlefield and patriot grave to every living heart and hearth stone all over this broad land, will yet swell the chorus of the Union, when again touched, as surely they will be, by the better angels of our nature."

—ABRAHAM LINCOLN, FIRST INAUGURAL ADDRESS

Capping Lincoln's woes, his arrival in Washington after his 1,904-mile (3,064 km) train trip was marred when two separate sources warned of a possible assassination attempt as he passed through Southern-leaning Baltimore. Acting on the advice of security chief Allan Pinkerton, the President donned a cloak and slouch hat and switched trains in the middle of the night, arriving in Washington secretly on Feb. 23. Northerners and Southerners alike derided what one newspaper called the President-elect's "surreptitious nocturnal dodging."

On March 4, Lincoln stood on the steps of the U.S. Capitol and addressed the citizens of both a reduced Union and the "rebel power." He laid out his policy, urging the seceded states to return to the Union and promising, "There needs to be no bloodshed or violence, and there shall be none unless it be forced upon the national authority. The power confided to me will be used to hold, occupy, and possess the property and places belonging to the Government." He concluded with a memorable peroration that sought to remind all Americans of the "mystic chords of memory" that bound them in the Union.

True to his word, Davis' first act as President of the C.S.A. was to send a peace commission to Washington in March: Lincoln refused to meet its members, in line with his strategy of not recognizing the Confederacy as an independent entity. But on his first morning in office, Lincoln met with a military crisis he could not ignore: U.S. government property—Fort Sumter in South Carolina—was close to falling victim to a rebel siege. ■

DUELING INAUGURALS *Two weeks after Davis took the oath of office as President of the Confederacy, Abraham Lincoln was sworn in as President of the United States, on March 4, 1861. But Lincoln would preside over a diminished Union, for seven states had seceded by the time he took the oath. In order, they were: South Carolina, Mississippi, Florida, Alabama, Georgia, Louisiana and Texas. Four more states—Virginia, Arkansas, Tennessee and North Carolina—joined them following the April 12 attack on Fort Sumter in Charleston, S.C. One of Lincoln's primary concerns in his first months in office was to secure Union control over three border states—Kentucky, Missouri and Maryland, adjacent to the District of Columbia—whose residents were deeply divided over their allegiance to North or South. The Capitol dome was under construction, above, on Inauguration Day, as the old "Bulfinch dome" was replaced by the far larger one designed by Thomas J. Walter*

Clash at Fort Sumter

APRIL 12, 1861

The first salvo of the war is fired in the first state to secede from the Union, at a Federal fort in Charleston, South Carolina

FACING A REBELLION AGAINST THE UNION on the day he was sworn into office, President Abraham Lincoln extended an olive branch to Americans living in the Southern states in his Inaugural Address, but he also drew a line in the sand, pledging to exert his executive powers to maintain possession of all U.S. Government property. When Lincoln walked into his new office the next morning, he found a telegram on his desk that immediately tested his resolve on this issue. The communiqué was from Major Robert Anderson, commander of the U.S. Army garrison in Charleston, S.C., home of some of the most rabid secessionists in the South.

Since South Carolina seceded from the Union early in December, Anderson's garrison had been threatened and harassed by local "Fire-eaters"—so much so that late in the same month, the Kentucky-born Anderson moved the Federal garrison from Fort Moultrie, its home base on Sullivan's Island in Charleston Harbor, to Fort Sumter, a stronger and more easily defended facility in the center of the harbor. That decision electrified Union supporters in the North, as the Southern states had seized the momentum in the current crisis with their rapid-fire series of secessions.

But Anderson's Federal troops, if celebrated in the North, now found themselves island-bound and encircled by hostile forces, who fired their artillery at ships attempting to bring necessities to the fort. Unless he was resupplied with provisions within six weeks, Anderson wrote Lincoln early in March, he must surrender Fort Sumter to the rebels.

In the months since his election, Lincoln had held his cards closely to his chest, refusing to speculate on how the Union would deal with seceding states. Modern-day historians have described this balancing act as "masterly inactivity." But the crisis at Fort Sumter signaled that the time for inactivity was past: action was demanded. Yet Lincoln's new government was disorganized, and its lines of authority were unclear. After days of debate, Lincoln made a decision: on April 6, he ordered the U.S. Navy to send a fleet of ships to resupply and relieve the Federal garrison. A second relief expedition was dispatched to Fort Pickens at Pensacola, Fla., a similar U.S. Government stronghold surrounded by rebels.

Lincoln's show of force played into the hands of Confederate President Jefferson Davis, who was seeking to create a tipping-point incident that would decisively spur Southern states still hesitant to secede—especially the

WAR'S FIRST SALVO *The antagonists at Fort Sumter knew each other well long before the war. Union commander Robert Anderson, at left, was one of Confederate General P.G.T. Beauregard's instructors at West Point in the 1830s, and both officers distinguished themselves in the Mexican War. Beauregard, born just outside New Orleans, spent years strengthening the city's defenses before he was named as the new superintendent of West Point in January 1861. But Louisiana seceded from the Union only days later, and Beauregard soon threw in his lot with the rebellion.*

Beauregard and the Kentucky-born Anderson maintained a good relationship during the crisis at Fort Sumter, and when Anderson surrendered, Beauregard released him, allowing him to take along the tattered 33-star flag that had flown over the fort, shown at top left. Beauregard would go on to play a significant role in the First Battle of Bull Run (Manassas) and Shiloh; he also helped design the famed Stars and Bars of the Confederate battle flag. Above, Fort Sumter under fire.

wealthiest state in the South, Virginia—into joining the Confederate cause.

On April 11, as the Northern supply fleet drew near Charleston, a delegation of rebels brought Anderson a message from the Confederate commanding officer, General P.G.T. Beauregard: Withdraw from the island, or face the consequences. Anderson refused, the rebel emissaries withdrew—and in the early hours of the next morning, the first salvo of the war was fired. Its target was not only the Federal garrison at Fort Sumter: the Southern rebels were attacking the very concept of the United States, former colonies joined since 1776 in rebellion against Brit-

ain, then united by the Articles of Confederation in 1781 and the U.S. Constitution in 1787.

Outmanned, outgunned and out of supplies, Anderson's garrison surrendered around 2:30 p.m. on April 13. Lincoln argued that no state could secede from the Union without the consent of all the others, and he called the war to come an internal revolt rather than a contest between two independent states. That distinction was important, but what was more significant was that the divisions that had been simmering for decades had now ignited: shots had been fired at a U.S. fort, and its flag had been hauled down. America's Civil War had begun. ■

AFTER THE BATTLE *This picture of the interior of Fort Sumter was taken the day after the Union surrender. Locals called it Evacuation Day, echoing the term used by Bostonians to describe the withdrawal of British forces from their city on March 17, 1776. The facility was badly damaged during the 34 hours of bombardment, with shells descending on it at the rate of two per minute*

CORBIS

Center of the Storm

Charleston, S.C., was one of the South's great port cities, and as such, it had been strongly fortified against foreign invaders in the first decades of the 19th century. Batteries ringed the inner harbor, which was home to three large forts: Moultrie, Johnson and Sumter. An estimated 5,500 rebel troops surrounded Sumter and its 85 Union officers and men.

As shown in this map made by Union cartographer Robert Sneden, Fort Sumter, in the center of the harbor, was within firing distance of 15 separate batteries. The Southern assault began about 4:30 on the morning of April 12, when a mortar fired from Fort Johnson burst over the harbor, a signal to open fire. The barrage from three sides quickly set fire to the fort.

That morning, the first few ships of the Union's relief fleet approached the harbor; the convoy was late, having been scattered by a severe storm. But the supply ships were no match for the land-based rebel batteries, and on April 13, following 34 hours of constant shelling, Anderson surrendered. General Beauregard allowed the commander and his men safe passage back to the North.

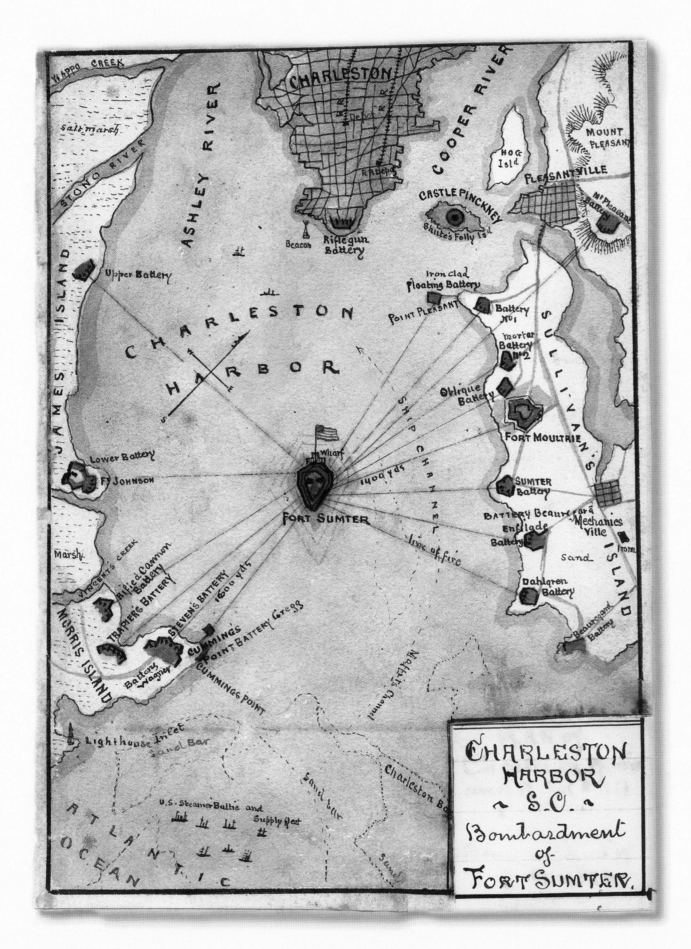

Americans Go to War

North and South struggle to turn state militias into real armies

Country Cousins

In June 1861 these men of the Third Arkansas Infantry Regiment mustered in Arkadelphia, Ark. Scorned as "country boys" when they arrived in Vicksburg, Miss., to apply to join the Confederate Army, they were turned down. But political connections obtained a place for them in Robert E. Lee's Army of Northern Virginia. The only Arkansans to serve on the Eastern front distinguished themselves at some of the war's pivotal moments, fighting at the sunken road at Antietam and at Devil's Den at Gettysburg.

White House Duty

When the war broke out in April 1861, neither side was prepared for the four years of battle that would follow. In Washington, new President Abraham Lincoln, sworn in the previous month, found himself isolated and surrounded by Maryland, a border state where many Southern sympathizers lived, particularly in Baltimore.

After Fort Sumter was taken, the capital was essentially unguarded until Union troops began arriving late in April. Here, Clay's Battalion, irregular troops raised by Kentucky politician and slavery foe Cassius M. Clay, stand guard outside the White House.

Protecting the Iron Horse

Workers erect wooden palisades on Duke Street in Alexandria, Va., to protect the Orange & Alexandria railroad tracks in 1861. The line was fought over throughout the conflict and was a frequent target of cavalry raids. The war offered the spectacle of cavalry divisions concentrating on gaining control of the technology that would ultimately make them obsolete.

Empire State Warriors

Soldiers of the 22nd New York State Militia posed for a portrait outside a wigwam-style tent at Harpers Ferry, Va., in 1861. Like many other soldiers who enlisted in state militias, these men from northern New York State were later folded into the Union Army as a more formal infantry regiment that saw action at the Second Battle of Bull Run and Fredericksburg.

Young Hero

Ohio boy Johnny Clem became the toast of the North after the Battle of Shiloh, in which the drummer boy supposedly was knocked unconscious when an artillery shell tore through his drum. The story is almost certainly false, having been conflated with the song *The Drummer Boy of Shiloh,* written by William S. Hays.

But if Clem did not serve at Shiloh, his actual experiences during the war are just as fascinating as the myth. When only 10 he sought to enlist in the Union Army; allowed to do so at 12, he was spoiled by the older troops. He saw action at the Battle of Chickamauga in eastern Tennessee in 1863 , where he is said to have gone to battle bearing a musket cut down to his size. As the story goes, he shot a Confederate officer who asked him to surrender.

After that battle, Clem was promoted to sergeant, becoming the youngest soldier ever to be a noncommissioned officer in the U.S. Army. Later he was captured by Confederate cavalry in Georgia, but he went free in a prisoner exchange, after Confederate newspapers lampooned hapless Yankees who "have to send their babies out to fight us." Nationally famous by war's end, Clem graduated high school in 1870 and joined the Army again, retiring in 1915 as the last Civil War veteran to do so; he was awarded the rank of Major General.

Called to Serve

Brothers Private Henry L. Larrabee and First Sergeant Herbert E. Larrabee served in the 17th Massachusetts Infantry Regiment. The group lost 21 men in battle in the war, and 151 to disease.

The Things They Carried

Private Albert H. Davis of New Hampshire shows off what the well-equipped Union soldier carried: a bedroll, canteen, and haversack, along with an 1841 Mississippi musket with bayonet.

Sharp-Dressed Man

The tasseled cap worn by Emery Eugene Kingin of the 4th Michigan Infantry was regulation for Zouave regiments, but his shirt and trousers appear to be nonstandard issue.

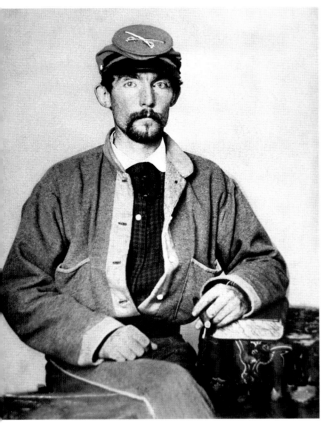

Horse Soldier

Private John Lawson Wrenn of the First Regiment of the North Carolina Cavalry served under J.E.B. Stuart, whose "Tarheels" fought in more than 160 actions.

Before the Rifle

Private Thomas Taylor served in the Louisiana Infantry, the "Tigers." His musket barrel had no grooves, unlike more accurate rifles that followed.

Gone Too Soon

The war was short for Maximilian Cabanas. The young Texan died in a Northern prison camp at age 16.

Georgia Warriors

These three young men enlisted in Company D of the Third Regiment of the Georgia Volunteer Infantry on April 26, 1861, two weeks after the clash at Fort Sumter. The two soldiers on the left, Columbus C. Taylor and Jas. D. Jackson, were killed at the Battle of Malvern Hill on July 1, 1862, at the end of the Northern invasion of Virginia known as the Peninsula Campaign. The soldier on the right, James H. Porter, served in a railroad detachment and was mustered out of the army in January 1862. This photo was taken near Richmond, Va., in the winter of 1861-62.

The Third Georgia Regiment served in the Army of Northern Virginia, seeing action in almost every major battle in the Eastern theater, including Fredericksburg, Gettysburg, Spotsylvania and the Wilderness.

The First Battle Of Bull Run

JULY 21, 1861

A Union Army finally invades Virginia, but it retreats in disarray as its green troops and cautious generals are whipped by the rebels

LIKE THE POWERFUL LOCOMOTIVES THAT played a major role in the Civil War, the two opposing sides in the conflict required a good deal of huffing and chuffing, stoking and priming before they could work up the full head of steam required to wage war. The last major U.S. conflict had been the highly successful campaign fought against Mexico in 1846-48. That conflict had gone well for the Americans, but following the victory, both the U.S. Army and Navy had lapsed into complacency. There was no better symbol of the state of the Union's military forces than its leader, General Winfield Scott. He was not only a hero of the Mexican War, he was also a veteran of the War of 1812. Turning 75 years old in 1861, "Old Fuss and Feathers" was known for falling asleep in meetings.

The rebels of the South, of course, had no standing army or navy to call upon when the war commenced, and voluntary state militias initially filled the gaps. The first months of the war were an exercise in shaking off torpor. Both sides spent them assembling men, munitions and supplies and attempting to mold them into a cohesive fighting force—for before they could make war, Abraham Lincoln and Jefferson Davis had to make armies.

The wake-up call came at a critical railroad nexus some 33 miles (53 km) west and slightly south of Washington in northern Virginia, Manassas Junction, in a battle Southerners named after that location and Northern commanders chose to call Bull Run. In many ways, this initial contest foreshadowed many that would follow in the next four years: it was fought on Southern soil, centered on a

key transportation junction, involved heavy loss of life and was won when the outnumbered Confederate commanders and armies proved much more able and nimble than their Union counterparts. And though the battle has come down through history as a great Southern victory, it was also the first of many engagements in which the winning side squandered a chance to follow up on a successful battle and deal a mortal blow to the foe.

When months went by following the fall of Fort Sumter with very little military activity, Northerners began clamoring that the battle must be taken to the rebels. Top Union commanders resisted, advising against sending untrained armies into the fray, but President Lincoln strongly believed it was important for the Union to strike a blow as early as possible against the Confederacy. And the calendar was working against him as well: the Northern recruits who had responded to his call for volunteers after Fort Sumter had signed up for only a single 90-day term, which would expire by late summer. On June 29, Lincoln forced the hand of his cautious military advisors, ordering his generals to mount an offensive in Virginia.

The task fell to Major General Irvin McDowell, a Mexican War veteran who led an army of 35,000 men out of Washington toward Manassas; if the Union could

AFTERMATH *In March 1862, eight months after the initial Battle of Bull Run, Union soldiers returned to Manassas Junction after the Confederates withdrew from the area to defend Richmond from the Union invasion expected that summer. At right, Northern troops examine positions fortified by the South*

win control of this key transportation nexus, Lincoln and his generals agreed, perhaps they could isolate the rebel capital, Richmond, some 102 miles (164 k) to the southeast of the railway junction.

Facing McDowell was the hero of Fort Sumter, General Pierre G.T. Beauregard, whose Army of the Potomac consisted of some 22,000 men. Another large Confederate army was not far away: General Joseph Johnston's Army of the Shenandoah, some 10,000 strong, was stationed west of Manassas, and McDowell expected a second Union army, led by Major General Robert Patterson, would keep them bottled up.

Patterson failed to do so, and this setback would determine the outcome of the battle. In a development that would be repeated many times in the years to come, the Southern armies, fighting to defend their homeland, easily eluded the Northern "invaders." While McDowell's army slowly clanked its way across northern Virginia—its painful progress carefully monitored by Confederate outposts—Johnston's brigades slipped past those of Patterson.

A WALL OF STONE On the day of battle, July 21, the green Union troops carried out a surprise attack on the Confederates' left flank that almost carried the day, but the arrival of Johnston's divisions at the battlefield at a critical moment helped win the day for the rebels. As the Confederates retreated uphill near Henry House, home of bedridden widow Judith Henry, a heroic stand by one of these late-arriving brigades from the Shenandoah Valley—Virginia troops under the command of General Thomas Jonathan Jackson—held the line for the Confederates, allowing them to regroup. The tide of battle had turned, and the legend of the South's "Stonewall Brigade" was born.

The emboldened Southerners now mounted a furious countercharge, and for the first time in the war the famed "rebel yell" was heard on the battlefield. The wildly keening sound, sometimes compared to the wail of a banshee, unnerved the Northerners, whose retreat turned into an ignominious, unruly flight. (The actual sound of the rebel yell has been lost to history:

WHO'S WHO? *The two sides in the conflict were so ill prepared for combat early in the war that their uniforms were not, well, uniform. Early on, troops of both sides fought in the Zouave garments worn by French troops in tropical Africa. At Bull Run, Southern soldiers attired in blue were mistaken for friendly troops by Union forces, who held their fire, allowing the rebels to gain a superior position. After Bull Run, both sides hurried to outfit their troops in their now-familiar blue and gray uniforms*

47

according to one Union veteran:"if you claim you heard it and weren't scared that means you never heard it.")

A SOLDIER'S VIEW Corporal Samuel J. English of the Second Rhode Island Volunteers described the scene that followed in a letter home. "The R.I. regiments, the New York 71st and the New Hampshire 2nd were drawn into a line to cover the retreat, but an officer galloped wildly into the column crying the enemy is upon us, and off they started like a flock of sheep every man for himself and the devil take the hindermost; while the rebels' shot and shell fell like rain among our exhausted troops. As we gained the cover of the woods the stampede became even more frightful, for the baggage wagons and ambulances became entangled with the artillery and rendered the scene even more dreadful than the battle, while the plunging of the horses broke the lines of our infantry, and prevented any successful formation out of the question."

As they retreated in a mob up the Warrenton Turnpike toward Washington, the panic-stricken Union troops collided with well-dressed Northern sight-seers, some of whom had arrived at the battlefield bearing picnic baskets, as if attending a sporting match. For months, Confederates would amuse themselves with exaggerated tales of the North's "Great Skedaddle" from Bull Run.

There was no amusement in Washington when Lincoln and his Cabinet received the news of the Union debacle. Alerted by Secretary of State William H. Seward, Lincoln went to the telegraph office at the War Department in the early evening, where he read a dispatch from a Federal captain of engineers: "The day is lost. Save Washington and the remnants of this army ... The routed troops will not re-form."

Embarrassment turned to dismay when hosts of disorganized, beaten soldiers began trudging into the capital. The war's first great battle had served notice that the Southern insurrection, despite the wishful thinking of Union supporters, would not be put down in days or even months. Indeed, it would be eight long months before another Union Army dared to venture into Virginia. ∎

★

The Commanders at Bull Run
Savvy Confederate generals hand the Union a stunning setback

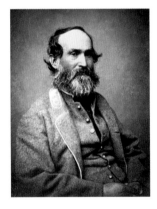

JUBAL EARLY

The West Point graduate from Virginia served in the Seminole Wars before turning to a law practice. Forty-four in 1861, he initially opposed secession but soon joined the rebel cause. He came to attention for his courage at Bull Run and rapidly rose under the patronage of Robert E. Lee, taking part in most of the key battles in the Eastern theater, including Gettysburg.

JOSEPH JOHNSTON

The Virginian was 54 in 1861 and a veteran of both the Mexican and Seminole Wars. He resigned his post as brigadier general to join the Confederate army, the highest-ranking Union officer to do so. Wounded while commanding Southern troops in the Peninsular Campaign, upon his recovery he was sent to be the Confederates' top general in the West.

THOMAS J. JACKSON

Jackson, 37 in 1861, was an obscure, eccentric professor at the Virginia Military Institute who would soon become one of the war's greatest leaders. "There stands Jackson like a stone wall," General Barnard Bee is said to have cried at Bull Run. "Rally behind the Virginians!" Jackson had earned the nickname that he would carry into history.

IRVIN MCDOWELL

Forty-two in 1861, McDowell was an Ohio-born West Point graduate (where one classmate was his Bull Run foe, P.G.T. Beauregard) who had served with distinction in the Mexican War. He was replaced after his defeat at Bull Run by George McClellan, but in an ironic twist of fate, he shared the blame for the North's second defeat at Bull Run, in the battle of 1862.

★

A Union Disaster

Robert Knox Sneden, a Union cartographer, made this sketch of the course of the battle at Bull Run, where Union troops attacked Confederates guarding the railroad hub at Manassas Junction. The battle is recalled as an unseemly rout of the North. But the Union came close to winning, thanks to Irvin McDowell's decision to hold off attacking P.G.T. Beauregard's well-entrenched troops along Bull Run around Blackburn's Ford. Instead, McDowell sent half his men north and west of the railroad lines that were his primary objective and attacked Beauregard's left flank, which was exposed and lightly manned. However, the Union flanking march allowed time for the troops of General Joseph Johnston's Army of the Shenandoah to begin arriving by rail at Manassas Junction—a most timely appearance.

On the morning of July 21, McDowell's army crossed Bull Run at Sudley Ford, far west of where Beauregard expected the attack. The Yankees easily rolled back the Confederate troops, who retreated to the east. A second wave of Union troops, led by General William Tecumseh Sherman, began flooding across the Stone Bridge, and the day looked dark for the Confederates. Yet it was here that General Thomas J. Jackson's troops from Virginia, among Johnston's late arrivals, made their stand, stopping the advancing Yankees in their tracks. As Johnston's full army poured onto the field, the Southerners now turned the tide, attacking the Union troops and sending them fleeing pell-mell back across the river and, in some cases, all the way to Washington. The rebels could have pursued and done more damage to the Union troops, but they chose to hold their position.

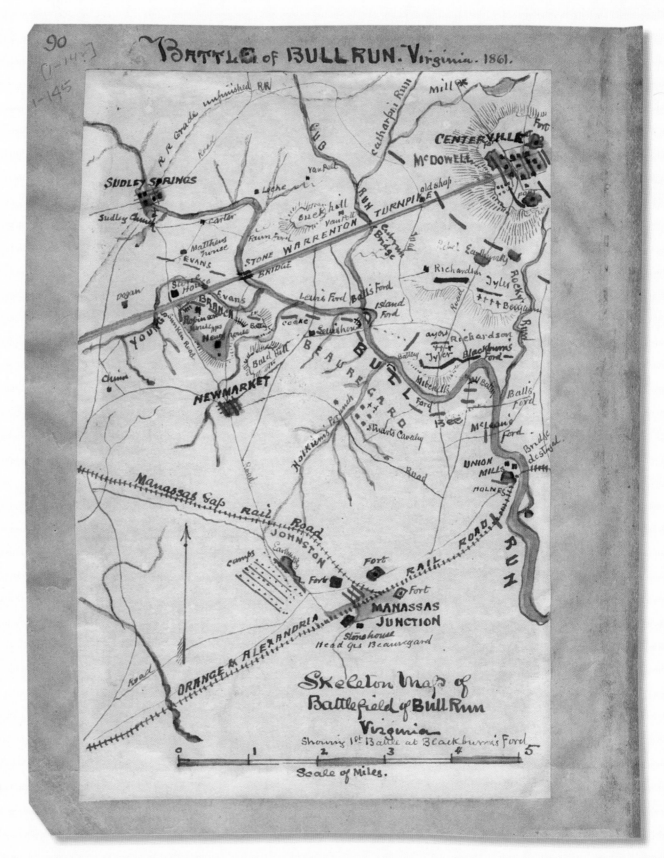

The Battle of Wilson's Creek

AUGUST 10, 1861

Confederates advance into Missouri and tangle with Union troops as North and South vie to control the border states

AMONG THE COMPELLING ISSUES THAT Abraham Lincoln faced as he struggled to get his bearings early in his presidency was the status of the border states. These three hotbeds of turmoil were far from peas in a pod. Missouri, a frontier state on the nation's far Western border, was equally divided between slavery's foes and advocates; it had been rocked in the 1850s by the battles over the future of Kansas, the territory to its west. Kentucky, a mountain state notched between Ohio to the north and Tennessee to the south, looked both ways in its cultural and political leanings. Maryland was home to the U.S. capital in the District of Columbia, but it was also a slave state that was a hotbed of Southern sympathizers.

Lincoln knew that control of Kentucky and Missouri would be vital to the Union war effort. His first task was to select a commander in this theater, the Department of the West, and he believed he had the right man in John C. Frémont, the noted explorer who in the 1856 election had been the first presidential candidate of the Republican Party. Lincoln appointed Frémont to command a large area west of the Mississippi (which modern historians of the war call the Trans-Mississippi West), as well as Kentucky. Illinois was soon added to Frémont's brief as well.

There was one problem, however: Frémont was ardent in his pursuit of glory. His shenanigans as he tried to wrest control of California from Mexico in 1846 as a young U.S. Army officer ended in a court martial for mutiny and a guilty verdict, though he was later pardoned. But his adventures as an explorer had won him national attention and the nickname "The Pathfinder"—even though, in the course of his journeys, he had led men to their death as his zeal for renown outpaced his common sense.

Frémont was based in St. Louis, and his first concern was Missouri, parts of which leaned strongly secessionist. The Army officer who held the temporary command in St. Louis before Frémont was appointed, Brigadier General Nathaniel Lyon, was a Connecticut-born foe of slavery who was eager to take the war to the rebels. Acting largely on his own, he had already taken prisoners at a camp of Southern-leaning militias ordered by Governor Claiborne Fox Jackson to gather outside St. Louis.

When Frémont took charge, he faced a pair of immediate threats: Lyon was now moving out of St. Louis to counter an army of pro-South Missourians led by Major General Sterling Price, a former governor of the state. An even larger threat was bubbling in Illinois, where 6,000 Confederates were advancing upriver, aiming for Cairo, the key location where the Ohio River flows into the Mississippi, then lightly held by Union troops.

Frémont made the right choice, sending Union reinforcements to Cairo and instructing Lyon to retreat for the moment, since Frémont had no more troops to send him. But as it turned out, Lyon was just as foolhardy as Frémont: ignoring his superior's wishes, he continued his advance toward Springfield, hoping to head off Price, who had now met up with Brigadier General Benjamin McCulloch, a Texan who led a battle-ready group of soldiers from Arkansas, Louisiana and Texas. That brought the total number of Southern troops in the area to more than 13,000, while Lyon only had 5,500 men.

On Aug. 9, Lyon and his subordinate officer, Colonel Franz Sigel, a German-born leader popular with St. Louis' strongly pro-Union German immigrant population, approached the rebel forces, camped along Wilson's Creek some 12 miles (19 km) southwest of Springfield. Though he was outnumbered 2 to 1, Lyon devised a non-standard battle plan that would later be made famous by Robert E.

THE GENERALS *Sterling Price, top, was a Mexican War hero and former Missouri governor who sided with the secessionists.*

The Union's Nathaniel Lyon, bottom, harassed militia units ordered by Missouri's pro-South Governor Claiborne Fox Jackson to gather outside St. Louis, then moved against Price's troops, sending them in retreat to central and then southwest Missouri

BORDER WAR *Confusion prevailed at times during the Battle of Wilson's Creek, the war's second major conflict. As at Bull Run, similar uniforms on opposing sides added to the disarray. Union troops under Franz Sigel were wearing gray, as were Louisiana rebels under Benjamin McCulloch, who penetrated close to Sigel's artillery as Union troops held their fire.*

Above, General Nathaniel Lyon is killed while rallying Union troops on horseback. He was the first Union general to die in the war

Lee: he would divide his forces, sending Sigel's units that night on a flanking march to approach McCulloch's rebels from the south, while he would attack Price's divisions head on from the north the next morning.

On the day of battle, Lyon's tactics seemed to be succeeding, as he attacked at dawn and his troops pressed Price hard. But Price's men rallied as the fighting surged around high ground soon named Bloody Hill. To the south, rebel troops, in particular the Louisiana Pelicans, took Sigel's artillery positions by storm, then headed for Bloody Hill to aid Price. When Lyon mounted his horse to rally his men, he was shot and killed, and the beaten Union soldiers retreated to Springfield. The second major battle of the war ended in a Confederate victory, but Missouri's future was still in play.

On Aug. 30, Frémont attempted to take charge of that future, declaring martial law across the state and claiming he would execute any rebels he found, seize their property and free their slaves. In short, Frémont was issuing a sort of one-man Emancipation Proclamation, without even consulting Lincoln. This was a step much too far, much too early: in the fight to win the hearts and minds of border-state citizens, it was likely to drive many Missouri and Kentucky residents into the Confederate camp. Lincoln was forced to revoke Frémont's orders, and on Nov. 2, the President removed the rash commander.

But Frémont's impetuosity sometimes paid dividends, and it did so in this case. Before he departed his post, he appointed a disgraced former U.S. Army officer who had only recently rejoined the military to lead the Union troops at Cairo. That officer, Ulysses S. Grant, would soon emerge as the leader Lincoln needed to beat the rebels. ■

51

1862

———◆———

"We have driven McClellan out of his fortifications & pursued him 20 miles, taking 50 pieces of artillery & tens of thousands prisoners. Still he claims that he has gained a great victory. The art of lying can go no farther."

—D.H. HILL, CONFEDERATE BRIGADIER GENERAL, DURING THE UNION'S PENINSULA CAMPAIGN IN VIRGINIA

INTRUDERS *In March 1862, the Confederates abandoned their position at Manassas Junction, Va., site of the July 1861 rebel victory, as they prepared for a Union invasion of Virginia, the Peninsula Campaign. Below, local children observe Union cavalry soldiers across Manassas Creek. In August 1862 a second great battle would be fought on this site*

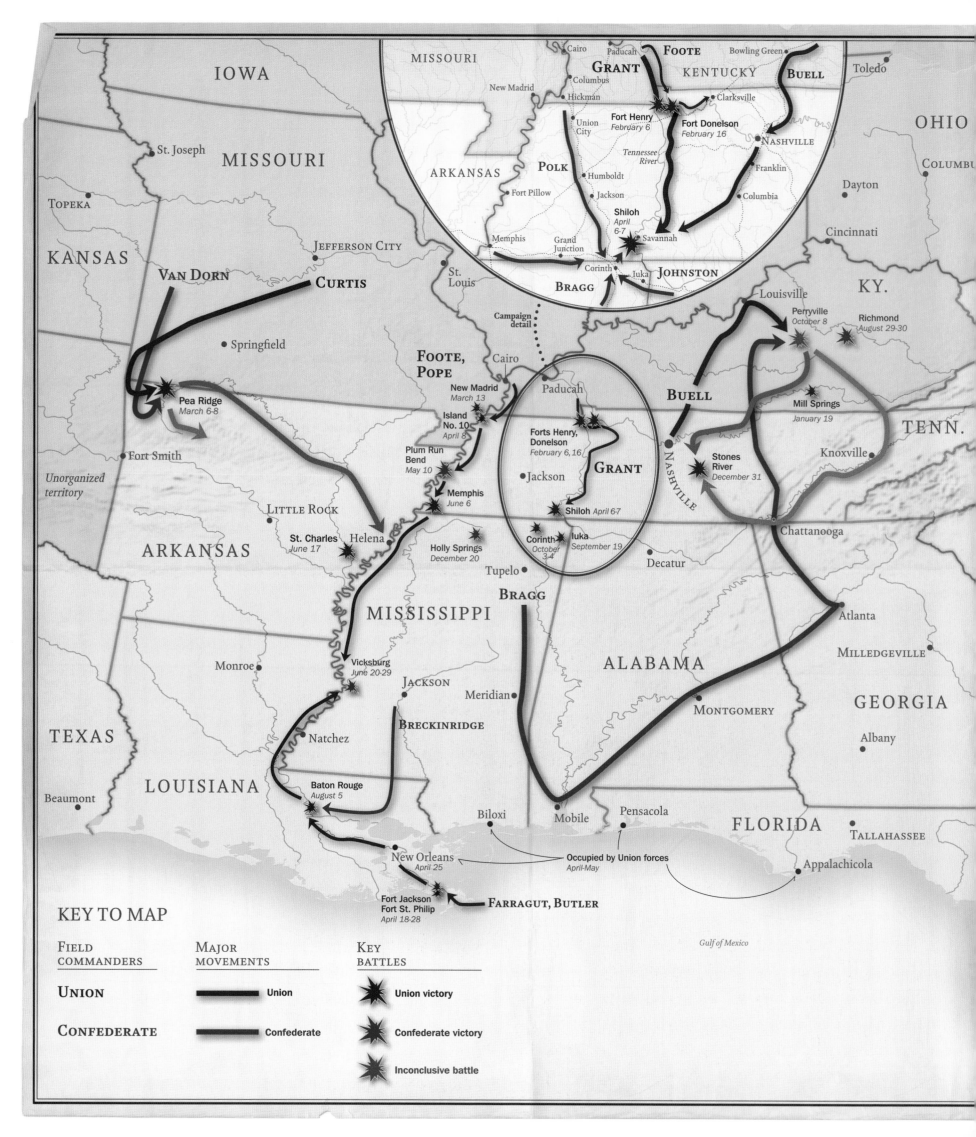

IOWA

MISSOURI

Cairo
Paducah
Bowling Green
Toledo

GRANT
FOOTE
KENTUCKY
BUELL

Columbus
Clarksville

New Madrid

Hickman

Union City
Fort Henry
February 6
Fort Donelson
February 16
NASHVILLE

ARKANSAS
POLK
Tennessee River
Franklin

Fort Pillow
Humboldt
Columbia

Jackson

MISSOURI

Memphis
Grand Junction
Shiloh
April 6-7
Savannah

St. Joseph

Corinth
Iuka
JOHNSTON

Topeka
MISSOURI
Jefferson City
BRAGG

Cincinnati

KANSAS
VAN DORN
CURTIS
St. Louis
KY.

Louisville

Springfield
FOOTE, POPE
Cairo
Perryville
October 8
Richmond
August 29-30

Pea Ridge
March 6-8
New Madrid
March 13
Paducah
BUELL

Fort Smith
Island No. 10
April 8
Forts Henry, Donelson
February 6, 16
Mill Springs
January 19

Plum Run Bend
May 10
Nashville
TENN.

GRANT
Knoxville

Unorganized territory
Jackson
Stones River
December 31

LITTLE ROCK
Memphis
June 6
Shiloh *April 6-7*

St. Charles
June 17
Helena
Holly Springs
December 20
Corinth
October 3-4
Iuka
September 19
Chattanooga

ARKANSAS
Tupelo
Decatur

MISSISSIPPI
BRAGG
Atlanta

Monroe
MILLEDGEVILLE

Vicksburg
June 20-29
ALABAMA
GEORGIA

TEXAS
JACKSON
Meridian

Natchez
BRECKINRIDGE
MONTGOMERY
Albany

LOUISIANA
Baton Rouge
August 5

Beaumont
Biloxi
Mobile
Pensacola
FLORIDA
TALLAHASSEE

New Orleans
April 25
Occupied by Union forces
April-May
Appalachicola

Fort Jackson
Fort St. Philip
April 18-28
FARRAGUT, BUTLER

Gulf of Mexico

KEY TO MAP

FIELD COMMANDERS	MAJOR MOVEMENTS	KEY BATTLES
UNION	Union	Union victory
CONFEDERATE	Confederate	Confederate victory
		Inconclusive battle

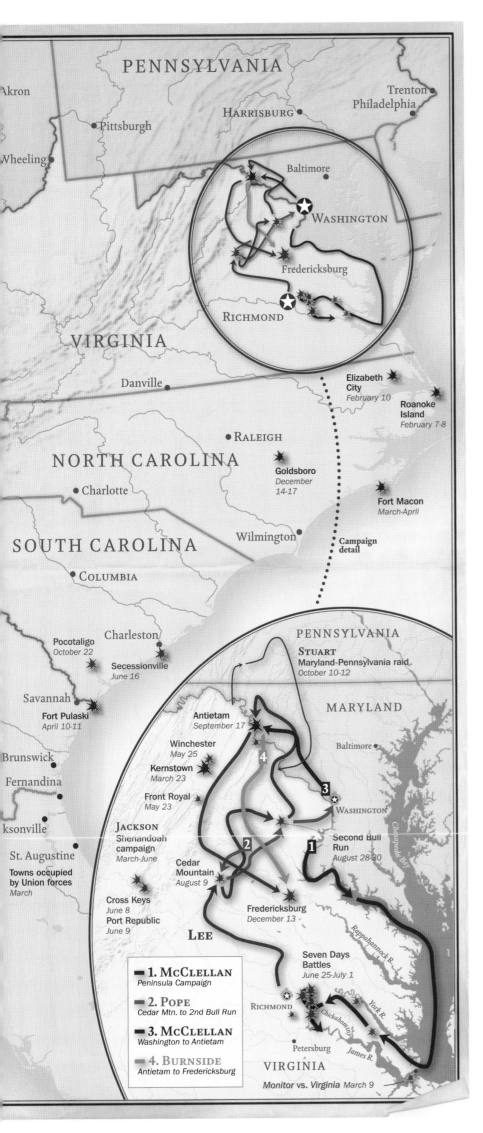

Towns occupied
by Union forces
March

1. **McClellan**
   Peninsula Campaign

2. **Pope**
   Cedar Mtn. to 2nd Bull Run

3. **McClellan**
   Washington to Antietam

4. **Burnside**
   Antietam to Fredericksburg

Monitor vs. Virginia March 9

1862
Situation Report

After a year of few battles, the war begins in earnest when the North invades Virginia in March and the South invades Maryland in September. In the West, the Union makes significant advances in Tennessee.

Feb. 6 Union General U.S. Grant captures Fort Henry in Tennessee. Ten days later he takes control of an important rebel fortress on the Cumberland River, Fort Donelson.

March 9 At Hampton Roads off the Virginia coast, the C.S.A. ironclad *Virginia* battles the Union ironclad *Monitor* to a draw, ushering in a new age of nautical warfare.

March 17 The Peninsula Campaign begins as General George McClellan's Army of the Potomac advances from Washington onto the Virginia Peninsula, aiming to attack the Confederate capital, Richmond, from the southeast.

April 6-7 A Confederate surprise attack on Grant's unprepared troops at Shiloh on the Tennessee River results in a major battle in which the Union troops weather an initial beating and then drive the rebels from the field.

April 25 Union ships under the command of Flag Officer David Farragut capture New Orleans, a major seaport.

May 8-June 9 General Stonewall Jackson outwits three Union armies in the Shenandoah Valley Campaign.

May 31 In the Battle of Seven Pines, rebels beat Union troops outside Richmond. General Robert E. Lee assumes command of the Army of Northern Virginia the next day.

June 25-July 1 In the Seven Days Battles, Lee drives McClellan's troops away from Richmond. The North wins a battle at Malvern Hill on July 1, but the Peninsula Campaign fails and the Union troops return to Washington.

Aug. 28-30 Union troops under General John Pope are defeated in the Second Battle of Bull Run.

Sept. 17 After Lee's surprise invasion of Maryland on Sept. 4, the armies collide at Antietam. Lee is defeated, but most of his army escapes. Lincoln issues a preliminary Emancipation Proclamation on Sept. 22.

Dec. 13 New Union General Ambrose Burnside invades Virginia but is badly beaten at the Battle of Fredericksburg.

The War at Sea

As a Union blockade of rebel ports begins to turn the screws on the South's economy, a brilliant dash wins New Orleans for the North

THE CIVIL WAR IS REMEMBERED FOR ITS great battles on land—Shiloh and Antietam and Gettysburg. But many students of the war argue that the Union's eventual triumph was in large part due to its victories on water, from the North's naval blockade of Southern ports to its battles to control the waterways of the West. Surprisingly enough, the vision behind the Union's maritime strategy was put forth very early in the conflict, not by a leader of the U.S. Navy but by top Army commander General Winfield Scott.

In May 1861, only a month after the war began, Scott outlined a strategy in which the Union would wage economic war on the South by blockading its ports, thus strangling the region's income from its vital cotton exports and denying it the imported goods needed to wage war. Critics derided this proposed strategy, calling it the "Anaconda Plan," and the name stuck. Scott's corollary proposal was to establish Union control of the entire length of the Mississippi River, cutting the Deep South off from the area known as the Trans-Mississippi West.

Even before Scott proposed this strategy, President Lincoln had acted to begin a blockade of Southern ports, issuing an order to do so on April 19, 1861, one week after the war began with the shelling of Fort Sumter. But releasing the order was one thing, fulfilling it quite another. At the time, the U.S. Navy consisted of some 90 ships—on paper. In truth, only 42 ships were seaworthy, and many Navy officers were defecting to the South. So the blockade began with an improvised flotilla of merchant and fishing ships hastily outfitted with armor and cannon. But Lincoln's Secretary of the Navy, Gideon Welles, proved an energetic and effective administrator and builder: by war's end, the U.S. Navy consisted of 671 ships.

The Atlantic Coast, closest to England and France, the

DAVID FARRAGUT *The aggressive seaman served as a midshipman in the War of 1812 when he was only 11 years old. His well-connected foster brother, David Dixon Porter, helped win him command of the fleet he led to the capture of New Orleans. At left is a contemporary illustration of Farragut's ships trading salvos with the guns of Forts Jackson and St. Philip*

South's primary trading partners, was the focus of the blockade. To maintain it, the North would need local coaling stations for its steam-driven warships, so as to avoid long refueling voyages. In 1861 a series of Union attacks met with success, as small Southern forts near Cape Hatteras, N.C., and Port Royal, S.C., fell to Northern troops. In 1862 the North launched a far more extensive operation, supervised by General Ambrose Burnside, that involved coordinating a flotilla of some 60 ships with 13,000 Army troops in an attack on the key port of Roanoke, N.C. Burnside succeeded: the North captured the key port and took control of major local railroad lines.

The Northern blockade soon began to exert its strangling effect on Southern commerce, spawning one of the war's most colorful sideshows, as Southern ships—"blockade runners"—vied to elude the Union craft patrolling rebel harbors. Historians recognize the blockade as an important component of eventual Union victory, though debate still rages over the full extent of its impact. But there is no debate about another naval triumph that occurred early in 1862: when Flag Officer David G. Farragut captured the South's largest city, the great port of New Orleans, he dealt a crippling blow to the rebellion.

New Orleans was guarded by twin forts at the mouth of the Mississippi, Fort Jackson on the west bank and, slightly upstream, Fort St. Philip on the east. Between them a heavy iron chain stretched across the river, linked to hulks of obsolete ships deliberately sunk to create a barrier. On April 18, 1862, Farragut's fleet of 17 ships drew close to Fort Jackson and began shelling the fortresses,

whose batteries of heavy cannon fired back. When five days of Union shelling failed to damage the installations, Farragut resorted to a gamble: he sent two gunboats to ram the chain and breach it. When it snapped, Farragut ordered his fleet to run the gauntlet of fire between the two forts. For 90 hellish minutes, beginning about 2 a.m. on April 24, the Union ships exchanged fire with the guns in the fortresses and with a rebel defending fleet that included two ironclad ships, one not quite completed. Yet all but one of the Union ships survived the passage: the rebels' primary defensive barrier had been bypassed.

On April 25 Farragut sent a delegation to accept the surrender of the city, which had been only lightly defended by local militiamen who had now withdrawn. Soon 15,000 federal troops, marching upstream from the Gulf, joined Farragut's force, and General Benjamin Butler took control of the graceful old city. The Confederate grip on the Mississippi had been loosened but not completely broken: it would be 15 months before General Grant captured the last rebel stronghold, at Vicksburg, Miss. But with New Orleans in Union hands, the South's chances of winning the conflict had been sharply reduced. ■

> "[General Benjamin Butler is] a brutal tyrant … sent … to oppress, rob, assault and trample upon our people in every manner which the most fiendish ingenuity and most wanton cruelty could devise."
>
> —ALEXANDER WALKER, SOUTHERN JOURNALIST, ABOUT THE UNION GENERAL IN COMMAND OF OCCUPIED NEW ORLEANS

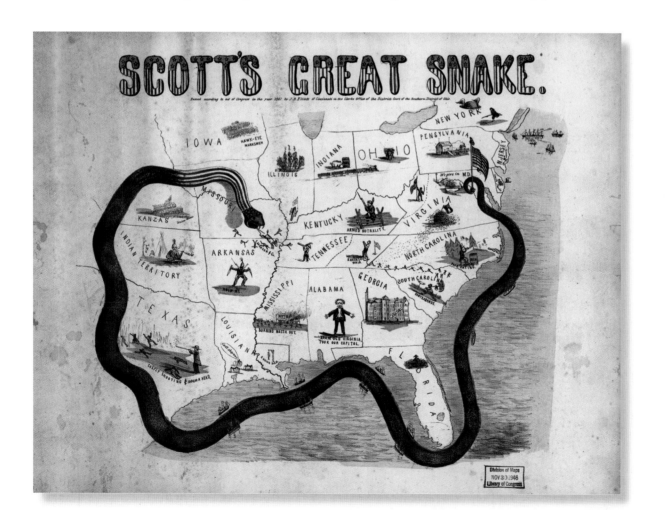

THROTTLING THE REBELS *This Northern cartoon mocked General Winfield Scott's proposed strategy of quelling the rebellion by a blockade of coastal ports as unworkable, but as the Union gradually applied more and more pressure to the flow of goods into and out of the South, the results were felt both on the battlefield and in Southern towns and cities. By war's end, the blockade was a critical part of the "total war" strategy championed by General U.S. Grant and other leaders, which advocated not only attacking the rebel troops but also laying waste to their infrastructure of farms, bridges, ports and railroads.*

Control of the Mississippi was a primary element of the Anaconda Plan. The capture of New Orleans relatively early in the war was a major Union victory, and when Grant took control of Vicksburg, Miss., 15 months later, the Confederacy was effectively partitioned into a patchwork of small, independent elements that could be beaten on the battlefield

IRONCLAD DISAGREEMENT
The Monitor *and* Virginia *trade fire at close quarters. The Union vessel, in the foreground, was described by some as a "cheesebox on a raft." Others called it "a tin can on a shingle"*

Floating Fortresses Usher in a New Kind of Naval War

Two futuristic vessels put on a show off the Virginia coast—but no winner is declared

The most renowned naval duel of the Civil War ended in a draw, when two highly innovative ironclad ships clashed in a four-hour skirmish off Hampton Roads, Va., early in 1862, with neither striking a knockout blow. The Northern blockade of rebel ports was particularly galling here, for it was the sea lane by which rebel leaders in the capital of Richmond communicated with the outside world. To break the Union cordon, Southern naval architects envisioned a powerful new craft. They raised the remains of the warship U.S.S. *Merrimack,* scuttled by Northern sailors when they evacuated the U.S. Navy yards at Norfolk, Va. The ship was renamed the C.S.S. *Virginia* and was covered in iron plates, slope-sided to deflect gunfire. Designed to be a floating battering ram, the big ship was 275 ft. (84 m) long, far larger than the 175-ft. ironclads used by General U.S. Grant on the Western rivers in 1862. Yet its size and weight made it sluggish in the water.

When Northern leaders got wind of these developments, they commissioned a contest to design an ironclad vessel that could take on the *Virginia.* The winner was Swedish-born naval engineer John Ericsson, who was forced to build a smaller ship than he hoped to in order to meet the *Virginia's* projected completion date. His U.S.S. *Monitor* was far more advanced in design than the *Virginia:* most of its bulk was below the waterline, leaving only a small pilothouse and a large turret with two guns on its deck. The turret was the most remarkable aspect of the ship, for it revolved. The *Monitor's* crew could thus find the best line of fire on a foe simply by rotating the turret, rather than by turning the entire ship. But the vessel's design proved far from seaworthy, and the Union Navy was forced to tow the craft to face the *Virginia* at Hampton Roads.

On March 8 the *Virginia,* on its maiden voyage, rammed one Union ship and sank her, then drove a second aground, where it burned. That night the *Monitor* arrived at Hampton Roads, and the next afternoon the two ships pounded each other relentlessly, in a classic matchup of agility vs. sheer muscle. Neither ship prevailed, and the *Monitor* finally withdrew after a shell exploded on its pilothouse, temporarily blinding the ship's commander, Lieutenant John Worden. The *Virginia* also retired, and the two ships never again met in combat. Confederates claimed to have won the sea battle, but they lost the larger naval war: the Union blockade of Hampton Roads continued. The *Virginia* was blown apart and scuttled when the Union took control of Norfolk in May 1862. The *Monitor* sank in heavy seas on Dec. 31, 1862, off Cape Hatteras, though the Union would build more advanced versions of the craft later in the war. The wreck of the *Monitor* was located in 1973, and its revolutionary turret was brought to the surface in 2002.

A Sailor's Life
Civil War ships married old technology to new—and changed flags frequently

Powder Monkey

Apprentice sailors on warships assigned to keeping cannoneers supplied with gunpowder were dubbed "powder monkeys." This young man aboard the U.S.S. *New Hampshire,* circa 1864-65, seems to have the poise of an old hand. The *New Hampshire* was one of the Union ships helping maintain the naval blockade of the harbor at Port Royal S.C., midway between Charleson, S.C. and Savannah, Ga. Though primarily a store ship that carried supplies, as a Navy vessel it carried a battery of guns. Its history was unusual: it was commissioned in 1816 as a 74-gun warship to be named the U.S.S. *Alabama,* and though it was ready to be put to sea in 1825, it was kept in drydock for decades, as the U.S. Navy engaged in few conflicts during that period. The ship was completed, renamed the *New Hampshire* and launched in 1864.

Artillery Drill

Perhaps showing off for visitors, well-dressed sailors on a Union ship, most likely the U.S.S. *Hunchback,* run through a gun drill with a light cannon suited for top-deck duty. The craft was not really a warship: it was built as a New York City ferryboat in 1852 but was purchased by the U.S. Navy and refitted as a gunboat late in 1861. Renamed the *Hunchback,* it saw extensive duty as a blockade ship off North Carolina and supported land assaults on Confederate forts in the area. After the war it was decommissioned and returned to ferry duty in New York City with a new name honoring a landlubber: *General Grant.*

Shifting Allegiances

Many ships of the Civil War era, like the U.S.S. *Hendrick Hudson* at left, were hybrid craft that combined the old technology of sailing ships with the modern steam engine. The ship changed flags during the war: originally built as a merchantman in Brooklyn, N.Y., in 1859, it was seized by the Confederacy in 1862, renamed the C.S.S. *Florida* and put into service as a blockade runner. Only months later, it was captured by the aptly named U.S.S. *Pursuit* and was put on blockade duty around Florida as the *Hendrick Hudson*.

For the remainder of the war, the *Hudson* plied the coastal waters of Florida, where it captured several blockade runners and took part in various land expeditions. The ship was lost at sea off Havana, Cuba, in 1867.

Dining al Fresco

Sailors aboard the U.S.S. *Monitor* await their meal; though most daily life aboard the ship was conducted belowdecks, when possible it was preferable to let the smoke from the cooking fire vent into the open air. One sailor stands atop the revolutionary rotating gun turret that distinguished the ship.

Built in great haste in the Greeenpoint district of Brooklyn, N.Y. (then an independent city), the *Monitor* carried a crew of some 60 officers and men. But its unique design, the first of its kind, proved unsafe on the open sea: its flat top deck was easily swamped by large ocean waves. When the *Monitor* sank, only 10 months after it was launched, it was amid a gale and high seas off Cape Hatteras, N.C. Sixteen crew members died.

The *Monitor* design was more successful on rivers, where waves were not high. Later in the war, updated versions of the craft served the Union well in campaigns along the Mississippi and on the James River in Virginia; their top decks sloped to help repel enemy fire.

River War in the West

A tough general's campaign wins Union control of key waterways, but the South surprises the North in the Battle of Shiloh

FOR UNION SUPPORTERS, THE year 1861 brought all too few opportunities for celebration. The year's largest battle, at Bull Run, had ended in a humiliating rout, and the new commander of the Army of the Potomac, General George B. McClellan, seemed incapable of mounting an offensive against the rebels, whose capital, Richmond, Va., was only 107 miles (172 km) south of Washington, D.C. So when the first glimmers of good news for the North arrived from the Western theater early in 1862, they were greeted with an outburst of enthusiasm.

Like the war in the Eastern theater, the conflicts in the West revolved around the control of transportation lines, in this case the region's rivers, the primary thoroughfares for shipping food, livestock, timber, iron—and now, soldiers and guns. A second major goal involved politics. President Abraham Lincoln believed it was essential to maintain Union control of the border state of Kentucky, which was deeply divided between supporters of the U.S.A. and the C.S.A., and he hoped to wrest military control of secessionist Tennessee from the rebels as well.

In the first few months of 1862, Union soldiers and sailors managed to win a series of engagements that helped establish Union control of key rivers in Kentucky and Tennessee and the essential Mississippi River port city of New Orleans. Along the way, a pair of heroes emerged

for the North: the unflappable naval commander Flag Officer David G. Farragut, 61, and the grinding, no-nonsense Army general Ulysses S. Grant, 40.

While Confederates in the Eastern theater generally assumed a defensive posture, the rebels in the West, eager to win control of Kentucky, seized the initiative. The resourceful and energetic Confederate commander in the region, General Albert Sidney (A.S.) Johnston, sent troops from Tennessee to occupy Bowling Green, Ky., and he ordered the creation of a new stronghold, Fort Henry, along the Tennessee River. At the same time, he bulked up the defenses of two other important river forts, the first at Columbus, Ky., overlooking the eastern shore of the Mississippi River, and the second at Fort Donelson along the Cumberland River, guarding access to the Tennessee capital, Nashville.

The Union commander in the theater, General Henry Halleck, had the right man to upset the Confederates' plans: General Grant, who had been placed in charge of the Union stronghold at Cairo, Ill., some 25 miles (40 km) upriver from Columbus, by General John Frémont before

REINFORCEMENTS *Steamboats are docked at Pittsburg Landing after the Battle of Shiloh, where the arrival of Union troops from the Army of the Ohio on such ships turned the tide in the North's favor. Above, General Grant poses for a portrait in 1861*

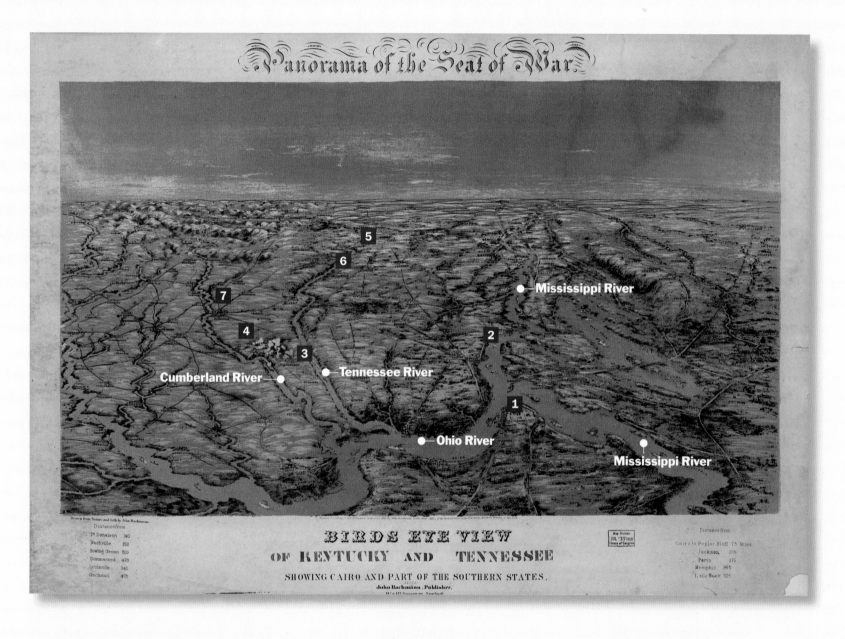

Battle to Control the Rivers

To celebrate the Union's successes in the Western theater, commercial illustrator John Bachmann created this bird's-eye view of the region where General U.S. Grant campaigned in the winter and spring of 1862. The map looks southeast from Grant's headquarters at Cairo, Ill., the key confluence where the Ohio River, flowing southwest, joins the Mississippi, flowing south. Upstream from Cairo are two more confluences, where the Tennessee and Cumberland rivers flow into the Ohio. Down the Mississippi on the eastern shore was the well-fortified Southern stronghold at Columbus, Ky.

Grant bypassed Columbus by moving his camp up the Ohio to Paducah, Ky., and launching an attack on Fort Henry on the Tennessee River. When that fortress fell, Grant marched his troops overland and laid siege to the much stronger Fort Donelson on the Cumberland River, which he also captured. But as Grant traveled deeper into rebel territory, he was surprised at Pittsburg Landing and came close to losing his army before reinforcements arrived.

1 CAIRO, ILL.
U.S. Grant commanded some 20,000 men here, at a key junction of the Ohio and Mississippi rivers. His goal: beat back Southern armies to ensure Union control of Kentucky and Tennessee. Rebel armies were commanded by A.S. Johnston.

2 COLUMBUS, KY.
This major Confederate stronghold helped the South control the lower Mississippi, vital to the rebels' trade. Rather than assault it head on, Grant chose to bypass it and drive deeply into Tennessee, splitting apart two Southern armies.

3 FORT HENRY, TENN.
The South built this new fort in order to control access to the Tennessee River, but it was located in a low-lying position and proved very difficult to defend. Floodwaters helped swamp the fort's guns even as ironclad Union gunboats attacked, and it fell quickly to the North on Feb. 6.

4 FORT DONELSON, TENN.
From Fort Henry, Grant quickly marched cross-country to encircle the rebel stronghold of Fort Donelson on the Cumberland. On Feb. 16, 13,000 rebel troops surrendered after a failed attempt to break the siege.

5 CORINTH, MISS.
After dispatching some 17,000 men under Simon Buckner in a failed bid to hold Fort Donelson, rebel commander Johnston withdrew to Corinth, leaving the prize of Nashville (7) to the Union.

6 PITTSBURG LANDING, TENN.
Johnston struck Grant hard here on April 6, catching the Union general completely by surprise and coming close to scoring a game-changing victory. But the timely arrival of additional Union troops that night helped Grant fight the rebels to a standstill.

the onetime presidential candidate was removed from command in the West by Lincoln in favor of Halleck. But Halleck and Grant would battle each other in the days to come, as Halleck questioned Grant's impetuosity and worried about his reputation for hard drinking.

On Nov. 7, 1861, the ever aggressive Grant had launched an attack on a new Confederate outpost at Belmont, Mo., just across the Mississippi from Columbus, aiming to use the fort as the base for an assault on Columbus. Grant's 3,000 troops, landed by Union vessels, won control of the camp, but the South struck back when General Leonidas Polk sent reinforcements across the Mississippi from Columbus. Having determined he could not take heavily-fortified Columbus, Grant conducted an orderly withdrawal. But he had left his calling card with the rebels.

Now, as the new year began, Grant cooked up an audacious plan to win control of the key rivers of Tennessee. He proposed bypassing Columbus and sending the 15,000 men of his Army of the Tennessee to attack Fort Henry on the Tennessee River, then taking on the larger rebel post at Fort Donelson on the Cumberland River. Halleck was dubious, but urged by Lincoln, he agreed. Early in February, Grant moved his base from

Cairo to Paducah, Ky., and began sending his troops up the Tennessee via steamboat. On Feb. 6 he launched his attack on Fort Henry, led by four innovative new naval fighting vessels: ironclad warships commanded by U.S. Navy Flag Officer Andrew Foote. The salvos from the ironclads quickly overwhelmed Fort Henry's defenses. The North had won a clear, relatively easy victory.

Now Grant pressed on, marching his men across a 12-mile (19 km) isthmus that separated the Tennessee River from the Cumberland. Within days, the Northern troops had completely surrounded Fort Donelsen. The troops inside were led by a weak commander appointed for political reasons, Brigadier General John Floyd, and second-in-command General Gideon Pillow. They had been joined by some 17,000 troops led by General Simon Buckner, sent by General Johnston to reinforce Floyd's men and help stave off Grant's army.

On Feb. 14 Grant sent Foote's ironclads to test the fort's defenses; this time the well-entrenched rebels repelled the assault. The same day, 10,000 more Union troops arrived to reinforce the siege. That night the trapped Confederates tried to break through the Union lines. Despite early success, Floyd's timidity proved fatal for the Confeder-

HEAVY METAL *In this contemporary illustration, four Union ironclad gunboats attack Fort Henry while shells fall in the river around them. The boats were designed by naval architect Samuel Pook and built by Indiana engineer James B. Eads, who supervised the 4,000 men who constructed them in four months. Resembling fortified barges, the larger boats were 175 ft. long and 50 ft. wide (53 x 15 m)*

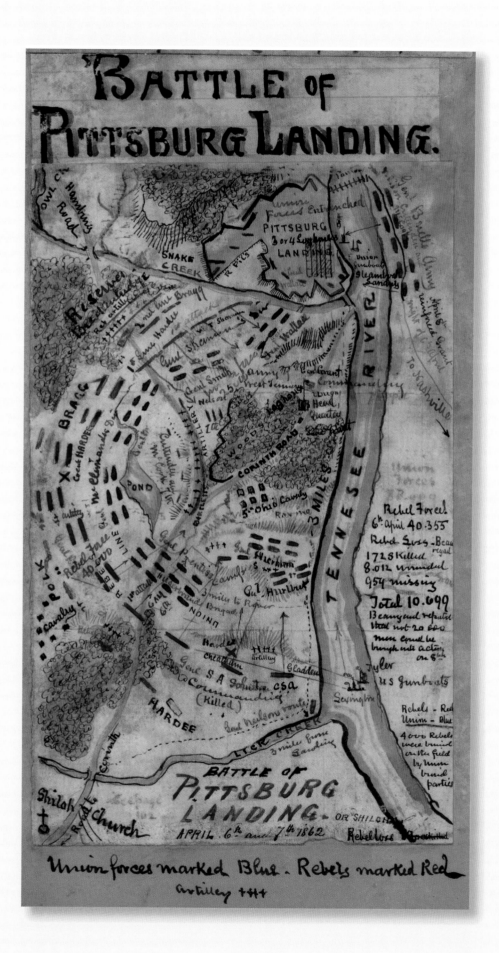

A Hornet's Nest at Pittsburg Landing

His victories at Forts Henry and Donelson made General Ulysses S. Grant a hero to civilians in the North, but within weeks of these triumphs, Grant was caught napping as he led his men further up the Tennessee River, hot on the trail of the withdrawing Southern commander, General A.S. Johnston. The Confederate's retreat was a strategic gambit, intended to lure Grant deep into rebel territory. Grant, awaiting the arrival of the Army of the Ohio under Major General Don Carlos Buell, was so convinced the Southerners were bent on digging in at Corinth, Miss., that on April 1 he set up camp on the far side of the Tennessee, rather than leaving the river as a natural barrier between his troops and Johnston's.

On April 6, Johnston sprang his trap, sending some 44,000 rebel troops to attack Grant's unsuspecting soldiers on a lazy Sunday morning. The brunt of the surprise onslaught near Shiloh Church fell on the troops led by Generals William Tecumseh Sherman and Benjamin Prentiss. The Union soldiers fell back and finally formed a defensive line along a sunken wagon road, where rebels under General Braxton Bragg launched a furious assault upon the site they began calling the "Hornet's Nest."

This was the high point of the rebel attack. Within hours, General Johnston was shot dead while rallying his troops at the front line. General P.G.T. Beauregard, hero of Fort Sumter, replaced him—and proved to be a hesitant leader. Prentiss's troops at the Hornet's Nest ultimately surrendered, but their valiant stand had provided time for Grant to establish a strong artillery line above the sunken road—and for Buell's Army of the Ohio troops to arrive, borne by steamboats. Watching the fresh Union troops cross the river that night, Confederate cavalry officer General Nathan Bedford Forrest feared that his side would lose the battle. He was right: the next morning, Grant orchestrated a stunning Union counterattack that drove the Confederates from the field and back to Corinth, though the Union troops were too exhausted to follow.

The battle shocked the nation: on each side more than 10,000 men had been killed or wounded in what was quickly recognized as the bloodiest day of battle yet to be fought on American soil. Beauregard was now denounced by Southerners. Grant, so recently the toast of the North, was also strongly criticized, and some voices called for him to be removed. President Lincoln disagreed. "I can't spare this man," he declared. "He fights."

> "There will be no fight at Pittsburg Landing. We will have to go to Corinth, where the rebels are fortified."
>
> —U.S. GRANT,
> TO A SUBORDINATE
> OFFICER

ates, most of whom were forced back into the fort by a strong Union counterattack led by troops under General Charles F. Smith, Grant's onetime teacher at West Point.

As for Floyd, he and Pillow found escape routes on the river and fled, leaving 13,000 men under Buckner inside the fort. When an angry Buckner sent envoys to discuss peace terms with Grant, the Union general rejected their offer with a brusque response: "No terms except an unconditional and immediate surrender can be accepted."

Unconditional surrender! After months of watching the endless dillydallying of Union commanders in the East, Northerners were thrilled by these eight defiant syllables—and soon newspapers were lionizing U.S. Grant as "Unconditional Surrender" Grant. When all the Confederate troops indeed surrendered on Feb. 16, the North had finally won its first great victory on land. Kentucky seemed safe for the Union—and now Grant could see his way toward controlling Tennessee as well.

General Johnston wasn't about to to let that happen. Regrouping at Corinth, Miss., he lured Grant into following him further down the river, then did just what his opponent would have done: he hurled his troops in a massive surprise assault against Grant's unprepared soldiers at Pittsburg Landing on the Tennessee River. In the next two days, the fighting around Shiloh Church would reach a level of ferocity and bloodshed new to the war. The battle Southerners called Pittsburg Landing and Northerners called Shiloh was the first of the great Civil War land battles, pitting some 65,000 Union troops against some 45,000 rebels. Like other battles that followed, it was marked by confusion among commanding officers; great valor by soldiers; and a shifting, complex flow of battle that saw the Confederates win a resounding victory on the first day of their surprise attack, only to have their gains negated by the timely arrival of Union reinforcements on the second day.

On April 7, after two days of intense struggle, the two sides were holding much the same positions as they had before the battle began—but the Union had suffered some 13,000 casualties and the Confederates almost 11,000. Most important, Grant's armies had held the field to fight another day. His campaign had handed the North a victory of major importance in a critical region—and more good news would soon arrive from New Orleans. ■

SKETCH OF THE BATTLE AT SHILOH
Artist Henri Lovie made this sketch of events along the Union left wing on the afternoon of April 6, the first day of the battle, near a peach orchard where Confederate commander General A.S. Johnston was slain the same day. Astride the horse is Union Colonel H.B. Reed of the 44th Indiana Infantry Regiment. Lovie's scrawled title for the sketch is on the reverse: "The woods on fire."

The real-time drawing is a rough draft created for potential use in a more polished version for the magazine Frank Leslie's Illustrated Newspaper. *It is one of more than 650 such sketches collected by the magazine's art director Joseph Becker (1841-1910). A selection of more than 135 of the sketches was exhibited for the first time in "First Hand: Civil-War–Era Drawings from the Becker Collection" at the McMullen Museum of Art at Boston College in 2009*

A Soldier's Life

As in all major wars, troops spend most of their time behind the lines

Dinner Party

Photographer Timothy O'Sullivan captured these officers of the Army of the Potomac enjoying a leisurely repast while in winter quarters at Brandy Station, Va., either in late 1863 or 1864. A young African American, perhaps a former "contraband" liberated by the Emancipation Proclamation, stands by to attend them.

Camp Followers

Wives and children sometimes followed their husbands to war, particularly in the early period of the conflict. The image at right, from 1861, may be a family portrait; the soldier was a member of the 31st Pennsylvania Infantry Regiment, attached to the Army of the Potomac in Washington.

Skinny-Dipping

Not only was basic hygiene lacking during the Civil War, but the relationship between cleanliness and good health was not yet understood; in France, Louis Pasteur was just beginning to study germ theory. But hot, dirty men could clean off in a stream, as these Union soldiers are doing at the North Anna River in Virginia. The ruins of a train trestle can be seen in the distance.

A Time for Prayer

Father Thomas H. Mooney poses with soldiers from the 69th New York State Militia while saying a Sunday Mass. This unit was made up almost entirely of Irish-American immigrants and was dubbed the "Fighting 69th." Its troops famously did not panic at the First Battle of Bull Run and helped form a rear guard.

Clip Joint

Soldiers from the Army of the Potomac gather at a camp barbershop in 1862. There was ample downtime for McClellan's troops early in the year, before they invaded Virginia in the Peninsula Campaign. But the soldiers fled Virginia, fighting a rear-guard action in the Seven Days Battles at the end of June; faced a formidable foe when they fought Robert E. Lee's troops at Antietam in September; then ended the year with the grisly slaughter at the Battle of Fredericksburg in December.

Theater of Battle

A group of Confederates and well-dressed "sports" gather outside a group of tents near the war's end, when Northern troops under General U.S. Grant were besieging General Cadmus M. Wilcox's forces in Petersburg, Va., in 1864-65. Two African-American men hold roosters at the ready for a cockfight.

Evergreen boughs were widely used as roofing during the war; they offered fresh fragrance and were believed to help ward off disease.

Read All About It

An enterprising vendor offers a precious item amid the fog of war: newspapers. The picture was taken by Alexander Gardner in the late summer or fall of 1863, outside a Union camp under the command of General George G. Meade. Thanks to the telegraph, Civil War newspapers were able to cover events with a much briefer lag time than in any previous conflict—although the printed product sometimes traveled at the speed of a horse.

Potluck Supper

Officers of the Union Army may have dined while seated around a table with a server standing at the ready, but for enlisted men, meals were more casual. These soldiers, shown in 1861, are from the 71st New York Volunteers, a company founded by nativist Know-Nothings in the 1850s. The unit's founders would likely have had little use for the Irish-American soldiers in the same Union Army, shown earlier, who attended Mass on Sunday.

Downtime

With blankets hanging from clotheslines around their camp, Union soldiers write letters and mend garments on a lazy day, perhaps a Sunday afternoon, in 1861.

Card Game

Officers of the 114th Pennsylvania Infantry Regiment while away the hours during the lengthy Siege of Petersburg in 1864-65, below. If these men from the Army of the Potomac joined their unit at its founding, in 1861, they may have served at Antietam, Fredericksburg, Chancellorsville and Gettysburg, among other major battles of the war.

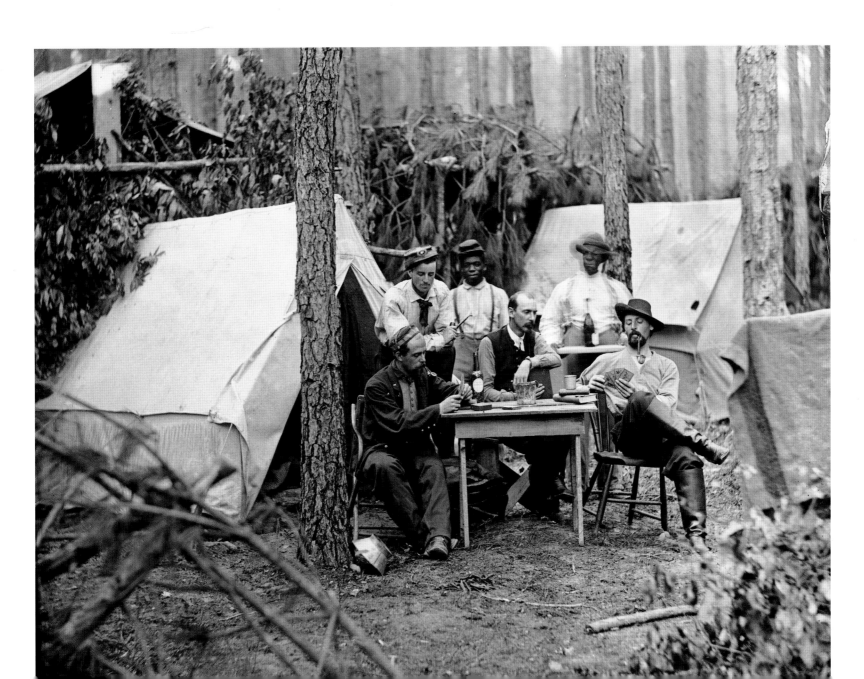

The Peninsula Campaign

Prodded by President Lincoln, General McClellan's Army of the Potomac invades Virginia but is repelled by agile rebel defenders

THINK OF IT AS A 19TH CENTURY D-DAY: on March 17, 1862, Union General George B. McClellan launched one of the largest land-sea operations in the history of warfare as he led his Army of the Potomac across Chesapeake Bay and into secessionist Virginia in a sweeping left-hook assault on the Confederate capital of Richmond. The invading force was vast and mighty: an armada of some 400 ships and barges bore some 120,000 men, more than 15,000 animals, 1,200 wagons, 44 artillery batteries and a host of support personnel into the fray. (On D-day, the Allied invasion force that landed at Normandy numbered some 150,000 men, borne by more than 5,000 craft.)

The campaign that followed would be a disaster for the Union, whose movements were constrained by overblown estimates of Southern strength; whose leader, McClellan, was far too cautious and timid; and whose clanking, lumbering approach to warfare proved no match for the much nimbler Confederates. At one point, Brigadier General J.E.B. Stuart's rebel cavalry unit literally ran rings around the Union Army. In short, the four-month-long campaign was the First Battle of Bull Run writ large. And like Bull Run, it ended in a humiliating retreat for the North.

After the disaster at Bull Run, President Abraham Lincoln had appointed McClellan to lead the new Army of the Potomac, and the young general had bulked up Washington's defenses and shaped his novice soldiers into a proud, cohesive unit. But he seemed content to do no more. As the months dragged by, the Union's failure to launch a new attack on the Confederacy, whose capital at Richmond was only 107 miles (172 km) away, caused

J.E.B. STUART *Assigned by Robert E. Lee to probe the Union Army's right flank on June 12, the Southern cavalry commander led 1,200 horsemen in a complete circuit of McClellan's army, a feat that made him an instant hero throughout the South.*

At left is the Grapevine Bridge across the Chickahominy River, used by Union troops to cross the flood-swollen stream during the Battle of Fair Oaks, helping avoid a Confederate rout

75

consternation in the North, sent signals of weakness to watching European nations—and gave Lincoln fits.

Lincoln prodded. He cajoled. He scolded. He wrote memos. Yet the Commander in Chief could not get McClellan's vast Army of the Potomac to budge. Finally, early in 1862, McClellan unveiled his strategy for attacking Richmond. He would send his invading army by sea to the mouth of the Rappahannock River, some 80 miles (128 km) south of Manassas, Va., where General Joseph Johnston's army had been fortifying its position since the battle in July 1861. The Union would thus advance on Richmond from the east, forcing Johnston to move his force to meet it. But the plan had a flaw: it would leave Washington undefended. Lincoln was quick to see that; he approved the strategy with the stipulation that McClellan leave 40,000 troops behind to guard the capital.

The plan had another flaw: it couldn't be kept secret. When Johnston got wind of it, he withdrew from Manassas and moved his troops 40 miles (64 km) south along the river. The Union plan would have to be changed, yet Lincoln continued to insist that an attack must be launched. The President favored a direct overland assault; McClellan argued for a seaborne invasion of the Virginia peninsula where the James and York rivers met, some 70 miles (113 km) southeast of Richmond. Lincoln reluctantly agreed, again insisting that McClellan assign troops to guard Washington, and he showed his ongoing frustration with McClellan by removing him from overall command of the Union Army and leaving him in charge only of the Army of the Potomac, claiming that the general needed to focus all his energies on the coming invasion.

When Johnston's army evacuated Manassas, Union troops moved in—and so did Union newspaper reporters, who discovered that the huge force McClellan had long proclaimed was defending the key railroad junction had never existed. McClellan had declared Johnston's army to be 150,000 strong; it numbered some 45,000. McClellan had warned of the rebels' massive armaments, but most of their "cannons" turned out to be wooden logs, some painted to resemble artillery. Both North and South laughed at these "Quaker cannons." Yet McClellan would continue to consistently overestimate his foe's resources.

When the Army of the Potomac finally landed on the peninsula, McClellan didn't send his men into battle. Instead, he settled in for a leisurely siege of the Confederate fort at Yorktown. After all, he argued, it was defended by a force larger than his attacking army, then numbering about 55,000. In truth, General John B. Magruder commanded only some 13,000 rebel troops in the fort, but he staged a highly theatrical show of force, marching his troops here and there to give the appearance of great numbers, while artillery units raised a din worthy of a multitude of cannons. Once again, McClellan was bamboozled: his army camped outside Yorktown for a month, giving Johnston the time to move his entire army between McClellan and Richmond before he ordered York-

SMOKE AND MIRRORS *At left, when Confederate troops withdrew from Centreville, Va., near Manassas, in 1862, Union soldiers discovered that their much feared cannons were simply logs— a.k.a. "Quaker cannons."*

At right, the observation balloon Intrepid, *brainchild of "Professor" Thaddeus S.C. Lowe, is inflated to survey troop placements during the Battle of Fair Oaks. This was one of the first times such balloons had been employed in warfare*

Scenes from the Peninsula Campaign

The Union brings vast resources to its invasion of Virginia, only to be driven back in retreat

RISING STAR *Captain George Armstrong Custer, right, a Union cavalry officer, poses with Confederate prisoner Lieutenant James B. Washington at Fair Oaks, Va. The two young officers had been good friends at West Point*

THE EMPIRE STRIKES BACK *This photograph of a Union artillery depot on the beach near Yorktown, where the Army of the Potomac was laying siege to a Confederate fort, suggests the vast scale of the invasion that began on March 17, 1862. General McClellan had spent the months since the First Battle of Bull Run in July 1861 preparing his troops for the campaign*

THE CAISSONS, ROLLING ALONG *Artillery batteries led by Major Horatio G. Gibson, part of the Army of the Potomac's Horse Artillery Brigade, prepare to move into position near Fair Oaks, Va. The rapid movement of such light-artillery companies—when the ground was dry— would play a significant role in many of the larger battles of the war*

THE FALLEN *Union soldiers wounded at the Battle of Savage's Station, one of the running series of major clashes at the end of the Peninsula Campaign, are laid out to receive treatment at a field hospital. The Union lost 919 men in the June 29 battle; the South lost 450. Although neither side could claim a victory, the strong Southern offensive that would soon drive Union troops back to Washington continued*

A Rearguard Action

The last week of June 1862 found the Union's Army of the Potomac engaged in a desperate bid to withdraw intact from the invasion of Virginia launched in March. General George B. McClellan's troops had been repelled in their closest approach to the Confederate capital, Richmond, in the Battle of Seven Pines on May 31–June 1.

McClellan then took more than three weeks to mount a probing attack of the much enhanced defenses of Richmond built by new Southern commander Robert E. Lee. The South won that battle on July 25, at Oak Grove, then launched a devastating counterattack, hammering Union troops day after day and sending them into full retreat in a campaign called the Seven Days Battles.

Lee pounded Union forces at Mechanicsville, Gaines's Mill, Savage's Station and Glendale, driving them back. The Northern troops finally found high ground at Malvern Hill on the James River and dug in, supported by gunboats on the river. In the battle that followed, Lee hurled wave after wave of Southern troops (in red) uphill against well-entrenched Union troops led by General Fitz-John Porter. At battle's end, more than 5,000 rebels were dead and some 3,000 Northerners. The Union had won a battle—and the chance to evacuate Virginia—but it had lost the campaign.

town evacuated on the night of May 3-4. A similar sort of operation was taking place to the west, in the Shenandoah Valley, where a small force of General Stonewall Jackson's pesky rebels kept two Union armies busy chasing them around the hills and hollers, foiling their plans to move on Richmond from the west *(see following story)*.

As McClellan's army finally moved forward in late May, Mother Nature stepped in to aid Richmond's defense. Spring rains had bedeviled Union troops throughout the campaign; now the raging Chickahominy River washed away many of the bridges Union engineers had built across it, dividing the Army of the Potomac into two parts. Prodded by Jefferson Davis, and by General Robert E. Lee, a new military adviser to Davis who had his ear, Johnston now launched a counterattack on the Union troops south of the Chickahominy.

The result was a confused battle fought in swampy muck and mud about seven miles (11 km) east of Richmond. The Southerners called it the Battle of Fair Oaks, the Northerners the Battle of Seven Pines. By any name, it was a mess, with Southern generals, for a change, failing to coordinate their attack well, and Union soldiers showing initiative, when stalwart troops under Major General John Sedgwick crossed the Chickahominy over the fragile Grapevine Bridge to aid their trapped colleagues. The battle ended in a draw, with the North holding its position and the rebels withdrawing, at a price of some 5,000 Union casualties and some 6,000 Confederate dead and

wounded. Chief among the rebel casualties was Johnston, wounded in two places. Davis named Lee to replace him.

True to form, McClellan now hunkered down, again fearing that he was outnumbered and outgunned (in truth, he now commanded 105,000 men to Lee's 87,000). While he dithered, rebel cavalry officer Stuart led his men on a reconnaissance mission that took them entirely around the Northern army—a feat that again had the South laughing at the plodding and hapless North.

When McClellan finally ventured to send his men to test Lee's troops, at Oak Grove on July 25, they were stopped cold, and Lee sent his armies on the attack. In a bloody series of encounters known as the Seven Days Battles, rebel armies now drove McClellan's forces reeling back across the Chickahominy all the way to the James River. The rebels beat the Yankees at Mechanicsville on June 26 and again at Gaines's Mill on the 27th. McClellan's forces were now in full retreat, taking more losses at Savage's Station on the 29th and Glendale on the 30th.

The Union troops finally found a defensible position at Malvern Hill, where they slaughtered rebel soldiers whom Lee unwisely ordered to charge them. This victory allowed McClellan the chance to withdraw all his troops back to Harrison's Landing on the James River. A month later, the staggering remnants of the Army of the Potomac boarded U.S. Navy ships and returned to Washington. It would be three more years before Union troops would again draw so close to the Confederate capital. ■

BIG GUNS *Below left, Union soldiers from the 1st Connecticut Heavy Artillery Regiment stand by their massive mortars, each weighing some 8.5 tons. They could hurl the big cannonballs behind them some two miles.*

Below right, Confederate soldiers demonstrate that cotton was not only the heart of the Southern economy: bales of the stuff made excellent bulwarks against such cannonballs inside besieged Yorktown

Jackson's Shenandoah Valley Campaign

The wily Confederate general runs rings around his Northern foes, offering a master class in the art of military logistics and surprise

THOMAS JONATHAN JACKSON IS NOT ONLY one of the great military leaders of the Civil War; he is also an American original, a legendary eccentric who alternately inspired, bedeviled and browbeat his troops, even as he won their lasting devotion. Anticipating some of the great guerrilla warriors of the 20th century, he hewed to a military strategy based on the power of speed and uncertainty. "Always mystify, mislead, and surprise the enemy," he argued. And he put his teachings into practice so well that he succeeded in mystifying his own soldiers, misleading his subordinate officers and surprising generations of historians who have studied his campaigns.

When the war began, Jackson, 37, had been teaching at the Virginia Military Institute for 10 years, where he was regarded as an uninspiring disciplinarian by his students, even though the West Point graduate had distinguished himself in combat during the Mexican War. He found his footing in the Civil War as a martinet who drove his men relentlessly, demanding more effort from his troops than any other commander in the conflict. The rewards were prodigious: at the First Battle of Bull Run in 1861, it was the stand put up by Jackson's late-arriving "Stonewall Dvision" from the Shenandoah Valley that finally put the brakes on a Union breakthrough, giving the Confederates a chance to regroup and mount a counterattack.

In March 1862, as General George B. McClellan's Army of the Potomac invaded eastern Virginia in the Peninsula Campaign, Major General Nathaniel P. Banks was assigned to expel Jackson from the Shenandoah Valley, so that General Irvin McDowell's men could converge on Richmond from the west in tandem with McClellan's major thrust from the east. Instead, it was Jackson who went on the offensive. On March 23, he attacked what he thought was a small Union force only to find it was really the rear guard of Banks' large army. The Battle of First Kernstown was a defeat, but Jackson's men withdrew in good order, even after suffering more than 700 casualties.

By May, a third Union force, led by General John C. Frémont, was assembling in western Virginia, bound for east Tennessee in a poorly conceived campaign that aimed to take control of that key area for the Union. A single division of Banks' army remained in the region. Confederate President Jefferson Davis' new military adviser, General Robert E. Lee, suggested that by continuing to take the offensive in the Shenandoah Valley, Jackson's divisions might keep McDowell's and Banks' men tied down in the area while disrupting Frémont's plans.

In the weeks to come, Jackson would employ speed and surprise to defeat portions of these three Union armies with a force less than one-half their combined size, foiling their plans and helping guarantee the failure of McClellan's invasion. In part, Jackson's success hinged on superior intelligence, for his topographical engineer Jedediah Hotchkiss had drawn up a magnificently detailed map of the Shenandoah Valley, some 8½ ft. (2.5 m) long, that gave Jackson a god's-eye view of the terrain compared with his relatively blind Union counterparts.

Jackson began his campaign in characteristic style, by misleading both the Union commanders and his own troops. Early in May he marched his men east, feigning an attempt to join the fighting against McClellan. But when the soldiers reached Charlottesville, Jackson put them in train cars that carried them right back to the valley. Civil War chronicler Shelby Foote recounts that when the train began rolling west rather than east, the rebel troops gave a mighty cheer. On May 8 they utterly surprised and defeated some of Frémont's troops at the small town of

ONE OF A KIND *The curious eccentricities of Stonewall Jackson helped cement his legend. Famously devout, he prayed frequently and ostentatiously. He sucked lemons to fight indigestion and claimed to be allergic to pepper; he wore a shabby coat and cap more befitting a tramp than a general. His troops swore that he was so exalted in battle that his eyes gleamed with an indigo flame: they dubbed him "Old Blue Light"*

McDowell. Jackson next outfoxed Banks, sending his cavalry under General Turner Ashby straight at Banks' position at Strasburg while leading his "foot cavalry" on a flanking march to Banks' left; the pincer movement ended in a rout of Union troops at Front Royal, putting Jackson in position to whip all of Banks' remaining force.

Banks now led his army on a hasty retreat to its base camp at Winchester, 20 miles (32 km) north. When he turned to fight Jackson's larger force on May 25, the Northerners were beaten and retreated to the Potomac, leaving the hungry Southerners to feast on Northern food, gather much needed medical supplies—and take charge of 2,000 Union prisoners and 9,000 Union rifles. For months, the men of the Stonewall Brigade lampooned the Union commander as "Commissary Banks."

Now President Lincoln ordered McDowell and Frémont to pursue Jackson—ending dreams of a coordinated Union attack on Richmond. Jackson's ragged troops won a hair-raising race back to Strasburg, barely eluding their pursuers. As the pursuit continued, Ashby's expert cavalry troops held off the Union troops in a rearguard action, though Ashby himself was killed in a skirmish.

Halting at Port Republic, Jackson gambled, dividing his troops to take on the Union armies separately. Rebels under his feisty subordinate, Major General Richard S. Ewell, held off Frémont's larger force at the Battle of Cross Keys on June 8, and the next day Jackson's men whipped McDowell's army in the Battle of Port Republic. Both Northern armies, badly beaten, withdrew in defeat.

The Shenandoah Valley Campaign, one of the most famous series of engagements ever fought by Americans, was over. The Confederates had defeated divisions from three separate Union armies in five battles, losing none. Jackson's 10,000 men and Ewell's 7,000 had kept some 33,000 Federal troops in a dither and had disrupted two major Union campaigns. The Stonewall Brigade had not only traipsed up and down the valley, 646 miles (1040 km) in 48 days—it had also marched into legend. ∎

George B. McClellan

The leader of the Army of the Potomac was a master of the parade ground who hated to get his soldiers' splendid uniforms dirty

OBSERVERS OF THE CIVIL WAR ARE STILL stumped by the character and career of George B. McClellan, the Union general who seemed to possess all the qualities needed in a commanding officer—except the desire to command. The story of the North's first two years at war boils down to the long battle between McClellan and his civilian superior, Abraham Lincoln, for control of the Union's Eastern armies and over the creation of the strategies they would use to defeat the Confederate rebels—and to Lincoln's growing disillusionment with McClellan's interest in committing to conflict.

Lincoln's struggles to get McClellan to fight would be echoed in the 1940s, when Joseph Stilwell, the U.S. general serving as military liaison to American ally Chiang Kaishek, could not persuade the Chinese Nationalist leader to summon his troops into battle. Florid Senator Tom Connally of Texas memorably summed up Generalissimo Chiang's timidity: Chiang, he said, engaged in "too much 'issimo-ing' and not enough generaling."

And so it was with McClellan, whose mastery of martial "issimo-ing" no one doubted, including Lincoln, who once said of the vainglorious general: "If he can't fight himself, he excels in making others ready to fight." Indeed, McClellan's soldiers in the Army of the Potomac loved the general they called "Little Mac," cheering him wildly as he rode among them on his frequent inspections. McClellan excelled at drilling his men, at building camaraderie, at staging lavish parades to show their strength. But when it came time to order his troops into battle, time after time McClellan dithered and dawdled. He famously overestimated both the numbers of the rebel troops he faced and the armaments they bore. And when victory did come his way, he didn't capitalize upon it.

McClellan treated Lincoln with contempt bordering on insubordination in public and with outright ridicule in private. In a letter to his wife Ellen, he referred to the President as "nothing more than a well-meaning baboon"; in others, repeatedly, Lincoln is "the gorilla." On an infamous occasion in November 1861, Lincoln, Secretary of State William Seward and Lincoln's aide John Hay called upon McClellan at his home in Washington and were taken to a parlor, where they waited for some time. The men heard the general arrive, pass their door and trudge upstairs; some 30 minutes later they were told that McClellan had retired and would not receive them.

Small wonder that both observers from his era and historians who have studied his career vie to revile McClellan in the strongest terms. Lincoln's secretaries, John Nicolay and Hay, derided him as "the little Napoleon." In a 1950 book review, TIME described the general as "a stuffed tunic, an ambitious parade-ground dandy whose timidity in combat was close kin to cowardice." Historian Kenneth P. Williams wrote in his multivolume study *Lincoln Finds a General*: "No blow by [Stonewall] Jackson could be quite as paralyzing as an order by McClellan."

How did it come to this? McClellan was a man who achieved greatness—at least in his own estimation—when history thrust it upon him. But he also had a head start. He was born into a prominent Philadelphia family in 1826, and his well-connected father, an ophthalmologist, used his contacts to have his son matriculate at West Point in 1842, before he reached the enrollment age of 16. He graduated second of his class of 59 in 1846, just as the Mexican War was getting under way. Trained as an engineer, he served with distinction in the war and made a positive impression on a man who became a mentor and ultimately a rival, General Winfield Scott.

After his return from Mexico, the young officer engaged in a variety of engineering and surveying duties

> "He [General McClellan] is an admirable engineer, but he seems to have a special talent for a stationary engine."
>
> —ABRAHAM LINCOLN

POSING *McClellan made a fine show as a general in this photograph from 1863, but his critics, including Lincoln, began to see him as nothing but show. Visiting Antietam after McClellan failed to follow up on his surprise victory, Lincoln described the encamped Union Army as "McClellan's bodyguard"*

for the Army, which included tracing the Red River to its sources and seeking the best locations for transcontinental railroad passes through the Rockies. Along the way, he began to reveal some of the attributes that would distinguish his Civil War command: he was well liked by soldiers but held scarcely concealed contempt for superiors, especially nonmilitary superiors. He was a good engineer, but he proved easily susceptible to faulty intelligence and was poorly versed in topography.

In 1855 McClellan was handed a chance to broaden his view of strategy when he was asked to serve as an observer of the Crimean War, where he saw siege tactics at

Sevastopol, Russian cavalry maneuvers, even the new rifled muskets that would prove so deadly in the Civil War. In 1857 he resigned his commission to accept a position as chief engineer and vice president of the Illinois Central Railroad, capitalizing on his earlier railway explorations.

McClellan supported Stephen Douglas in the 1860 presidential campaign—radical Republicans would later accuse the general of harboring a soft spot for slavery—but when war came, he rejoined the Army. Thanks to his sterling past and good connections, he was commissioned as a major general, second in rank only to General Scott. As commander of the Army of the Ohio, he scored some minor successes against Confederates in western Virginia early in the war. When the rebels took control of Fort Sumter, Lincoln called for 75,000 volunteers to form a new Army of the Potomac, and he summoned McClellan to whip them into fighting shape.

McClellan exulted in his new status. "By some strange operation of magic," he wrote to his wife, "I seem to have become the power of the land." But as the months went by and McClellan found excuse after excuse for not leading his men into battle, the magic faded. Forced at last into advancing into Virginia, he allowed the army to become bogged down in the disastrous Peninsula Campaign, which ended in ignominious retreat.

Then McClellan was handed a victory by a most unexpected source: Robert E. Lee, who led his army into Maryland and into defeat at Antietam. Yet McClellan proved hesitant even in success, squandering the chance to follow Lee's army and carve it into pieces. Lincoln visited him after the battle and scolded him for his caution, then relieved him of his command. McClellan assured his wife that "history's verdict" would exonerate him. Two years later, the two men would do battle again: McClellan ran as the Democratic candidate for the presidency against Lincoln, who easily beat his old foe. Tellingly, 78% of the soldiers in the Union Army voted for Lincoln.

After the war McClellan traveled abroad, worked again in engineering and the railroad industry and served a single term as governor of New Jersey. He wrote his memoirs, *McClellan's Own Story,* which were published posthumously after his sudden death at only 58 in 1885. The *Atlantic Monthly* plowed through the pages of this master of "issimo" and rendered history's verdict: "His egotism is simply colossal—there is no other word for it." ■

The Second Battle of Bull Run

AUG. 29-30, 1862

For the Union, it's déjà vu all over again at Manassas, as Robert E. Lee's superb tactics send Northern troops reeling in retreat

THE SECOND BATTLE OF BULL RUN, OR Second Manassas, as the South called it, in many ways anticipated the Battle of Fredericksburg that would be fought later in 1862: it was a one-off sideshow under a new Union general that concluded in a convincing Southern victory. But this debacle for the North also illustrated the underlying reason for the Union's final victory in the conflict: an overwhelming dominance in men, arms and resources, against which all the South's valorous troops and superb generals would prove useless in the long run.

Preparations for the battle began even as General George B. McClellan was mounting his massive invasion of eastern Virginia, the Peninsula Campaign. This was by far the largest military action ever undertaken by the U.S. Government, yet at the same time, the Union, rich in manpower, was raising another major force to fight in the Eastern theater, the new Army of Virginia, led by General John Pope, 40. This self-satisfied young officer had distinguished himself in the war's Western theater and had been summoned to Washington, where he impressed President Lincoln with his confidence and apparent mastery of military strategy. Lincoln was rapidly losing faith in McClellan and was actively seeking generals prepared to take

BULL RUN REDUX *At top left, troops of the 41st New York Infantry Regiment pose at Manassas. Southern armies retreated from the key railway junction early in 1862, moving 41 miles (66 km) south to Culpeper as McClellan's invasion loomed and Northern troops moved in.*

At top right, Union troops view train tracks torn up by Jackson's troops during the 1862 battle

HUBRIS *General John Pope, whose ego seemed a match for that of rival George B. McClellan, was played like a fiddle by Robert E. Lee at Manassas. During the battle, his subordinate, General Fitz-John Porter, did not follow Pope's order to attack Longstreet's troops, leading to Porter's being court-martialed and cashiered*

the fight to the enemy. Pope appeared to be such a man.

Pope arrived in the East with a bang, issuing a proclamation that, bizarrely, painted his new charges as cowards, boasting, "I have come to you from the West, where we have always seen the backs of our enemies." Having shot himself in one foot, he took aim on the other, saying that he would execute any rebel sympathizers, even civilians, he encountered—a threat that so enraged mild-mannered General Robert E. Lee that he vowed to Stonewall Jackson that they must suppress this Union "miscreant."

Now that he had staved off McClellan's clumsy invasion on Richmond from the east, Lee decided to go on the offensive, taking the battle to Pope's army to his north and west, then moving into Maryland. He ordered Jackson to advance north against troops led by his recent foe from the Shenandoah Valley, General Nathaniel P. Banks. The two tangled at Cedar Mountain outside Culpeper, Va., on Aug. 9, with Jackson taking severe losses before rallying his men and ending the fight in a draw.

With Jackson keeping Banks engaged, Lee and his other top subordinate, General James Longstreet, began moving directly against Pope, whose Army of the Virginia, some 32,000 strong, was being reinforced by General Fitz-John Porter's veterans of the Peninsula Campaign. Now Lee hatched one of the tactical gambits that became his hallmark: defying military convention, he divided his army, roughly the size of Pope's, into two parts, sending Jackson on a wide flanking march around the north and west of Pope, camped at Manassas, while Lee's main army, under Longstreet, advanced head-on toward Pope's camp.

Pope simply could not conceive of such a daring strategy. When Jackson engaged his right flank, Pope withdrew the divisions standing between Longstreet's army and his own and sent them against Jackson, thinking that his army constituted the primary Confederate attack. On Aug. 29, Pope directed his full might at Jackson, whose "foot cavalry" went into Stonewall mode, suffering major losses as they valiantly hunkered down and kept Pope's army engaged. The next morning Lee sprung his trap: he hurled Longstreet's troops against Pope's almost entirely exposed left flank, held down by only 8,000 men.

Gotcha! Longstreet's divisions mowed through the Union left, sending Northern troops in full retreat past landmarks of the First Battle of Bull Run: Henry House and the Stone Bridge, scene of their humiliation a little more than 13 months before. "It's another Bull Run!" declared Union General Philip Kearny, who would die in a rearguard action at Chantilly on Sept. 1. It wasn't, exactly: the Northerners kept better order than in their first rout, but once again they had tasted defeat at Manassas. ■

The Battle of Antietam

SEPTEMBER 17, 1862

In a day of horrible bloodletting, the Army of the Potomac stops Robert E. Lee's troops in Maryland, then allows them to escape

HIS TROOPS WERE EXHAUSTED BY THE strain of repelling the Army of the Potomac's invasion of Virginia and their subsequent victory at the Second Battle of Bull Run. His supply wagons were bare, for northern Virginia's farms and fields had been stripped of crops and livestock after months of nonstop warfare. Many of his civilian commanders and his own subordinates advised him to give his troops a chance to heal and regroup. But Robert E. Lee—demonstrating the vast gulf that separated him from his overly cautious Union counterpart, George B. McClellan—decided in August 1862 that he must continue his invasion of Maryland, taking the battle to his enemies, with an eye to capturing much needed food and supplies, severing railroad access to Washington, possibly winning Maryland for the Confederacy and demonstrating conclusively to Europeans that a new state was taking shape in America.

The weeks that followed would prove to be one of the great turning points in the war. Lee seized the initiative with his daring invasion. His armies again proved far more agile than those of the North, and he seemed at times to be toying with the Army of the Potomac. But he was eventually forced to face the full extent of Northern power in a pitched battle near Antietam Creek, some 83 miles (133 km) northwest of Washington. The result was a mutual slaughter that remains the bloodiest day of combat ever fought on American soil, followed by the withdrawal of Lee's battered army, which might have been effectively destroyed had it not been for McClellan's failure to pursue it in the aftermath of the battle.

COMRADES *Above, Union officers on the staff of General Fitz-John Porter included Lieutenant George Armstrong Custer, lower right. At right, bodies lie in the field near the Dunker Church, scene of some of the heaviest fighting of the battle, as entrenched Confederate troops faced a series of Union attacks. The Dunkers were a sect of German Baptists who preached pacifism*

Indeed, the reverberations of Antietam would resound long after the fighting, for President Abraham Lincoln took advantage of this technical victory for the North to act on two issues that would have major consequences: he removed McClellan from command for good, and he issued the Emancipation Proclamation. With the latter, he made explicit a view he had long held: the war was being fought not over states' rights but over the need to end slavery on American soil—all American soil—once and for all.

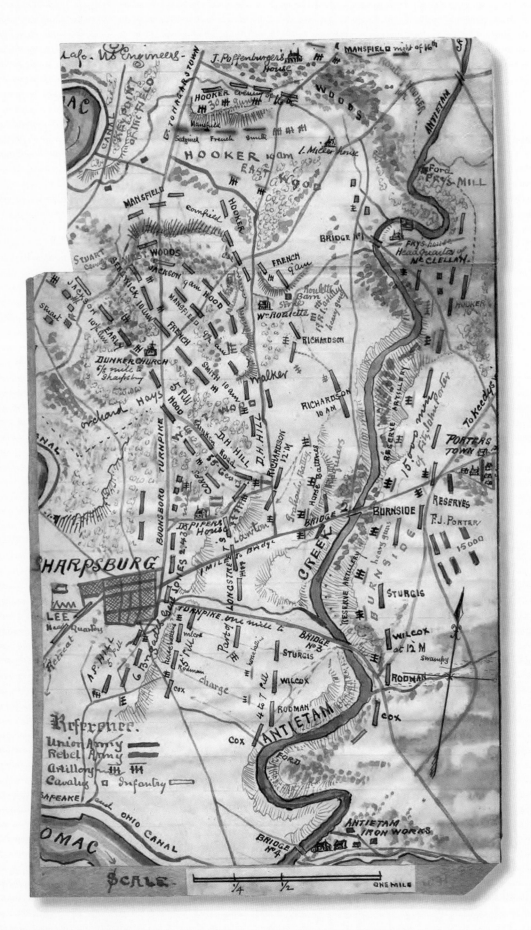

The Killing Fields

In the battle along Antietam Creek, the topography, the tacticsof the commanders and the sheer valor of the troops on both sides turned the pastures between the creek and the town of Sharpsburg into highly efficient killing pens, where soldiers where slaughtered by the thousands.

The battle unfolded in three main stages, beginning on the Union right, where General Joseph Hooker's divisions suffered horrific casualties as they drove troops on the Confederate left reeling back, with heavy action seen in a pasture called the Cornfield near the Dunker Church. But the Union attack was not well coordinated, proceeding by fits and starts, and when McClellan refused to send in the reserves he was withholding in hopes of a breakthrough, Lee was able to shift divisions to reinforce his endangered left flank.

By midday the most frenzied fighting was taking place in a sunken farm road near the Dunker Church, later christened "Bloody Lane." The Northern troops achieved a breakthrough here—and, true to form, McClellan failed to capitalize on it, again refusing to send in his reserves. In the early afternoon there was finally action on the Union left flank. General Ambrose Burnside's men had fought bitterly for hours to win control of a bridge across the creek, delaying McClellan's planned two-pronged thrust. Some Southerners on the scene and later historians argued that Union troops could have forded the creek simply by wading across it; that charge is likely false.

When control of the bridge was won, Burnside's divisions joined the fray and beat back the rebels. But for the third time, McClellan refused to exploit a breakthrough with his reserves, allowing time for Confederate General A.P. Hill's troops to arrive on the double-quick from Harpers Ferry, stemming the advance. Finally, the guns stopped sounding. As the sun set, the two armies took stock of their losses: 23,000 men lay dead or wounded.

> "Those in whose judgment I rely tell me that I fought the battle splendidly & that it was a masterpiece of art."
>
> —GEORGE B. MCCLELLAN,
> IN A LETTER TO HIS WIFE

On Sept. 4, Lee's weary legions—officially some 55,000 strong but losing soldiers daily to hunger and illness—crossed the Potomac some 35 miles upstream of Washington. Lee had hoped for support from Marylanders, but his ragtag divisions met with a cool response. Meanwhile, Lee divided his army, one of his favorite stratagems, and sent two-thirds of his men to secure his rear, dispatching Stonewall Jackson to attack the Union-held garrison at Harpers Ferry, a key transportation nexus, to ensure his path back to Virginia.

The Union was still reeling from its second defeat at Bull Run, and General John Pope was highly unpopular with his troops. So Lincoln sacked the preening general and resorted to a man he had little faith in. To the horror of many of his closest advisers, he put McClellan in charge of the Army of the Potomac once more, hoping to restore its vigor. Pope's Army of Virginia was folded into the Army of the Potomac. And sure enough, the troops were delighted to have "Little Mac" back in charge.

And for once, McClellan seemed to have not only a su-perior force but also good fortune on his side. On Sept. 13, near the town of Frederick, two Union soldiers stumbled upon a military man's dream: Lee's strategic plan for the invasion, wrapped around three cigars and apparently dropped by a careless Southern officer. "Here is a paper with which if I cannot whip 'Bobbie Lee' I will be willing to go home," McClellan crowed. But the cautious general soon brought his exuberance under control, and despite now knowing that Lee had divided his army, which could thus potentially be beaten in parts, he delayed forward movement for 18 hours, squandering the advantage of surprise. As usual, McClellan, commanding perhaps more than 80,000 troops, convinced himself that Lee's legions vastly outnumbered his; in truth, with his forces divided, Lee at the moment commanded only some 30,000 men. The Union delay gave the Confederates time to assume a defensive posture at South Mountain, where they held off the North's eventual assault, while Jackson's fast-moving army won control of Harpers Ferry.

Lee now decided that his best option was to take a

★

The Commanders at Antietam
The Army of the Potomac fails to engage all its forces and the battle ends in a draw

A.P. HILL

The Virginian was a West Point graduate who served in the Mexican War. After joining the Confederates, he fought well in the Peninsula Campaign and in the Second Battle of Bull Run, and he quickly became one of Robert E. Lee's most trusted lieutenants, under Stonewall Jackson. He was killed in battle just seven days before the Confederate surrender in 1865.

JAMES LONGSTREET

Lee called Longstreet his "Old War Horse," and the West Point graduate from South Carolina indeed served with distinction in many major battles. But after Lee and Longstreet disagreed on strategy at Gettysburg—and especially after the war, when Longstreet criticized the revered Lee in his memoirs—he fell out of favor with many in the South.

FITZ-JOHN PORTER

Porter was born in New Hampshire to a family long on U.S. Navy officers, but he chose an Army career. Rising to serve as one of General McClellan's top generals, he became a whipping boy for the Union defeat at the Second Battle of Bull Run and was court-martialed and cashiered; he fought for 23 years to exonerate his name.

JOSEPH HOOKER

The Massachusetts man had a familiar c.v.: West Point and the Mexican War. Ambitious for power, he distinguished himself at Antietam, where he was forced to step aside with a foot wound, and finally was given a chance to lead the Army of the Potomac. But Lee whipped him at Chancellorsville, where he again was injured, and he ended the war on the Western front.

★

stand: after all, his troops had whipped the North in the Peninsula Campaign, in the Shenandoah Valley and at the Second Battle of Bull Run. He little doubted he could do the same again. The position he selected was near Sharpsburg, about a mile north of the Potomac. Sept. 15 found his men erecting fortifications on the high ground along Antietam Creek, a shallow stream outside Sharpsburg that flowed into the Potomac. To his rear, Jackson's divisions, who had taken Harpers Ferry, were marching quickly toward Sharpsburg, even as Union forces began arriving on the far side of the creek.

On Sept. 16, McClellan had a chance to attack Lee's three divisions before the other Southern troops arrived. Instead, he spent the day making battle plans. Once again he had wasted an opportunity to seize the initiative and attack a far weaker foe.

THE FOG OF WAR The Battle of Antietam took place on a single day, Sept. 17. When it ended, some 23,000 men from both sides had fallen on the battlefield, either dead or wounded. The fighting, all participants agreed, had a frenzied, maddened quality experienced in no other battle. Its landmarks—the Dunker Church, the Cornfield, Bloody Lane, the Burnside Bridge—have entered American history. So has its toll: this was the single bloodiest day of battle in the American experience. The casualties suffered here were more than three times those of D-day.

McClellan's plan of attack against the Southern defense involved a two-pronged offensive: a large strike by General Joseph Hooker's divisions on the Confederate left flank, commanded by Stonewall Jackson, now on the scene. This charge would work in tandem with an assault by General Ambrose Burnside's troops on the Confederate right, held by General James Longstreet. McClellan, in the center, held 20,000 troops in reserve in hopes of exploiting any breakthrough on his wings.

Hooker's troops launched their attack on the Confederate left early in the morning, crossing Antietam Creek on an undefended bridge and pushing back troops from Georgia commanded by Colonel Marcellus Douglass in a series of intense charges in the Cornfield, a 30-acre plot surrounded by woods, near the Dunker Church. As Union Major Rufus Dawes wrote, "The men are loading and firing with demoniacal fury and shouting and laughing hysterically, and the whole field before us is covered with rebels fleeing for life, into the woods." Another Union soldier recalled, "It was a squirrel hunt on a large scale, as you could see our men creep along from tree to tree."

Jackson was forced to commit his reserves, and General John Bell Hood's units mowed down Union troops along Hagerstown Turnpike like a scythe, said one observer.

LIBRARY OF CONGRESS PRINTS AND PHOTOGRAPHS DIVISION

UNEQUAL IN DEATH *Two soldiers are dead, but only one— the Union trooper—has been buried in this Alexander Gardner photograph taken after the battle. When Mathew Brady exhibited the images his team had taken at Antietam at an exhibit in New York City, they illustrated the wages of war as never before seen by civilians. Said the New York* Times: *"Mr. Brady has done something to bring home to us the terrible reality and earnestness of war. If he has not brought bodies and laid them in our door-yards and along streets, he has done something very like it"*

Those troops, in turn, were cut down by federal artillery when they moved forward into the Cornfield. Waves of successive Union charges were rolled back there, until the men on both sides were exhausted. When Jackson asked Hood how the battle was faring, Hood replied that his entire division was "dead in the field."

McClellan, too, had reinforcements at his command: several Union divisions and the cavalry waited behind the lines. The most intense fighting now moved toward the center of the battlefield, along a sunken farm road: "Bloody Lane," it would soon be christened. "What a bloody place was that sunken road as we advanced," Sergeant Charles A. Hale of New Hampshire wrote in a letter home "the fences were down on both sides, and the dead and wounded men were literally piled in there in heaps. As we went over them in crossing the road, a wounded reb made a thrust at me with his bayonet; turning my head to look at him, I saw that he was badly hurt, and kept on."

As the Union advance continued, McClellan had a chance to drive a wedge directly into the relatively unprotected Confederate center. He decided not to risk it, declaring, "It would not be prudent to make the attack."

After a slow start, the battle was now raging on the Confederate right, where Burnside's troops had finally captured a key bridge over Antietam Creek and were poised to control the road to the only ford across the Potomac, Lee's escape route. Once again McClellan had the chance to send fresh troops into the fray to press the advantage, but he held General Fitz-John Porter's troops in reserve after Porter told him, "I command the last reserve of the last Army of the Republic." So instead of fresh Union troops tipping the balance on the Confederate right, it was a batch of new Southern arrivals, General A.P. Hill's troops hurrying from Harpers Ferry, who surged against the Union left and halted Burnside's advance.

The battle was over: the soldiers who lived through it told of the horror they felt that night as they heard their wounded comrades screaming for help on the battlefield. The next day, McClellan had a golden opportunity to smash the pitiful remnants of Lee's army. Incredibly, he did not do so: an undeclared truce reigned over the scene of carnage, allowing both sides to treat their injured.

THE AFTERMATH History records Antietam as a Union victory, for Lee, who could ill afford it, suffered more casualties than McClellan, and the whipped rebels soon withdrew across the Potomac. McClellan was quick to declare himself the hero of the day, but Lincoln, his Cabinet and many observers in the North were shocked that once again the general had allowed Lee's army to squirm out of his grasp just at the moment when it was most helpless;

some Northerners began to question whether McClellan had any interest in beating the South at all.

In early October, as McClellan's inert army remained on the battlefield, Lincoln visited the general and surveyed his troops: it was on this occasion that he referred to the Army of the Potomac as "McClellan's bodyguard." Meeting face to face in the officer's tent, the President strongly advised the general against overcaution and once again urged him to take the offensive against Lee.

The visit did no good: McClellan's army remained immobile. Weeks later, he wrote the President that his horses were worn out. Lincoln wired back, "Will you pardon me for asking what the horses of your army have done since the battle of Antietam that fatigues anything?"

Lincoln, at least, was fatigued: on Nov. 5 he replaced McClellan with Burnside, and "Little Mac" left the Army. But in the meantime, the President used the Union stand and Lee's retreat to strike a different kind of blow against the South: on Sept. 22, he surprised Americans of all stripes by issuing the Emancipation Proclamation. ∎

SHOWDOWN *President Lincoln meets with General McClellan near the battlefield on Oct. 3, 1862, 16 days after the battle. Lincoln had long since lost patience with McClellan's failure to engage the Confederates actively, and five weeks later he relieved the general of his command. The two would square off as presidential candidates in the 1864 election*

Scenes from Antietam

A quiet creek in Maryland sees
the war's deadliest day of battle

HIGH SIGNS *Brady photographer Timothy O'Sullivan took this photograph of a Union signal tower overlooking the battlefield along Antietam Creek from a perch on nearby Elk Mountain*

CALM BEFORE THE STORM *Soldiers of the 93rd New York Infantry Regiment pose for Alexander Gardner's camera at Antietam on Sept. 16, the day before the battle. For these soldiers, there would be no fighting: they were among the 20,000 troops that General McClellan could have ordered into the battle but chose not to, squandering a chance for a major victory*

VALLEY OF DEATH *The sunken road near the Dunker Church was the scene of some of the deadliest fighting at Antietam, as rebel troops defended against a series of Union charges. As many as 5,600 men from both sides died or were wounded in the four-hour fight along "Bloody Lane," the first 1,000-yd. (914 m) of the road*

TENDING THE WOUNDED *General Lee left many of his casualties behind, entrusting them to the charity of his enemies after the battle. Above, Dr. Anthony Hurd of the 14th Indiana Volunteers moves among the tents and improvised shelters that made up his field hospital after the battle, where he tended to the wounded of both armies*

Free at Last

After the Union victory at Antietam, President Lincoln issues the
Emancipation Proclamation, freeing the slaves in the rebel states

ON MARCH 4, 1865, ABRAHAM LINCOLN was sworn in for a new term as President, and in his Second Inaugural Address he reviewed the origins of the nation's great internal conflict. "One-eighth of the whole population were colored slaves, not distributed generally over the Union, but localized in the southern part of it," he recalled of the 1850s. "These slaves constituted a peculiar and powerful interest. All knew that this interest was somehow the cause of the war." Lincoln, of course, had been the prophet who most clearly foresaw that the na-

tion's deep divisions over the morality of slavery must be resolved. In the speech that had first brought him to national attention, he had declared in 1858, "'A house divided against itself cannot stand.' I believe this government cannot endure permanently half slave and half free. I do not expect the Union to be dissolved—I do not expect the house to fall—but I do expect it will cease to be divided. It will become all one thing or all the other."

The war represented the South's attempt to dissolve the Union and the North's attempt to hold it together. But Lincoln understood that there would be no resolution to his nation's ailment unless the root of the infection—slavery—was overthrown, once and for all. As a politician, he had frequently expressed his ardent desire to see slavery ended, but he had never joined the Abolitionists, who were viewed by many Americans as extremists. As President, one of his primary goals was to hold together a fragile political coalition that included radical Abolitionists and mainstream Republicans who hated slavery, as well as Northern Democrats who supported the war but took no interest in Southern slavery. Foreign eyes were also watching: most Britons strongly supported abolition, and Lincoln needed to keep England from recognizing the Confederacy as an independent state.

In modern political parlance, Lincoln was out in front of some of his Northern constituents. And he was aware that the great work of uniting America after the horrific war would hinge upon the cooperation of well-meaning citizens of the South. So in his first months in office he consistently described his primary goal as the preservation of the Union rather than the freeing of the slaves.

In his First Inaugural Address, Lincoln declared to the secessionist states of the South, "I have no purpose,

directly or indirectly, to interfere with the institution of slavery in the States where it exists. I believe I have no lawful right to do so, and I have no inclination to do so." He reiterated this thought on Aug. 22, 1862, in a letter he wrote to New York City newspaper publisher Horace Greeley, stating, "My paramount object in this struggle *is* to save the Union, and is *not* either to save or to destroy slavery. If I could save the Union without freeing *any* slave I would do it and if I could save it by freeing *all* the slaves I would do it, and if I could save it by freeing some and leaving others alone I would also do that."

The letter seemed straightforward enough, but it was disingenuous, for Lincoln had already decided that the only way to save the Union was to free all the slaves, and he had written almost the entire text of the document with which he would do so, the Emancipation Proclamation. On July 22, 1862, he had startled his Cabinet members by reading them a draft of the decree. It did not promise to free slaves in the border states, for Lincoln feared it might drive these areas, where loyalty to the Union remained fragile, into the arms of the Confederates.

The Cabinet's reaction to the proposal was divided, but a clear majority favored it. Secretary of State William H. Seward advised that such a bold step must follow a clear military victory by the Union, and Lincoln agreed. Antietam, in which the North beat Lee's invading army and sent it in full retreat back to Virginia, gave him that success. Five days after the battle, on Sept. 22, the President issued a "preliminary" Emancipation Proclamation.

Lincoln wrote this historic document of political and social liberation in his role as Commander in Chief of the Union Army, and it reads more as a military dispatch than as a ringing declaration of human rights. Indeed, one purpose of the decree was to resolve an issue that had plagued the North since the war began: how to treat the slaves liberated from bondage during the course of military exercises, described as "contraband" by Union officers. Now it was clear that these individuals were "forever free." That proposition was later written into the U.S Constitution by the 13th Amendment, ratified on Dec. 6, 1865, which outlaws slavery in the United States.

Lincoln himself, it should be noted, shared some of the racist attitudes of his time. He feared that not all the freed slaves could ever be fully woven into the fabric of American society, and he championed far-fetched notions of compensating the former slaves and settling Americans of African origin in colonies in Africa and Central America. Yet in issuing the Emancipation Proclamation, which he later came to see as the crowning achievement of his presidency, he took the essential step toward resolving the cleavage that divided America's house. ■

NOW WHAT? *At left, slaves freed during the Union's campaigns in Virginia flee their former homes along the Rappahannock River in 1862. Such fugitives were termed "contraband" by Union officers, and early in the war, some Southern slaveholders visited Northern army camps to retrieve their property. The Emancipation Proclamation resolved the issue, freeing all slaves in the rebel states.*

At right is a handwritten copy of the proclamation, issued on Sept. 22, 1862

African Americans in the War

Unshackled from slavery, blacks fight to carve out a new place in U.S. society

Standing Tall

For Southerners, the appearance of former slaves dressed in the blue uniforms of Union troops and bearing arms was confirmation of their deepest fears for the future when the war began. Northern leaders understood the powerful impact of such images. In March 1863, President Lincoln wrote to Andrew Johnson, then military governor of Tennessee, "The bare sight of 50,000 armed and drilled black soldiers on the banks of the Mississippi, would end the rebellion at once." Above, members of one such group, the 107th Infantry, U.S. Colored Troops, from Louisville, Ky., pose while drilling at Fort Corcoran, Va., in 1864.

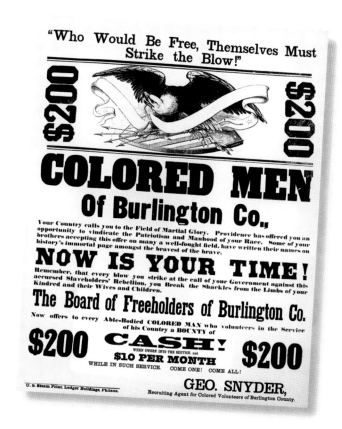

"Drummer" Jackson

This young man was a contraband—a former slave freed by Union armies—attached to the 79th Infantry, U.S. Colored Troops, based in Port Hudson, La. This photo of Jackson in a Union uniform was circulated widely in the North along with a picture showing the former slave in a disheveled state, as he appeared when freed. The before-and-after shots were among the Union's most popular and effective propaganda images.

To Arms!

At top right, a recruiting poster from Burlington County, N.J., is directed at Northern black men eager to join the Union Army and strike blows against "this accursed slaveholders' rebellion." Historian James McPherson estimates there were some 100,000 blacks in Union uniforms by 1864; at first they were paid less than white troops, but this injustice was righted by Congress in 1864.

Taking Aim

By 1864 African-American regiments were serving on a wide variety of fronts for the Union. At right, two sharpshooters were photographed in November of that year as they protected Northern positions at Dutch Gap, Va. Union engineers there were dredging a canal to facilitate Federal movements along the James River near Drewry's Bluff, some 8 miles (13 km) southeast of Richmond.

Kitchen Patrol

In addition to serving in uniform, freed blacks filled many rear-echelon positions for the Union Army. At left, a cook watches his pots at City Point, Va., during the long Siege of Petersburg in 1864-65. The background offers a fascinating backstage view of camp life: horses and wagons, a log cabin, tents, barrels filled with supplies—and the all-important railroad tracks.

On the Move

African-American contrabands arrive at a Union camp in this 1863 photo. In September of the previous year, President Lincoln declared such individuals "forever free" in the Emancipation Proclamation. At a time when wealth was measured in livestock and wagons, these exiles appear to have been better off than many other newly freed slaves.

A "Black Republic"

The workers at left are planting sweet potatoes at the Cassina Point Plantation on Edisto Island off the coast of South Carolina in 1862. According to Charles Spencer's history *Edisto Island, 1861-2006* (The History Press; 2008), after Southern leaders ordered Edisto evacuated in November 1861, whites fled the island and its black residents were among the first slaves freed in the war. Former slaves flocked to Edisto, which operated as a "Black Republic" for several months, until Union troops occupied it in February 1862.

Tending King Cotton

These former slaves were photographed at Fish Hall, a Hilton Head, S.C., plantation owned by the family of Emma Pope, the wife of Confederate General Thomas Drayton. The plantation was taken over by Union forces following the Northern victory over Drayton's forces in the Battle of Port Royal in November 1861. The workers at left were still planting, harvesting and ginning cotton but were now keeping the profits.

Duels in the Border Country

In a wide-open war in the critical states of the upper South, the Union takes Kentucky—but Tennessee remains a battleground

TODAY'S SPORTS FANS OFTEN NOTE THAT the "big market" teams of the East Coast draw more coverage than the teams of the smaller markets elsewhere. And so it was in the Civil War: Northern newspapers lavished attention on the campaigns in the Virginia theater, while coverage from the faraway Western front was often tardy and scant. As a result, generations of Civil War historians regarded Virginia and Maryland as the pilot house of the conflict. But today many scholars argue that the war's pivotal events took place along the Mississippi River and in the border regions of Kentucky and Tennessee, where steady Union advances first began to pave the way for the isolation of Richmond and eventual victory.

Events in 1862, early and late, shaped the course of the war in this theater. Kentucky never seceded and large portions of it were under Union control from early in the war (Abraham Lincoln remarked, "I *hope* to have God on my side, but I must have Kentucky"). Tennessee, despite strong Union sympathy in some regions, joined the Confederacy. And though U. S. Grant drove the rebels from their river strongholds in the state's west and the Union took control of Nashville early in the year, the central and eastern portions of the state were still rebel territory.

Parts of Mississippi, to the south, were also in play, and early in 1862 the Union ran up a string of victories in that rebel state and along the critical river that forms its western border. Under orders from Western theater commander General Henry W. Halleck, General John Pope and a Union fleet combined forces and took control of Island No. 10 on the lower Mississippi, a major Confederate position once considered impregnable, on April 7.

After the close-fought battle of Shiloh early in April, Union armies under Generals Pope, Henry Thomas and Don Carlos Buell—the McClellan of the West, a man who enjoyed the pageantry of war but disliked the nuisance of battle—moved against Corinth, a Union stronghold in northeastern Mississippi. Halleck, in command, won a major victory here on May 25, when the hero of Fort Sumter, General P.T. Beauregard, evacuated the city. A disgusted President Jefferson Davis soon replaced Beauregard with a close friend, General Braxton Bragg. The Confederates would mount an attempt to retake Corinth in October but would fail, and the city remained in Union hands for the duration of the conflict.

Another Union advance came on the Mississippi River, when a fleet under Flag Officer David Farragut, which had seized New Orleans for the North early in May, captured both Baton Rouge, La., and Natchez, Miss. Farragut next assaulted Vicksburg, Miss., site of the most powerful rebel fortress on the river, but his fleet was driven back.

On June 6 the North rejoiced at more good news, when Colonel Charles Ellet, who had refitted nine steamboats into ironclad rams, defeated a Confederate fleet in a major battle on the Mississippi outside Memphis, and the North took control of the fifth largest city in the Confederacy, a major transportation center. The South was left with only three major bases along the Mississippi: Vicksburg, as well as two smaller forts to its south.

The North had seized the initiative along almost the entire length of the river, in what one newspaper called "a deluge of victories." But when the Union Army launched its largest land operation of the year on this front, its momentum ran out. Halleck ordered Buell to lead a campaign to take Chattanooga, the linchpin of eastern Tennessee, located on the Tennessee River and a railway hub. But Confederate cavalry under Generals Nathan Bedford Forrest and John Hunt Morgan played havoc with Buell's supply lines. The rebel horsemen operated like guerrilla warriors, appearing out of nowhere to tear up railroad tracks and burn supply wagons, then melting back into the landscape, mosquitoes tormenting an elephant.

"Don't you belong to Bragg's army?"

—GENERAL BRAXTON BRAGG, TO A STRAGGLING SOLDIER AFTER STONES RIVER

"Bragg's army! Why, he's got no army! One half of it he shot in Kentucky, and the other half has been whipped to death at Murfreesboro!"

—THE SOLDIER'S RESPONSE; HE DID NOT RECOGNIZE BRAGG

YEAR-END BLOODLETTING
When blue and gray troops clashed at the Battle of Stones River at the beginning of 1863, it was the single deadliest battle of the war in terms of those killed as a percentage of those fighting. Philip Sheridan, only 31 and formerly a quartermaster, distinguished himself here and rose to become a significant Union leader

With Buell bogged down on the way to Chattanooga, his new counterpart, Bragg, was using the diversion created by the Confederate cavalry to mount an invasion of his own. On July 23, Bragg began sending the first of some 30,000 troops on a roundabout rail journey from Mississippi to Chattanooga. After completing the most extensive Confederate railroad movement of the war, he marched his men north into Kentucky, hoping to rally sympathetic locals to the rebel colors and take control of the Bluegrass State for the South, working in tandem with a separate army, 10,000 strong, led by General E. Kirby Smith. But new recruits were few, and Bragg's advance finally galvanized Buell, who marched to engage Bragg at the hamlet of Perryville, Ky. There, on Oct. 8, Union troops beat the outnumbered Southerners, beat them badly enough to send them retreating back to Tennessee.

The last major campaign of 1862 in this tumultuous theater was fought at year's end, after Buell had been replaced by General William Rosecrans. Prodded by Grant, Rosecrans launched a campaign against Bragg, encamped

at Murfreesboro, Tenn., some 33 miles (53 km) southeast of Nashville on the Stones River. Rosecrans commanded some 42,000 troops; Bragg, on the defensive, had 8,000 fewer men. The fight that followed raged over three days, into the new year. Once again, as at Shiloh, the fray began with a surprise assault by Bragg's rebels against Union soldiers as they ate breakfast in camp. But General Philip Sheridan rallied his troops to hold the center of the Union line, and a late Southern charge led by General John Breckinridge, a former Vice President of the U.S., failed. After a day's respite, Breckinridge's men again made a valiant charge against Union forces and were again mauled.

The Battle of Stones River, sometimes called the Battle of Murfreesboro, ended with 13,000 Union casualties and 10,200 among the Confederates. It is considered a Union victory, as Bragg now retreated once more. For the first half of 1863, Rosecrans and Bragg let their armies recuperate and regroup; it would be August 1863 before action once again heated up in eastern Tennessee, where the Union now clearly held the upper hand. ■

The Battle of Fredericksburg

DECEMBER 13, 1862

A new commander rouses Union troops to the offensive, but his plans for a surprise attack degenerate into a slaughter

FOR WANT OF ENGINEERS, A BRIDGE WASN'T built. For lack of the bridge, a river wasn't crossed on schedule. And for the resulting lack of surprise, thousands of Union soldiers found themselves marching uphill directly into the line of fire of the carefully positioned cannons of Robert E. Lee's artillery units until almost 12,500 of them fell as casualties in one of the most one-sided and needless slaughters of the war, the Battle of Fredericksburg.

Hovering in the air over this scene of carnage was the ghostly presence of a man who was not even there: General George B. McClellan, finally sacked by President Abraham Lincoln on Nov. 5, 1862, after his failure to pursue and destroy Lee's army following the Battle of Antietam. Replacing him as commander of the Army of the Potomac was General Ambrose Burnside, 38, who had distinguished himself in leading the land-sea invasion that had captured Roanoke, Va., for the Union earlier in

UPHILL BATTLE *The painting above, by Frederick Cavada, illustrates the task facing Union soldiers as they marched toward the Confederates, entrenched atop Marye's Heights. The line of rifle fire across the center shows the Confederate infantry position behind a stone wall along a sunken lane*

FREDERICKSBURG *The picture at right, perhaps taken before the permanent bridges across the Rappahannock were destroyed, gives a sense of the challenge faced by Union engineers as they attempted to erect pontoon bridges while Confederates entrenched in Fredericksburg directed withering fire at them*

1862 but had seemed a bit slow off the mark at Antietam.

His cheeks adorned by the manly muttonchops that his soldiers playfully dubbed "sideburns," the new commander was large and in charge: a big, bluff, hale man who exuded confidence and authority. He was thus physically suited for his new post, for he had been cast in the role of the anti-McClellan. Burnside understood that what the North and the White House needed now was not deliberation but decisiveness, not dithering but dispatch. In truth, however, he admired McClellan's superb air of command and felt himself unequal to his new role.

Yet dispatch was wanted, and that is what he provided. After simplifying McClellan's command structure, he got the Army of the Potomac—described after Antietam as an "inert mass" by Army commander Henry W. Halleck—on its feet and on the march. On Nov. 15, eight days after Burnside assumed command and almost two full months after Antietam, the Army of the Potomac finally tramped off to pursue Lee's Army of Northern Virginia.

Once his troops had escaped the butchery of Antietam, Lee had again divided his army, sending Stonewall Jackson's troops to their familiar stomping grounds in the Shenandoah Valley, while he settled with James Longstreet's divisions in Culpeper, Va., northwest of

Richmond. He may have believed that McClellan's lassitude was endemic amid Union Army officers and that there would be no more fighting until the spring, for with the Army of Northern Virginia divided, the path to the Confederate capital was only lightly defended.

It was this weakness that Burnside sought to exploit. If he moved quickly, only a natural barrier, the Rappahannock River, would stand between his army and Richmond. But all the bridges that spanned the river had been destroyed, so he called for Union engineers to meet him at Falmouth, Va., where they would build pontoon bridges to allow the army to cross the Rappahannock, take Fredericksburg and march on Richmond, 50 miles (80 km) to the south. But when Burnside's vanguard battalions quick-marched into Falmouth on Nov. 17, they found that the engineers had not arrived. A list of reasons worthy of a McClellan dispatch was delaying them: bad weather, bad roads, bad communications, bad administration.

So while Burnside cooled his heels, Lee gathered his troops to meet the challenge. By the time the Union bridge-builders finally began their work, on Dec. 11, the first wave of Lee's army had also begun arriving to prepare the defense of Fredericksburg.

Burnside's strategy, based on surprise, had failed. But

the North demanded dispatch, so he ordered the construction of six bridges across the Rappahannock, three near where Fredericksburg and Falmouth faced each other, and three more further downstream, where Jackson's troops were now arriving to join Lee's defense.

On Dec. 11, hunkered down in Fredericksburg as Federal artillery shells rained upon them, rebel troops sent withering fire at the exposed Union engineers as they drew into range, and the bridge-building effort stalled. So Burnside sent three regiments across the Rappahannock in boats in sufficient numbers to establish a beachhead.

A battle unusual for the Civil War followed: house-to-house, street-to-street combat within Fredericksburg, most of whose inhabitants had fled as the armies gathered. The Northerners gradually drove the rebels back, but the holding action had given General Longstreet's troops time to dig into a highly defensible position on Marye's Heights, the hills outside Fredericksburg, and for Jackson's army to arrive on the scene. As at Antietam, Lee was now offering the Union a rare chance to face off in a fixed position, but the advantage was all his.

With the element of surprise no longer in play, Burnside took an extra day, Dec. 12, to move his entire army across the Rappahannock and prepare his battle plan.

For whatever reason, order among the troops now broke down, and Union soldiers pillaged Fredericksburg, trashing and looting homes and stores in a drunken frenzy that disgraced both their cause and the midrank officers who allowed the crimes to proceed.

As Dec. 13 dawned—barely, for the day began amid heavy fog—the scene was set for the battle the Union had been seeking since Lee's army had escaped after Antietam. The Confederate general now had some 75,000 troops in the area, with Longstreet's army holding the Heights west of battered Fredericksburg along the Union right and center, and Jackson's troops holding uphill positions along the Union left. Burnside, commanding some 110,000 men, assigned Major General William B. Franklin's divisions to take on Jackson, while troops under Generals Joseph Hooker and Edwin Sumner would assault Longstreet's position. This challenge demanded marching briefly downhill, then emerging into an open field and moving uphill across meadows that had been carefully targeted by Longstreet's artillery batteries to create overlapping fields of fire: a killing cage. Union soldiers who survived the artillery shells would also face fire from Confederate troops well hidden behind a stone wall along a sunken lane—yes, another sunken lane that would soon be

WAGON TRAIN *Union covered wagons cross a pontoon bridge that spans the Rappahannock in May 1864, long after delays in building six such bridges at three crossings robbed the Union of the element of surprise and ruined Burnside's attempt to catch Lee napping*

LIBRARY OF CONGRESS PRINTS AND PHOTOGRAPHS DIVISION (2)

NEW BOSS *General Ambrose Burnside and two staff officers pose for Alexander Gardner's camera in November 1862. Though his army outnumbered Lee's, Burnside suffered almost 12,000 casualties at Fredericksburg to the South's fewer than 5,000*

bloody—from which they could pick off the Northerners.

The battle began on the Union left, where Burnside apparently intended to hurl a strong force against Jackson's famed Stonewall Brigade. But when General Franklin received Burnside's orders, he directed only a single division to lead the charge rather than assigning most of his troops to the attack. It may never be known whether this recipe for failure was the fault of Burnside's poorly written orders or was due to Franklin's well-known caution. Even so, after intense fighting, gritty Pennsylvania troops led by General George Meade battled to win a brief breakthrough in the middle of the Confederate line. But Franklin failed to exploit the opportunity, keeping his 20,000 reserve troops out of the action, even after receiving a direct order from Burnside to deploy them, and the fight there wound down in a stalemate by midafternoon.

The situation was different on the Union right, where Burnside brushed off the warning of brigade commander Colonel Rush Hawkins: "If you make the attack as contemplated, it will be the greatest slaughter of the war." He sent a first wave of Union soldiers, led by Brigadier General Nathan Kimball, marching into one of the most efficient death traps of the war; they were cut down by the Confederate artillery and riflemen. Another charge

was ordered, and more men marched to their doom. The Union troops knew that their valor and pluck had been questioned in both the North and South. Now they were determined to prove their courage, whatever the price.

A third charge followed, then a fourth. By day's end, 15 separate waves of Union soldiers had marched into the valley of death with no senior officer calling a halt to the carnage. "We are slaughtered like sheep, and no result but defeat," Union Captain William Nagle later wrote. From above, Lee watched the pageant of gore unfold with wonder: "It is well that war is so terrible," he remarked to Longstreet. "We would grow too fond of it."

When the guns fell silent, some 13,000 Federals were dead or wounded, more than at Antietam: "and no result but defeat." After a day's truce to clear the battlefield, Burnside's troops retreated in good order across the river. Lee's men also took their leave, many wearing new clothes. In a final grim coda to this scene of horror, Confederate troops who had arrived in Fredericksburg starving and clad in rags spent the night of the battle systematically stripping the clothing from the thousands of Union soldiers who lay dead on the battlefield. The rebels marched off to their winter quarters wearing the blood-spattered blue uniforms of the men they had slaughtered. ∎

1863

"Vicksburg was the only channel [at this time] connecting the parts of the Confederacy divided by the Mississippi. So long as it was held by the enemy, the free navigation of the river was prevented. Hence its importance."

—ULYSSES S. GRANT, *PERSONAL MEMOIRS*

RIVER WARS *The Union transport steamer* Missionary *makes a stop on the Tennessee River in 1863, the year both Vicksburg and Chattanooga fell to the Union. Like the railroads, steamships allowed generals to deploy troops much faster than in previous wars*

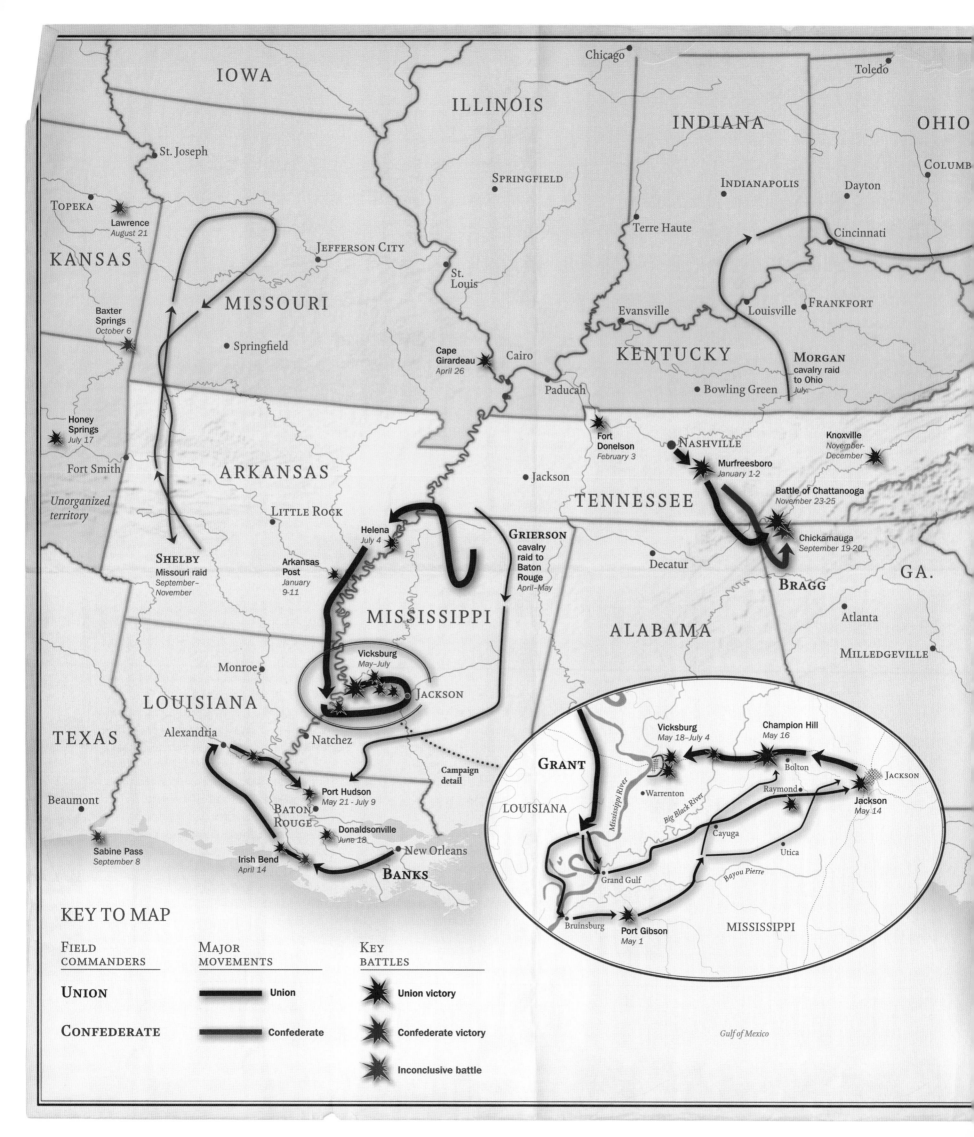

IOWA

ILLINOIS

INDIANA

OHIO

KANSAS

MISSOURI

Chicago

Toledo

St. Joseph

SPRINGFIELD

INDIANAPOLIS

Dayton

COLUMB

TOPEKA

Lawrence
August 21

Terre Haute

Cincinnati

JEFFERSON CITY

Baxter
Springs
October 6

Springfield

St.
Louis

Evansville

Louisville

FRANKFORT

KENTUCKY

Honey
Springs
July 17

Cape
Girardeau
April 26

Cairo

Paducah

Bowling Green

MORGAN
cavalry raid
to Ohio
July

Fort Smith

Unorganized
territory

ARKANSAS

Jackson

Fort
Donelson
February 3

NASHVILLE

Murfreesboro
January 1-2

Knoxville
November-
December

SHELBY
Missouri raid
September–
November

Helena
July 4

TENNESSEE

Battle of Chattanooga
November 23-25

LITTLE ROCK

GRIERSON
cavalry
raid to
Baton
Rouge
April–May

Decatur

Chickamauga
September 19-20

Arkansas
Post
January
9-11

GA.

BRAGG

MISSISSIPPI

ALABAMA

Atlanta

Monroe

Vicksburg
May–July

MILLEDGEVILLE

JACKSON

LOUISIANA

Natchez

Campaign
detail

TEXAS

Alexandria

Vicksburg
May 18–July 4

Champion Hill
May 16

GRANT

Bolton

JACKSON

Beaumont

Port Hudson
May 21 - July 9

BATON
ROUGE

Donaldsonville
June 18

LOUISIANA

Warrenton

Mississippi River

Big Black River

Raymond

Jackson
May 14

Sabine Pass
September 8

Irish Bend
April 14

New Orleans

BANKS

Cayuga

Utica

Grand Gulf

Bayou Pierre

Bruinsburg

Port Gibson
May 1

MISSISSIPPI

KEY TO MAP

FIELD
COMMANDERS

UNION

CONFEDERATE

MAJOR
MOVEMENTS

Union

Confederate

KEY
BATTLES

Union victory

Confederate victory

Inconclusive battle

Gulf of Mexico

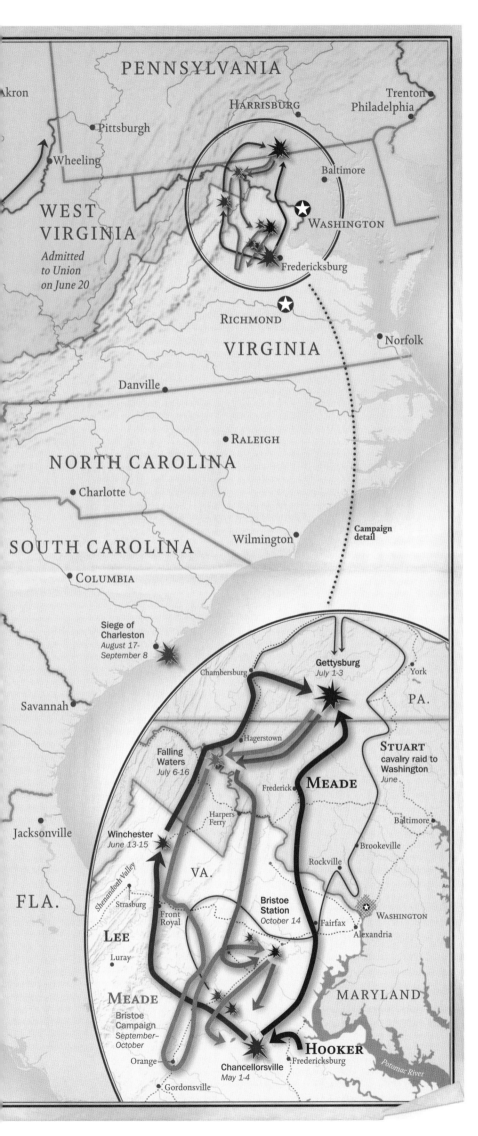

1863
Situation Report

In a watershed year of the war, General Ulysses S. Grant captures Vicksburg and Chattanooga for the Union, while General Robert E. Lee's invasion of Pennsylvania ends in disaster at Gettysburg

Jan. 1 The Emancipation Proclamation is officially issued.

March 3 With Union armies in need of soldiers, the U.S. Congress enacts a draft for men between the ages of 20 and 45. The act allows draftees to pay substitutes to serve.

May 1-4 Southern troops under Lee win a decisive victory at the Battle of Chancellorsville in northern Virginia, but Stonewall Jackson is wounded. He dies on May 10.

May-June Grant enters Mississippi and fights his way north, winning several battles, and placing the fortress city of Vicksburg under siege.

June 3 Lee's Army of Northern Virginia invades the North. On June 9, Union and Confederate horsemen clash at the Battle of Brandy Station in America's largest cavalry action.

July 1-3 In the war's largest battle, the new Army of the Potomac commander, General George G. Meade, wins a major victory over Lee's forces at Gettysburg. But as at Antietam in 1862, the rebels escape to fight another day.

July 4 In a consequential victory, Vicksburg surrenders to Grant, putting the entire Mississippi River in Union hands.

Sept. 13 General Meade's troops invade Virginia, beginning the Bristoe Campaign, which ends inconclusively.

Sept. 19-20 Confederates win the bloody Battle of Chickamauga in eastern Tennessee and trap a Union army in besieged Chattanooga, a gateway to the deep South.

Nov. 19 In his Gettysburg Address, Lincoln articulates the meaning and purpose of the war, aligning it with the founding American belief that all men are created equal.

Nov. 23-25 After Grant is put in charge in Chattanooga, Union victories drive Southern armies from the region, and the door opens for Northern advances into Georgia.

★

The Siege of Vicksburg

An irresistible force tackles an immovable object—and General Ulysses S. Grant wins control of the "Gibraltar of the West"

O F ALL THE BATTLES AND CAMPAIGNS of the Civil War, the siege of Vicksburg, Miss., remains uniquely touching. In a conflict considered the first modern war, here is a story as old as Homer's tale of Troy: the encirclement of an enemy fortress and the constriction of its lines of supply until its occupants are starved into surrender. The fight for Vicksburg also looked to the future, for it heralded a new phase of the war, in which its ravages would no longer be suffered only by its armies but would also be visited upon the citizens of the South. And it served notice, if more were needed, that the mastermind behind the Union triumph, General U. S. Grant, was the essential man President Abraham Lincoln had been seeking: a warrior who took on a job and would not rest until it was completed.

In 1863, Vicksburg was the most important city in the West. President Jefferson Davis called it "the nailhead that held the South's two halves together." Lincoln, who had made two journeys down the Mississippi from Illinois to New Orleans as a young man, chose a different metaphor: he described the graceful old city as the key to the

CITY ON A HILL *Vicksburg was divided into two sections, a gracious residential area atop the bluff and a busy working-class district along its wharves. Home to some 4,600 people in 1861, it had grown wealthy as a major port on the Mississippi. The large building atop the bluff is the Old Courthouse, built in 1858 and now a museum*

ISOLATED *The defense of Vicksburg was assigned in October 1862 to Lieutenant General John C. Pemberton, a Mexican War veteran suspected of pro-North sympathies by some, since he was born in Philadelphia*

West. "The war can never be brought to a close until that key is in our pocket," he declared. "I am acquainted with that region and know what I am talking about."

Flag Officer David Farragut had taken New Orleans for the Union in May 1862, and Grant had captured Forts Henry and Donelson to the north in Tennessee earlier that year. Vicksburg, seated regally along a bluff on the eastern shore of the Mississippi, was one of the last preserves of Confederate power on the river. Its big artillery batteries towered over the waterway, preventing Union vessels from passing up or down. Farragut tried on several occasions late in 1862 to take on the city's big guns from the river, but he was forced to withdraw his ships. Two other Confederate fortresses downstream of Vicksburg, one at Port Hudson, La., and the other at Grand Gulf, Miss., added to the rebels' domination of this stretch of the river.

Grant launched a tentative campaign against the Confederate "Gibraltar of the West" from Tennessee in October 1862, but he was driven back in December by South-

ern cavalry under Generals Nathan Bedford Forrest and Earl Van Dorn, who succeeded in disrupting his lines of supply. But when the year ended with a narrow Union victory at Stones River in Tennessee, Grant was once again free to direct his full attention to taking Vicksburg.

The enemy he faced was not only the rebel troops and guns within the fortified city but also the unique topography around it: to its north, vast stretches of marshy swamps, bogs and rivers made passage impossible. To the west was the river, where Union boats dared not venture. The south and east offered better approaches for Grant's armies—but how was he to get them there? The task called for moving the 45,000 troops divided between his two top subordinates, General William Tecumseh Sherman and General John A. McClernand (a Lincoln political appointee whom Grant did not trust) deep into rebel territory and into position to assail Vicksburg.

The Confederate armies defending the city were also led by two generals who had little faith in each other.

Aware of the battle to come, President Davis, a former U.S. Senator from Mississippi, had traveled west in December 1862 to hash out the lines of authority. He put General Joseph E. Johnston, wounded in the Peninsula Campaign and now recovered, in overall charge of the Western theater, and named Major General John C. Pemberton—a Philadelphia-born Yankee, no less—to lead the Army of the Mississippi, charging him to hold Vicksburg at all costs. But the two men were bitter rivals whose divisions would only aid the Union cause.

EARLY UNION MANEUVERS Grant approached the task of taking Vicksburg as a scientist might, undertaking four separate "experiments" as he searched for a way to direct the full extent of the Union forces, which included a fleet of ironclad gunboats and transport ships commanded by Admiral David Dixon Porter, against the rebel bulwark. The first was the digging of a cutoff canal across a peninsula that faced Vicksburg, to allow passage for Porter's vessels. Union soldiers toiled for months on the 1-mile (1.6 km) -long canal, but the work subjected them to the Confederate guns within Vicksburg and to even more deadly foes, diseases such as typhoid and dysentery that killed hundreds of soldiers. When the Mississippi repeatedly erased the men's efforts, work on the canal ceased.

At the same time, two more experiments were taking place amid the marshy mazes around Vicksburg: a pair of projected waterways aimed at bringing Porter's transport ships near Vicksburg from the north and west. But in both cases the cypress swamps proved impenetrable. The rebels stopped one of the attempts by erecting Fort Pemberton, a Confederate position that effectively blocked further Union progress in March.

The fourth experiment, an attempted passage by Porter's gunboats through Steele's Bayou, north of Vicksburg, also made no progress. Grant had absorbed the lesson: his final strategy for capturing Vicksburg called for marching his armies south through Louisiana on the west side of the river past the city, then transporting them across the waterway to approach the citadel from the south and east.

For the strategy to succeed, Porter's gunboats would have to steam past the big Confederate guns at Vicksburg so they could ferry the soldiers across the river. And the Union forces would have to take on two large Confederate armies: the 30,000 men inside Vicksburg commanded by Pemberton and the 30,000 more under Johnston, even now moving from Tennessee to the Mississippi capital, Jackson, 44 miles (72 km) east of Vicksburg.

Grant's plan was so daring and relied on so many variables falling into place, that his subordinates, including Sherman, considered it too risky. But Grant was acutely aware that his failure to achieve traction against Vicksburg was attracting criticism in the North: old charges that he was a drunkard had begun circulating again.

GRANT MOVES SOUTH On April 16, Grant's final campaign on the Mississippi began on a moonless night, when Porter's fleet of eight gunboats and three transports utterly surprised the Confederates inside Vicksburg. In a daring run, they plowed downstream past the city's big guns, which sank only a single transport. A few nights later, five of six more transports managed to slip past the batteries, and by month's end Grant had a full Union fleet and some 23,000 soldiers across the river from Bruinsburg, Miss.

Porter's fleet carried these divisions, led by McClernand, across the Mississippi on April 30. The crossing succeeded in large part because Grant diverted the rebels

OLD AND NEW *The battle to control the vital Mississippi saw action by warships of all stripes. The unidentified schooner at top, powered by sail, carried 13-in. (33 cm) mortars that pounded Southern forts along the lower Mississippi.*

An even more important role was played by powerful new ironclad gunboats like the U.S.S. Essex, bottom, a former steamboat ferry refitted for combat. It served in the Union campaigns at Fort Henry and Vicksburg

A City Encircled

Union mapmaker Robert Knox Sneden's depiction of Vicksburg shows its location along the east side of a huge bend in the Mississippi River, which made it highly defensible. Two major forts to its north secured the city against invasion from the land while also allowing Confederate artillery to fire from several angles at Union boats venturing downriver.

Union forces are shown in purple on the map; Confederate troops and fortifications are in red. In the months before Grant began his campaign against the city in the spring of 1862, Vicksburg's defenses were bulked up until it boasted the most elaborate entrenchments of any city in the South, including Richmond.

The Union gunboat fleet shown at the bottom of the map ensured that no Southern relief vessels could steam upriver to bring desperately need supplies into the city during the siege.

On June 7 a Confederate force diverted from Louisiana attacked a Union garrison at Milliken's Bend, some 15 miles (24 km) northwest of Vicksburg. The garrison was primarily defended by two regiments of newly trained African-American Union soldiers who fought with distinction and repelled the rebels.

During the 47-day siege, some 22,000 Union artillery shells were hurled into the city and against its defenses, although the toll on the city's inhabitants was not extensive: estimates of the number of civilians killed range from as few as 20 to more than 50.

Sneden shows 40,000 rebel troops inside the city; in reality, some 30,000 troops surrendered to General U.S. Grant on July 4, 1863, and were subsequently paroled.

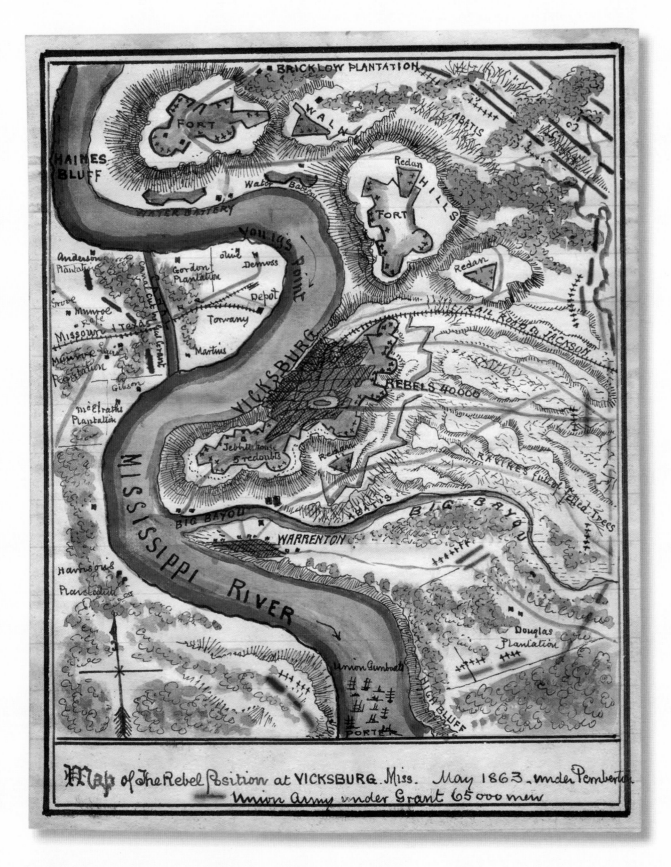

with a one-two punch: Sherman's army kept Confederate troops north of Vicksburg busy with a feigned main thrust that led Pemberton to send 3,000 troops to that area, rather than to oppose Grant in the south. Meanwhile, in the last two weeks of April, Major General Benjamin Grierson led 1,700 Union cavalrymen in a wide-ranging raid across Mississippi, spreading havoc, tearing up railroad tracks and burning supply depots in perhaps the most effective Northern cavalry action of the war.

Grant now had a large force in Mississippi, where the rebels had evacuated their fort at Grand Gulf; deep behind enemy lines with no means of supply, the Union troops lived off the land. Grant's first target was Port Gibson, 10 miles (16 km) east of the river, held by only 6,000 rebels. Grant took the fortress easily on May 1. His next move was a surprise: rather than marching directly on Vicksburg, he led his men northeast and captured Jackson, held by some 6,000 of Johnston's troops. Grant wanted to secure his eastern flank before taking on Vicksburg.

On May 16 the largest battle of the campaign took place at Champion Hill, midway between Jackson and Vicksburg, where Grant's army overwhelmed 20,000 rebels sent from Vicksburg by Pemberton. The Confederates fell back to the Big Black River, only 10 miles east of Vicksburg, and were again badly beaten, on May 17. The remnants of this army now withdrew inside Vicksburg, whose citizens were shocked by their plight as they filed in: the rebels were dirty, ragged, defeated. An emboldened Grant hurled his troops against Vicksburg's outer defenses on May 19, but the Confederate entrenchments proved as strong as he had feared, and the Union troops were repelled at a high cost in casualties. When another attack on May 22 proved just as futile, the Northerners hunkered down to conduct a siege of the city.

INSIDE THE CITY Five weeks before, on April 16, the ordeal of Vicksburg's citizens had begun to the strains of an orchestra. The local aristocrats had been holding a spring ball at one of the city's grand mansions; it ended in utter confusion and chaos as the city's batteries opened fire on Porter's gunboats, which in turn sent artillery shells roaring into the streets as they successfully steamed past the rebel defenses. In the weeks to come, as Grant's troops gradually surrounded the city, residents dug caves for shelter in the soft, loamy hillsides of the town; Union artillery guns were now close enough to begin unleashing a steady barrage of shells into the city. Some of the caves were a grotesque reflection of Southern grandeur: they were furnished with fine furniture, rugs and gas lamps.

The city was now defended by some 30,000 troops under Pemberton. Grant, whose armies were growing in size

FOXHOLES *Union troops from General John Logan's divisions dug out artillery shelters in the hills near Wexford Lodge outside Vicksburg, home of the Shirley family, which they occupied during the siege. As many as 500 similar caves were dug by residents inside the city; Union troops derided Vicksburg as "Prairie Dog Village." But when the city surrendered, the Northern troops entered its streets with a restraint that was commended in both North and South*

PORT CITY *Steamships crowd Vicksburg's wharves in a picture taken following the city's surrender to the Union. Before the war, the city was wealthy from the river trade: according to historian Lee Sandlin, "Its commercial district was able to support ... a grocery store selling fancy tinned goods from Europe, a milliner carrying fabrics from Asia, a perfumery stocked with scents from the Middle East, and a bookstore called Clarke's Literary Depot with the latest and raciest novels from New York, London, and Paris"*

as new units moved across the Mississippi, commanded some 80,000 men around it. After destroying the capital of Jackson, the Union troops had withdrawn, leaving its remains to Johnston, who held some 30,000 troops there. Vicksburg's hopes now rested with Johnston's so-called Army of Relief. But despite the frantic messages Johnston was receiving from Davis in Richmond, he was so spooked by Grant's force that he left Vicksburg to its fate.

As the siege continued, the people inside the city began to starve. Pet cats and dogs strangely disappeared; prices for necessities soared. As Lee Sandlin recounts in *Wicked River* (Pantheon; 2010), a lively survey of life on the Mississippi in the steamboat era: "Beef and pork were unobtainable. They were replaced ... by mule meat ... People were so desperate for salt that they were tearing apart the butchers' smokehouses so they could scrape out the salt from the ancient fat drippings that had soaked into the floorboards ... [by early July] the mule meat was gone from the butchers' windows; several memoirs claimed that it was replaced by neatly skinned rat carcasses."

As Union engineers tunneled under the city's defenses to detonate explosives, as a constant rain of artillery shells undercut rebel morale, and as Johnston's long-awaited Army of Relief failed to materialize, Pemberton's position became ever more untenable. On June 28, a group of Confederate soldiers delivered a message to their despised,

Pennsylvania-born commander: "If you can't feed us, you had better surrender ..." On July 4, Pemberton did so, bringing the city's ghastly sufferings to an end.

UNION TRIUMPH When Grant's victorious troops marched into the city, they behaved with a grace that reflected well upon their officers: there was no gloating, and the Northerners happily shared their rations with the soldiers and citizens, commending them on their valiant stand. Grant, famed for his tough policy of "unconditional surrender," decided that taking in hand some 30,000 rebel troops would create an administrative nightmare. He paroled the Southern troops, urging them to give up their fight and return to their homes. Most, but not all, did so.

Within days, Northern control of the Mississippi was cemented when rebels troops inside Port Hudson, 250 mi. (402 km) to the south, surrendered to a Union army. The South had been cut in two. President Lincoln, who now had his long-sought key in his pocket, painted the new state of affairs in the West in a phrase wrought for history: "The Father of Waters again goes unvexed to the Sea."

The citizens of Vicksburg were far from unvexed: it would be 82 more years, amid festivities marking the end of World War II in Europe in 1945, before Independence Day was celebrated once more by the inhabitants of this proud city on a hill. ∎

Scenes from Vicksburg

The starving city weathered the Union siege for 47 days

LEST WE FORGET *Proud of their city's courage during the siege, Vicksburg's citizens preserved some of the caves within which they took shelter during the ordeal. Above, an observer stands outside the entrance of one such cave in the 1890s*

SPOILS OF WAR *Two houses of worship, a Methodist church in the foreground at right and a Roman Catholic church at rear, preside over a large lot crowded with Confederate wagons and artillery captured by the Union when the city surrendered. Grant paroled 30,000 rebel troops*

HARD TIMES *As the Union grip around Vicksburg tightened, the city's straits were reflected in unusual ways. At left is a copy of the July 2 edition of the* Daily Citizen, *printed on wallpaper for lack of newsprint.*

Early on, the paper regularly declared that General Johnston's Army of Relief was on its way; by late June a writer was pleading, "Where is Johnston"?

BIG GUNS *Union gunners tend their mortars at Battery Sherman, named for General William T. Sherman, east of Vicksburg on the road to Jackson, Miss., the state capital. After Jackson was taken by Sherman's troops and devastated, Confederate commander General Joseph Johnston moved back into the city, but he did not act to relieve the Union siege. These mortars could hurl a 13-in. (33 cm) cannonball some 2,650 yds. (2.4 km)*

Ulysses S. Grant

If Lee was a patrician, the Union general was a plebe. But he won the war with a modest bearing, an iron will and an eye to the future

THE RIVAL GENERALS WHO COMMANDED the largest armies of the Civil War were perfectly cast for their roles. Robert E. Lee was every inch the Southern patriarch, his handsome face, well-groomed beard and erect posture always suggesting he was prepared for his portrait to be painted. Ulysses S. Grant, in contrast, paid little attention to his appearance—and it showed. War chronicler Shelby Foote quotes a journalist who wrote, "Grant has none of the solder's bearing about him, but is a man whom one would take for a country merchant or a village lawyer … there are a thousand men like him in personal appearance in the ranks." Congressman Elihu Washburne, who once spent six days with Grant on the move, told his fellow Representatives that Grant "took with him neither a horse nor an orderly nor a servant nor a camp-chest nor an overcoat nor a blanket nor even a clean shirt … he fared like the commonest soldier in his command, partaking of his rations and sleeping on the ground." Yet another writer called him "a plain businessman of the Republic."

When it came to war, Grant was indeed all business, and he conducted his business with such briskness and dispatch that by March of 1864, when President Abraham Lincoln summoned him from his triumphant campaigns in the West to become the new leader of all the Union armies, Congress voted to elevate Grant to the rank of Lieutenant General. The unprepossessing Ohioan thus became only the third American officer to hold that rank, following George Washington and Winfield Scott.

In an age of industry, Grant was the soul of industriousness. The Confederates, who celebrated time-honored agrarian values, conducted war in the past tense: J.E.B. Stuart went to battle on a warhorse, wearing a plume in his hat. Grant trained his gaze on the future: far more

than the Southerners, he made engineering central to the military process, astounding the South with the tactical advantages science could bring. During the Overland Campaign of 1864, Union engineers quickly erected a pontoon bridge across the James River that allowed Grant to bypass Lee's fortified positions and appear at his rear, after evading detection by the rebels for three days.

For Grant, war was a process, not a pageant. Stymied in trying to take Vicksburg, he embarked on a series of "experiments," creative navigational endeavors designed to open an unexpected avenue into the fortified city—and also to keep tens of thousands of encamped Union soldiers active and engaged in outwitting the enemy.

Grant's rise to the rank of Washington and Scott would have seemed highly unlikely as recently as 1860, when the West Point graduate, after experiencing a steep fall from grace, was struggling to support his wife and four children by working as an assistant in his father's tannery in Galena, Ill. In truth, this plain businessman of the Republic was never much of a success in the real world of business, and he had left a once promising career in the U.S. Army over allegations of drunkenness.

Born Hiram Ulysses Grant in Point Pleasant, Ohio, into an old family from Massachusetts, the young man received his new name by accident, when a local Congressman mistakenly stated his name as Ulysses S. Grant on his nomination to attend the U.S. Military Academy at West Point. After graduating from the academy in 1843, Grant, like almost every other important general in the Civil War, served in the Mexican War, where, despite his posting as a quartermaster, he was twice brevetted for bravery. He also learned much from closely observing the tactics of such leaders as Generals Zachary Taylor and Winfield Scott. Like Abraham Lincoln, then serving in Congress, Grant opposed the war as a land grab: he later

> "The most modest, the most disinterested and the most honest man I ever knew, with a temper that nothing could disturb … sincere, thoughtful, deep and gifted with courage that never faltered."
>
> —CHARLES A. DANA, IN HIS MEMOIRS OF THE WAR

turned the feeling, and when Buchanan believed he had evidence proving Grant had been drinking on the job, he asked the 32-year-old to either retire from the service or face a court martial. On July 31, 1854, Grant resigned his commission and soon returned to the Midwest.

The next seven years were a period of struggle for Grant: an attempt at farming failed, and for a time he worked as a bill collector in St. Louis before he settled into the tannery. When war broke out, Grant found his calling. After helping recruit a group of volunteers in Galena, he received a commission from the governor of Illinois to serve in the state militia. Energetic, experienced and assured, he rose quickly in the ranks. But along the way, he was dogged by rumors that he was a drunkard.

When he was Grant's superior, General Henry W. Halleck told President Lincoln that Grant had a drinking problem. The charge was so severe that Secretary of War Edwin Stanton sent his respected assistant, Charles A. Dana, to visit Grant in Tennessee. Dana's report was so positive about Grant's character and behavior that it actually helped propel him higher in the ranks. Most scholars today believe that Grant had a drinking problem prior to the war but successfully avoided the bottle during most of his wartime service, thanks in part to the assistance of loyal aides. Lincoln resolved the issue in his inimitable backwoods fashion, claiming that if he could find out whatever it was that Grant was supposed to be drinking, he would send barrels of the stuff to his other generals.

One must live an eventful life if serving two terms as President of the United States constitutes a let-down, but that is the case with Grant: the Civil War was his finest hour. Running on the motto "Let Us Have Peace," he was elected as a Republican in a landslide victory in 1868. And he tried to sow peace, with amnesty for former rebels, with his support of black freedmen and moderate forms of Reconstruction in the South, and with his surprisingly generous outreach to Native Americans. But though he was elected again in 1872, an economic crisis, the Panic of 1873, and revelations of corruption in his Administration made his final years in the presidency very bitter.

The old soldier spent his last years writing his memoirs, hoping to leave a financial legacy for his family, even as he suffered great pain from throat cancer. He completed the work only days before he died at 63 in 1885. To his grave, Grant never had the regal bearing of a Robert E. Lee. But the two men shared an inner gallantry that has earned them a place in the pantheon of American heroes. ■

REDEEMED *Forced to resign from the U.S. Army in 1854 over charges of drunkenness, Grant flailed in private life for seven years before finding his calling again when the war broke out. By 1864, when this picture was taken outside his tent at Cold Harbor, Va., Grant was showing the self-confidence and resolve of a man who has beaten his inner demons—as well as more than a few Confederate generals*

described it as "one of the most unjust [wars] ever waged by a stronger against a weaker nation."

In 1848 Grant married Julia Boggs Dent; the couple would have four children. He was posted to the Pacific Northwest in 1852, where he served as a quartermaster at Fort Vancouver in Washington State. After being posted to Fort Humboldt in California in 1854, Grant, now a captain, seems to have gone into serious depression: his wife and children were away in the Midwest, and he had lost most of his private capital when he was duped by a merchant in San Francisco. He despised his superior officer, Lieutenant Colonel Robert C. Buchanan, who re-

The Battle of Chancellorsville

MAY 1-4, 1863

The Army of the Potomac gets a new commander, but once again Robert E. Lee and Stonewall Jackson outfox a larger Union force

FOR THE SOLDIERS OF THE ARMY OF THE Potomac, the year 1863 began amid scenes that seemed eerily symbolic of the larger Union plight in the Eastern theater of the war: the men were bogged down, flailing forlack of direction and losing faith in their commanding officers. In mid-January, only one month after the Union debacle at the Battle of Fredericksburg, General Ambrose Burnside rousted his divisions from their winter quarters north of the Rappahannock River and sent them marching south again, aiming to take the battle to Robert E. Lee's exhausted Army of Northern Virginia one more time. But just as the men began to move, severe rainstorms turned dirt roads into swales of mud, and after two full days of misery and almost no progress, Burnside was forced to call a halt to the inept "Mud March."

Soon it was Burnside himself who was called to a halt by his superior, President Abraham Lincoln. The disaster at Fredericksburg and the Mud March, as well as rising levels of desertion in the Northern ranks due to Burnside's slack and inequitable administration of the Army, forced Lincoln to remove the commander he had put in

place less than two months before. The President named General Joseph Hooker, "Fighting Joe" to the soldiers, as the new commander of Union troops in the Eastern theater. And in his first months on the job, the general, who had served as a reliable subordinate officer in the Peninsula Campaign and at Antietam, proved a good choice, reducing corruption, improving camp cleanliness and food and reorganizing his cavalry to make it more independent, along Southern lines. He even commissioned new regimental badges, restoring morale among his charges.

Yet when Fighting Joe took the fight to the enemy in May 1863, the outcome would be depressingly familiar: in the Battle of Chancellorsville, Robert E. Lee and Stonewall Jackson utterly outwitted Hooker and sent his much larger army into the maneuver its soldiers now knew best—retreat.

Among his other changes, Hooker had improved the North's intelligence operations, and for the first time in this theater, a Union commander had an accurate tally of the forces arrayed there. Hooker's Army of the Potomac numbered some 130,000 troops, while Lee's Army of Northern Virginia, hunkered down in winter quarters around now well-fortified Fredericksburg, was about 60,000-strong, a bit smaller than usual, for Lee had sent General James Longstreet's army southeast to address Union movements along the Virginia coast.

Hooker began his spring offensive in promising fashion, employing tactics seldom used by his predecessors,

AFTERMATH *Brigadier General Herman Haupt, left, the resourceful engineer who supervised Union logistics, observes dead horses and an artillery caisson of the Washington Artillery of New Orleans atop Marye's Heights, Va. on May 3, after Northern troops finally took control of the Confederate position*

for he eschewed brute strength to focus on movement and surprise. His plan was to keep Lee in place at Fredericksburg while the vast majority of Union soldiers, some 70,000 men, would ford the Rappahannock upstream of the town and congregate at Chancellorsville, Va., a hamlet some 10 miles (16 km) northwest of Fredericksburg. They would then advance on Lee's lightly guarded rear, where he was least likely to expect a Union attack. Lee, it was hoped, would be pinned down during this movement by a smaller Union force under General John Sedgwick that would attempt to cross the river near Fredericksburg, drawing attention away from the main Union thrust. It was a plan worthy of Lee himself, but its success would demand stealth, subtlety and agility, qualities that Northern commanders had so far proved unable to muster.

Hooker's success in restoring discipline among his troops was evident when the soldiers crossed the Rappahannock in timely fashion at a number of fords west of Chancellorsville in the final days of April, then split into two wings and marched unopposed into the hamlet. But now Hooker faced an ally that time and again had aligned on the Southern side: the region's unique topography. The Northern commander had managed to land his army smack dab in an area locals called the Wilderness—a vast, dismal, second-growth forest of swamps, heavy underbrush and dense foliage. "I was not prepared to find it an almost impenetrable thicket," the general later admitted.

Hooker was unprepared regarding another important matter: he assumed Lee would abandon his position at Fredericksburg and retreat south toward Richmond when he realized the full extent of the Union forces now across the Rappahannock. But Lee decided to stand and

ROUND TWO *This stone wall along a sunken road at the foot of Marye's Heights was the scene of fierce fighting at both the Battle of Fredericksburg and the Battle of Chancellorsville five months later.*

Above, the wall is shown soon after the fighting ceased in the latter struggle, when Union soldiers under General John Sedgwick assaulted entrenched Confederates in one of the largest bayonet charges of the war. They routed the rebels and finally drove them from the heights above

SOLDIER'S REST *After Stonewall Jackson's death at Chancellorsville, the South was plunged into mourning. Some 20,000 people filed by his coffin, lying in state in Richmond, before Jackson was buried in Lexington, Va., at the Virginia Military Institute, right. The great commander's dying words have entered the American lexicon: "Let us cross over the river, and rest under the shade of the trees"*

"I retired from his presence with the belief that my commanding general was a whipped man."

—UNION GENERAL DARIUS COUCH, ON HOOKER

fight rather than fall back; he well knew that Northern superiority in numbers had seldom ensured a Union victory in the past. And Lee had yet another arrow in his quiver of surprises: he would not only dig in and resist Hooker's advance, but he would again challenge accepted military strategy by dividing his main force in two. Suspecting the move against Fredericksburg was a sideshow, Lee kept less than a third of his force in position to face the Federals under Sedgwick who were harassing his base camp, while he sent the rest of his troops, under Jackson, to tackle Hooker in the Wilderness outside Chancellorsville.

On May 1, Hooker's troops began moving on Fredericksburg from the west; the plan was working well. But when vanguard Union troops bumped up against some of Jackson's men moving in from Fredericksburg to challenge them, Fighting Joe seemed to lose his nerve. Despite his superiority in numbers, he decided to abandon the offensive and pull back to assume a defensive posture in the Wilderness—against the strong advice of his subordinates, who pleaded with him to stick to his plan. For whatever reason, the fight seemed to have gone out of Fighting Joe. For the next few days, he would remain inert and passive against foes who were alert and active.

Soon the rebels were again making hay with their superior knowledge of the local lay of the land. Major Jedediah Hotchkiss, the Confederate topographical engineer whose detailed map had helped Jackson run rings around three Union armies in the Shenandoah Valley a year before, located a plank road running through the Wilderness that might allow Jackson to move south of Chancellorsville and attack Hooker's unprotected western flank, just when the Union general was expecting an attack from the east—thus turning the tables on Hooker's flanking strategy. The ploy involved leaving only 15,000 Southern troops to face 72,000 Northerners while Jackson's men were on the march, but Lee again chose to divide his army, believing Jackson could execute the plan.

And he did: on May 2, Jackson's men pulled off one of war's riskiest maneuvers, a transit across the front line of another army. The 12-mile (19 km) hike ended in midafternoon; it was not entirely undetected, but when Hooker heard that the Stonewall Division was on the move, he convinced himself the Southerners must be retreating.

This was no retreat. Around 5:15 p.m., Jackson's men burst upon unsuspecting Northern troops on the Union right commanded by General Oliver O. Howard. Howling the rebel yell, they attacked across a 2-mile (3 km) front and pushed the Yankee line back by some 2 miles. In retrospect, this magnificent surprise assault came to seem a highwater mark for the South in the war. For that night, even as the rebels were rejoicing in their successful gambit, tragedy struck: Stonewall Jackson, reconnoitering the front lines in the Wilderness with a group of officers on horseback, was hit twice in the left arm by friendly fire, bullets fired by his own troops. That night his arm was amputated. Lee, who knew no one could replace Jackson, declared, "He has lost his left arm but I have lost my right." Jackson died of pneumonia eight days later.

The battle continued on May 3, with cavalry officer General J.E.B. Stuart filling in for Jackson, as the rebels continued to hammer the Federals in the Wilderness, using artillery located in an uphill position called the Hazel Grove that gave them a commanding advantage. Nine miles away, outside Fredericksburg on the second front, history was repeating itself as Sedgwick's Union troops faced obstacles that were all too familiar when they assaulted Confederates on Marye's Heights. As in the Battle of Fredericksburg, two Union charges were stopped by rebels massed behind the stone wall along the sunken road. But a third charge succeeded, and the cheering Northerners at last commanded Marye's Heights.

Back at Chancellorsville, Hooker was felled when a cannonball hit the mansion he was using as his headquarters and knocked him unconscious. But he was soon able to resume command, and he now ordered a withdrawal from the mansion, ceding victory in the Wilderness to the rebels. Soon Confederate troops were cheering as Robert E. Lee arrived at the mansion to take in the scene. When Lee learned of Sedgwick's surprising success at Fredericksburg, Lee dispatched troops who checked the Northern advance midway between the two towns. The rebels hit Sedgwick's men again the next day, May 4, and when that fight ended in a draw, Sedgwick retreated back across the Rappahannock. The next day, Hooker followed.

Another new Union general had managed, despite vast superiority in numbers, to lose another major battle. "My God! My God!" said Abraham Lincoln when he heard the news. "What will the country say?" ■

The Battle of Gettysburg

JULY 1-3, 1863

Robert E. Lee leads exhilarated Confederate troops in an invasion of the North, but his last great gamble ends in defeat and retreat

THE GREATEST BATTLE EVER FOUGHT ON American soil dazzles us with its onslaught of numbers: 165,000 men clashed here in a conflict that raged across three full days. When it was over, some 28,000 Confederate troops were dead, injured or missing and 23,000 on the Union side. In the war's largest artillery battle, more than 300 cannons dueled for hours; in its largest cavalry battle, some 20,500 horsemen contended. But in the end, all the swollen statistics of this pivotal battle resolve into focus around a single person, General Robert E. Lee. For this was Lee's battle, a self-inflicted wound: in modern terms, he owned Gettysburg, win or lose. This second Confederate invasion of the North, following the setback at Antietam in September 1862, was entirely Lee's brainchild.

The thoughtful general pitched his plan to President Jefferson Davis at a strategy session in Richmond on May 15, when the Confederates' top military minds were grappling with Grant's Vicksburg campaign and Union advances in Tennessee. The question: Should General James Longstreet's army be dispatched from Virginia to help take on Grant? No, said Lee. Rather than remain on the defensive in the West, he argued, the South should take the offensive in the East, surprising the Union with an unexpected strike in Pennsylvania, west of Washington.

As Lee ticked off the advantages of a surprise attack, his argument became more compelling. The rich farms and well-stocked storehouses of the North would address his primary problem: a lack of food and supplies for his soldiers. Moreover, the sudden appearance of 75,000 rebels in Union territory considered far from the front would deeply alarm the locals and rally thousands of increasingly skeptical Northerners to the cause of the Peace Democrats, or Copperheads, the growing anti-war party led by former Ohio Representative Clement Vallandigham. And the unexpected reversal of momentum would send a powerful message to the South's most important audience: diplomats in London and Paris who still refused to believe that the Confederacy was an emerging state rather than an upstart regional faction.

Lee also knew that another factor made an advance imperative: the stalemate on the Eastern front, now more than two years old, amounted to a war of attrition that favored the North, far richer in manpower and supplies. A dramatic action was needed, a bold stroke was called for—now. And what better time than in the wake of Chancellorsville, when the Northern armies had once again been humiliated by the smaller, more adept rebel forces?

Was Lee a victim of hubris? The word seems harsh for such a measured individual, but his confidence in himself, his leaders and his troops, so essential in a successful general, was deservedly high. After he had taken the reins of the Army of Northern Virginia during the Peninsula Campaign, his tough, swift troops had driven the larger Army of the Potomac retreating back to Washington. They had lost at Antietam but had escaped annihilation. They had then whipped the Yankees at Fredericksburg, at the Second Battle of Bull Run and at Chancellorsville.

GRIM REAPER *Timothy O'Sullivan is believed to have taken this photo of dead Federals at Gettysburg, "Harvest of Death," on July 6, three days after the battle concluded*

He and his gifted subordinates—J.E.B. Stuart, Longstreet, A.P. Hill, the late Stonewall Jackson—had watched a hapless quartet of Union generals test them and fail: McClellan and Burnside, Pope and Hooker. Lee believed he now led the single greatest fighting force on earth. But he was incorrect in thinking that this meant his troops could overcome any obstacle and win every battle.

GREENER PASTURES President Davis signed on to Lee's plan. Early in June, Lee led his troops northwest out of Fredericksbrug, with Major General Richard Ewell commanding the Stonewall Brigade in place of its recently deceased leader. Stuart's cavalry directed Northern eyes away from Lee's advancing units with a diversionary raid. Stuart's actions during the campaign have been heavily criticized: on the way north, the showy general insisted on holding a review of his 9,500 horseman, topped off with a mock charge. When Lee couldn't attend, Stuart put on the same show three days later, tiring his troops and horses.

Stuart wasn't expecting Union opposition to his raid, and he was unprepared when improving Northern cavalrymen, led by Major General Alfred Pleasonton and Major General John Buford, surprised him at Brandy Station outside Culpeper, in the largest mounted battle of the war. Stuart escaped the trap and set off on one of his typical exploits, a raid around the perimeter of Union positions. But this meant that he would be out of touch with Lee and unable to reconnoiter Northern troop movements early in the battle, one of his primary assignments.

Even so, the cavalry action succeeded in allowing the invasion to proceed. Now, as the Southerners crossed the Potomac, their spirits soared. Memoirs and letters of both rebels and Pennsylvanians paint the scene: under the warm June sunlight the rich farmlands unrolled in a vision of wealth that staggered the triumphant, barefoot rebels. The invasion was a picnic. It was a combination of all the entertainments of rustic America—a horse race, a chicken fry (with requisitioned chickens), a parade—and the prizes were everything that the North could offer.

The hungry rebel soldiers enjoyed the 25 barrels of sauerkraut they requisitioned at Chambersburg and the cherries that were ripening everywhere. They marched 15 to 20 miles a day without straggling, whooping and yelling as they went. The horses, well fed at last, carried their heads higher and pulled with a firmer step. At York, General William ("Extra Billy") Smith changed the bands' tune from *Dixie* to *Yankee Doodle,* and he even won smiles and cheers from some citizens when he made

> "Here we are, ladies, as rough and ragged as ever but back again to bother you."
>
> —A CONFEDERATE SOLDIER'S ALLEGED GREETING TO MARYLAND WOMEN

★

Officers Who Won Fame at Gettysburg

A brave rebel, a green commander and a former professor make history

GEORGE E. PICKETT

The great charge at Gettysburg bears his name, but two fellow generals, J. Johnston Pettigrew and Isaac R. Trimble, joined Pickett in leading the attack. After the war he fled to Canada briefly but returned to the U.S. in 1866. He was pardoned in 1874.

GEORGE G. MEADE

The West Point graduate, reared in Philadelphia, served in the Seminole Wars and in Mexico before the Civil War began. Thrust into command only three days before the Battle of Gettysburg, he performed skillfully and helped forge the Union victory.

JOSHUA CHAMBERLAIN

The former college professor was 34 years old when he led troops of the 20th Maine Infantry in a valiant bayonet charge at Little Round Top. After the war, the hero served as governor of Maine and then became president of Bowdoin College.

★

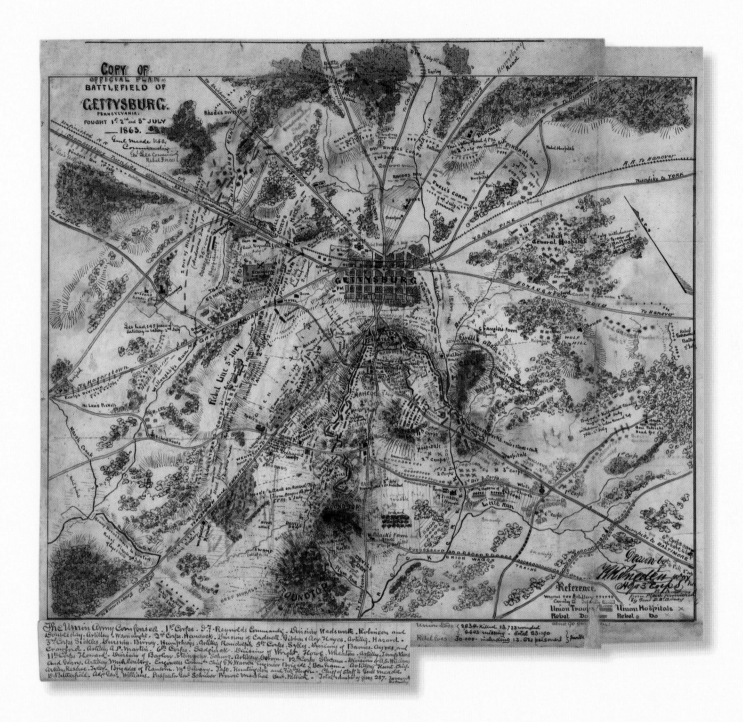

A Crescent of High Ground Saves the Union

This map of the battlefields at Gettysburg by Union cartographer Robert Knox Sneden shows the central line of battle a few miles outside the small town. On July 1 the Union troops, shown in purple, were driven south through the streets of the town by advancing Confederates, in red. But the Northerners dug in and built entrenchments in a superior defensive position on the high ground around Cemetery Ridge, aligned in a pattern often described as a fishhook, running from Devil's Den, at center right of the map, up toward the town, then curving south along Cemetery Ridge to Big Round Top and Little Round Top, at lower center. The battle raged all along this line for the next two days.

On July 2, as Longstreet attacked Union positions along the ridge, two desperate stands held back the rebel tide. Soldiers of the 20th Maine Infantry, led by Colonel Joshua Chamberlain, a professor of rhetoric at Bowdoin College, fired until they were out of bullets, then charged downhill at the rebels with bayonets fixed and held the field. To their left, the 1st Minnesota Regiment, outnumbered 8 to 1, charged an Alabama unit, losing 215 of 262 men, as they plugged a gap in the line. On July 3, in Pickett's Charge, 14,000 rebels undertook a gallant but ill-advised advance into the teeth of well-positioned Federal infantry and artillery; with their defeat, the battle gradually wound down.

them a comical speech: the weather was too warm in Virginia, he said, so the army had moved north.

The locals may have tittered, but when news of the invasion reached the big Eastern cities, the alarm bells began clanging. They sounded loudest in Washington, where Lincoln urged General Joseph Hooker to get his men quickly out of Frederick, Md., and onto Lee's trail. When Hooker dawdled, Lincoln took the bold step of replacing him even as a major battle loomed. The President chose General George Meade to command the Army of the Potomac in Hooker's place, and the Northern armies began marching toward Pennsylvania under their fourth commanding officer in a single year.

STOPPING FOR SHOES The buoyant Southerners were beginning to get a taste for luxuries unknown in Virginia, and on June 30, Brigadier General J. Johnston Pettigrew led the way to Gettysburg, Pa., a small town where a number of local roads connected, because he had heard that he could get shoes for his men there. General Hill, just back from conferring with Lee, assured Pettigrew that the Federals were still in Maryland, 16 miles (26 km) away.

Oops. The Federals *were* in Gettysburg, in the form of two brigades of cavalry led by Buford. This seasoned officer from Illinois had taken note of the high ground in and around Gettysburg and had already decided it would make a highly defensible position for the North. When Hill's unshod troops came marching toward Gettysburg the next morning, July 1, Buford's horsemen surprised them a bit north of the town and a fight erupted. It quickly grew in size and intensity as troops from both sides, drawn by the sound of gunfire, poured into the area.

The first day's fighting at Gettysburg was an impromptu skirmish that mushroomed into a major battle in an area where neither Lee nor Meade had expected it. Before either commander arrived on the scene, some 24,000 rebels were fighting 19,000 Federals tooth and nail. It was the Union troops who distinguished themselves early on this day, and none more so than the famed "Iron Brigade," Midwestern lads in distinctive black hats who shared the toughness and élan of the Southerners. Supporting Buford's thrust, they mauled rebel troops led by Confederate Major General Henry Heth.

When Lee arrived outside Gettysburg late that day, he organized a charge led by units under Generals Ewell and Hill that swept through the Union lines and sent the Federals scampering through the streets of the town. But under the strong leadership of General Winfield Scott Hancock, the Northerners regrouped and joined other divisions entrenching in the heights south of the town.

Assessing the surroundings, Lee realized that taking control of this high ground was crucial, and he gave Ewell the discretion to attack the Union position on Cemetery Hill, if possible, while the situation was still fluid. Ewell chose not do so. Generations of critics have opined that the man whose place Ewell had taken, Stonewall Jackson, would doubtless have seized the heights. Perhaps that's right. The fact remains: Union troops spent the night of July 1 creating fortifications and artillery positions along Cemetery Ridge and three miles (4.8 km) south to a pair of elevated knobs, Big Round Top and Little Round Top.

SCENES OF VALOR The Confederates were also making plans for July 2; after all, Lee had launched the invasion hoping to bring the Yankees onto a battlefield where his superior soldiers could lick them. Now he had the Federals in his sights, if not on the ground of his choosing. General Longstreet, commanding half of Lee's troops, knew the rebel position was perilous; he urged Lee to avoid a direct assault and attempt a flanking maneuver around the Union, forcing the Yankees to withdraw from their strong position and pursue. Yet Lee not only overruled his top lieutenant, he ordered Longstreet to lead the day's charge on the Union left at Little Round Top.

Longstreet, clearly angry with Lee, took his time getting his men prepared. Lee had wanted them to step off in the morning, but it was late afternoon before Longstreet's troops began their assault. To their surprise, they found the Union left was no longer at Little Round Top. Union Major General Dan Sickles had moved his men, without authorization, to a salient (protruding) position in front of the knob. This perch gave them a good overview of the battlefield but was detached from the main Union line, exposing them to attacks from two sides. When Longstreet's troops, 15,000 strong, swarmed into a peach orchard, across a wheatfield and up against a rocky area known as Devil's Den, where Sickles and his men had holed up, the fighting grew furious and deadly.

Sickles' insubordinate action unexpectedly threw a wrench into the rebel plan, as desperate stands by two Union regiments from Maine and Minnesota stopped advancing Confederates long enough to allow reinforcements to arrive and hold the position. As night fell and the casualties were counted, each side had suffered more than 9,000 dead or wounded, in addition to the 17,000 total casualties from the day before. And the worst day of fighting, July 3, was still ahead.

THE THIRD DAY The harrowing events of July 2 had proved Lee wrong and Longstreet right: the Union position along Cemetery Ridge was simply too strong to be successfully assailed. Yet in the Southern counsel of war

> "My heart was heavy. I could see the desperate and hopeless nature of the charge and the ... slaughter it would cause."
>
> —GENERAL JAMES LONGSTREET, AFTER THE WAR, ON FOLLOWING LEE'S COMMAND TO ORDER PICKETT'S CHARGE

A New Technology Records the War with an Unflinching Eye

Civil War photographers left an indelible record of the human cost of the conflict

The Civil War was the first major conflict to be fully reported by a new medium, photography, which in the 1860s was just emerging from its infancy. First developed in France and Britain in the late 1820s and 1830s, photography became a popular craze after Louis Daguerre perfected the Daguerreotype process, and *cartes de visite*—calling cards with photo portraits—were social essentials in polite society in Europe and America. When the Civil War war came, successful New York City portrait photographer Mathew Brady was inspired to document it, thus becoming one of the world's first photojournalists. "I had to go. A spirit in my feet said 'Go,' and I went," he later recalled.

Brady enlisted a corps of photographers, many of whose pictures appear in this book, including Alexander Gardner, Timothy O'Sullivan and George Barnard. These men followed the armies from camp to battleground, traveling with wagons outfitted as darkrooms. The images that resulted brought home the horror of war in new and ghastly detail. As Bob Zeller observes in his study of photography in the war, *The Blue and Gray in Black and White* (Praeger; 2005), "The Antietam photographs were the first images of American dead on the battlefield and their 'terrible distinctness' altered at once the vision of the conflict for those on the home front. If no other artifact of the Civil War existed … the Antietam photographs would be enough. Today, more than 140 years later, their impact is still visceral."

The photographers' documentation of the war was severely restricted by the limitations of the medium. Exposure times were very slow, and an image took 10 to 30 seconds to be fully captured—which explains why all the photos in this book show either the preparations for battles before they began or the results of battles after they stopped, but never the battle in progress.

If camera and film technology were still in their early stages, so were the ethics of photojournalism. In the most famous instance, Gardner, O'Sullivan and James Gibson first photographed a dead Confederate in the plate at left, then moved the body to a more picturesque location in Devil's Den, right, and took the famed image known as "Home of a Rebel Sharpshooter." However, Zeller argues that this is a unique instance, and that Civil War photographers did not routinely alter reality to create impact.

BEFORE *Historian Frederick Ray was the first to note, in 1961, that three cameramen photographed the dead Confederate soldier above in situ, then moved the body and arranged it for better composition*

AFTER *In recent decades, historians have retraced the exact positions of Civil War photographers as they focused on the battlefields. The soldier was moved 72 yds. (66 m) to his new position at Devil's Den, says Zeller*

Alfred Waud

Ordinary Americans encountered the war not only in photographs but also through the work of "special artists," who sketched events in pencil for magazines and newspapers. In today's terms, they were "embedded" with the troops. As *Harper's Weekly* reported, "They have made the weary marches and the dangerous voyages. They have shared the soldiers' fare; they have ridden and waded, and climbed and floundered ..."

One of the most gifted artist-journalists was London-born American Alfred Waud of *Harper's,* who once wrote that when he climbed a tree to sketch a battle, "rebel sharpshooters kept up a fire at me the whole time." At right are three of Waud's sketches of the Battle of Gettysburg: from left, a scene at Devil's Den, an attack by Confederate "Louisiana Tigers" troops, and the death of Union General John F. Reynolds.

late on July 2, Lee again insisted that the Confederates must launch a frontal assault on the 3rd. He seems to have simply refused to believe that his troops could not beat the Union men, whatever the odds. Again Longstreet stated his objections; again Lee insisted on the attack.

Early in the afternoon, Longstreet's artillery batteries, some 150 cannons strong, opened fire on the Union positions, and the Northern guns, roughly equal in number, answered back. The artillery duel lasted for two hours. One observer, Union Headquarters Aide Frank Haskell, later wrote, "We thought that at the second Bull Run, at the Antietam, and at Fredericksburg ... we had heard heavy cannonading; they were but holiday salutes compared with this ... great oaks heave down their massy branches ... as if the lightning smote them."

Finally the Union guns stopped, perhaps disabled or out of ammunition, and Longstreet ordered the attack. Leading the nine divisions that assembled were Generals Pettigrew, George Pickett and Isaac R. Trimble, but the assault entered history with Pickett's name on it. The men's impossible challenge: cross wide-open farmland to attack troops in uphill, entrenched positions. This was Fredericksburg with the roles reversed. It also became a scene of unmatched gallantry, as the rebel line, almost a mile wide, stepped off and marched directly into the Union guns—guns, it turned out, that had fallen silent as a ruse to invite the attack. When the Northern cannons again roared, and Union sharpshooters opened up on the exposed rebels, slaughter ensued. Of 14,000 men who made the charge, only 7,000 survived. After this carnage, the fighting slowed to a halt. When the final tally was taken, Gettysburg proved to be the deadliest battle in American history: some 51,000 men died, were injured or were unaccounted for when Independence Day 1863 dawned.

THE REACTION For the Northerners, Gettysburg indeed seemed like a kind of dawn, the beginning of the war's end. Newspapers called it Lee's Waterloo. On July 7, the exhilarating news arrived that Vicksburg had surrendered to U.S. Grant three days before, encouraging many voices to declare the war was almost over. But once again, victory would be incomplete. Like McClellan at Antietam, Meade failed to pursue Lee's beaten army as it retreated across the Potomac, though it was ripe for the picking. An angry Lincoln berated Meade, but the damage was done. As the President feared, despite Lee's overwhelming loss, the war would grind on for 21 more deadly months.

Lee was a superb strategist who concealed the soul of a riverboat gambler within the polished exterior that led later admirers to call him the "marble man." But this time he had rolled the dice and lost. Future generations would blame Stuart, Longstreet and Ewell for the South's greatest defeat. Each of those men could have performed better at Gettysburg, but Lee knew who was to blame. After his army was beaten, he passed slowly among his retreating, exhausted men, whose line stretched for more than 14 miles (23 km), begging them to keep their ranks and assuring them, "It was all my fault." ∎

OUTPOST OF MERCY *Personnel of the Sanitary Commission, the Union agency staffed primarily by women volunteers that assisted in the nursing of the injured and the disposition of the dead after battles, are shown at Camp Letterman, the hospital established by Union top medical officer Dr. Jonathan Letterman at Gettysburg. The facility treated some 4,000 wounded soldiers, regardless of their allegiance, following the battle*

The Gettysburg Address

Dedicating a cemetery at the battlefield, President Lincoln casts the war and the United States as agents to create human equality

POPULAR LORE DEPICTS ABRAHAM LINcoln as writing his most famous speech in haste on the train that carried him from Washington to Gettysburg, Pa., where he had been invited to deliver short remarks at the dedication of a cemetery for the fallen Union soldiers late in 1863. It's a fine story but off the mark: Lincoln biographer David Herbert Donald tells us that the President pondered the substance of his remarks for several weeks, struggling with its conclusion, before he wrote out the final copy on Nov. 18, when he left the capital for the next day's ceremony. Lincoln had come around to agreeing with some of his supporters, who had been urging him to articulate afresh the moral and political values that were driving the war—after all, it was his ability to do so that had won him the presidency in the first place.

At the ceremony, Lincoln's remarks followed a two-hour stemwinder delivered by famed orator Edward Everett that reads today as all frosting and no cake. The President's brief speech, delivered unamplified to a crowd of 15,000 people, appeared to move few at the time, but that's not surprising: the address packs so many powerful ideas into so few words that it remains a masterpiece of concision, revealing its import slowly.

BOUND FOR GLORY
These travelers passed through the Hanover, Pa., railroad depot on their way to nearby Gettysburg for the dedication of the cemetery on Nov. 19, 1863

FACE IN THE CROWD
In this rare picture of Lincoln at Gettysburg, the President is not wearing his signature stovepipe hat.

This image was for many years the only known photo of Lincoln at the ceremony, but in 2007 a photo researcher used modern techniques to magnify long-distance pictures of the ceremonial parade and found two images of Lincoln, taken from behind, riding into the site on horseback

Lincoln's words not only rose to the occasion; they surpassed it. The President set forth the purpose and meaning of the present conflict and went further, redefining the very purpose of the United States. America, he stressed, was not simply a political union of independent states; it was a nation—and what's more, a nation dedicated from its founding to human equality. He dated the birth of this new nation to the Declaration of Independence in 1776, which first stated the radically forward-looking ideal behind the American Revolution, the proposition that all men are created equal. In referring to the Declaration as the birth moment of the U.S., Lincoln was effectively bypassing the 1789 U.S. Constitution, a political document flawed by compromise, as reflected in its sotto voce but inescapable endorsement of human slavery.

Confidantes tell us that Lincoln himself was initially disappointed with the reception of his effort, but within days of its publication across the land, the speech began to be recognized as one of the most powerful statements of human rights and democratic values ever delivered. Critics in the South, as well as antiwar Copperheads in the North, did not agree; a Copperhead Chicago newspaper called it a "perversion of history." That view, however, remains a minority report. ∎

Lincoln's Gettysburg Address

Four score and seven years ago our fathers brought forth on this continent a new nation, conceived in liberty, and dedicated to the proposition that all men are created equal. Now we are engaged in a great civil war, testing whether that nation, or any nation, so conceived and so dedicated, can long endure. We are met on a great battle-field of that war. We have come to dedicate a portion of that field, as a final resting place for those who here gave their lives that that nation might live. It is altogether fitting and proper that we should do this.

But, in a larger sense, we cannot dedicate, we cannot consecrate, we cannot hallow this ground. The brave men, living and dead, who struggled here, have consecrated it, far above our poor power to add or detract. The world will little note, nor long remember what we say here, but it can never forget what they did here. It is for us the living, rather, to be dedicated here to the unfinished work which they who fought here have thus far so nobly advanced. It is rather for us to be here dedicated to the great task remaining before us—that from these honored dead we take increased devotion to that cause for which they gave the last full measure of devotion—that we here highly resolve that these dead shall not have died in vain—that this nation, under God, shall have a new birth of freedom—and that government of the people, by the people, for the people, shall not perish from the earth.

Caring for the Wounded

Doctors and nurses, overwhelmed by the carnage, race to aid the fallen

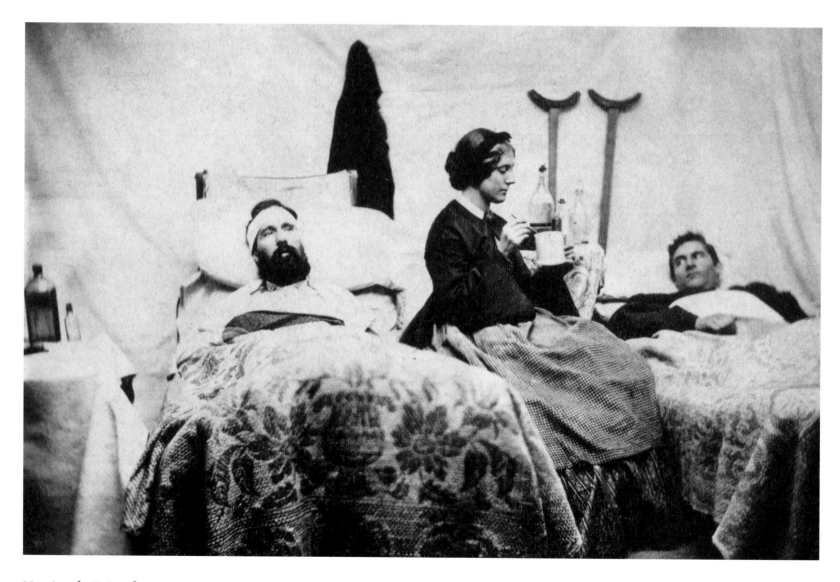

Nursing the Injured

Both North and South began the war with far too few doctors, surgeons and nurses to treat the wounded, and throughout the war, most female nurses were untrained volunteers. Above, a nurse tends to two wounded men in an undated photo. Dorothea Dix, a respected advocate for the mentally ill, was named superintendent of Union Army Nurses, but she clashed with male physicians and took great care to ensure that her charges would not be perceived as attractive: she ordered that all Union nurses be at least 30 years old, "plain" in appearance and wear drab dresses.

Retrieving Casualties

Above, soldiers from a Union Zouave division engage in a drill to practice removing casualties from the battlefield. Early in the war, medical evacuations were conducted in a haphazard manner, with soldiers randomly designated to carry the injured behind the lines. But as casualties mounted, Union Army of the Potomac medical director Jonathan Letterman systematized the process, with designated ambulances and stretcher-bearers following the combat and evacuating the wounded to field hospitals, helping reduce battlefield mortalities.

Amputating a Limb

The vast majority of nonfatal wounds were to the soldiers' arms and legs; after major battles, surgeons could be busy for days amputating limbs. Both antisepsis to prevent infection and antibiotics to cure it were unknown. "The septic sins of the time [were] responsible for this harvest of death and suffering," wrote medical historian George W. Adams. At left, a man holds a chloroform mask over the mouth of a patient before surgery at the Camp Letterman hospital after Gettysburg.

Hospital Laundry

Women volunteers, including several African Americans, hang laundry to dry behind a hospital in this photo, taken in Nashville in July 1863. Although antisepsis was not yet understood, nurses and doctors learned from the pioneering work of the famed British nurse Florence Nightingale in the Crimean War and did their best to maintain clean hospitals.

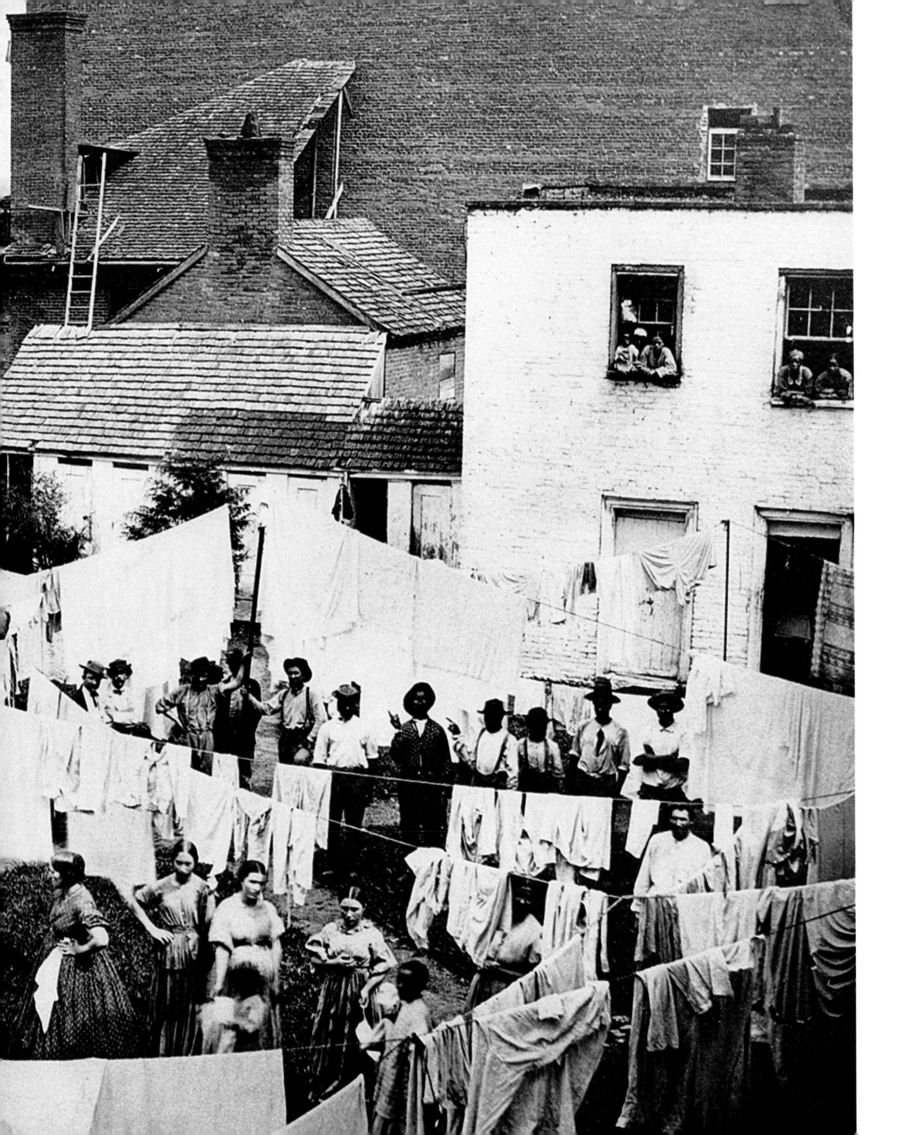

Mending After Fredericksburg

Wounded Union soldiers from the First New Jersey Brigade recuperate after the Battle of Fredericksburg in December 1862, one of the war's bloodiest conflicts. Despite the shocking toll of deaths from battle during the war, camp life was even more dangerous. In her book *This Republic of Suffering* (Random House, 2008), historian Drew Gilpin Faust notes that "twice as many soldiers died of disease as from battle wounds." In the camps, drinking water was often contaminated by nearby latrines, and diarrhea, dysentery, typhoid and malaria were rampant.

Field Pharmacy

Though some wounded soldiers were simply handed a bullet to bite on while undergoing an amputation, doctors widely used morphine, chloroform, ether—and liquor—to dull the senses during medical procedures. At right, a rolling field pharmacy sets up shop during an encampment of General George Thomas' Union troops in the Western theater.

A Union Hospital

Soldiers recuperate at the Armory Square Hospital in Washington, circa 1863; the veteran in the wheelchair has had a lower leg amputated. The 1,000-bed facility was at the center of a large medical complex erected in 1862 on the National Mall at the site now occupied by the Smithsonian National Air and Space Museum. It was demolished in 1964.

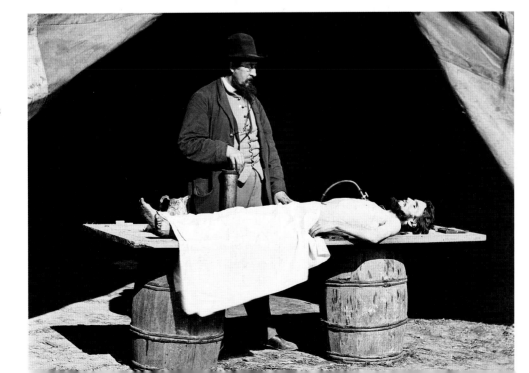

Embalming the Remains

Dr. Richard Burr, an embalming surgeon, prepares a body for the preservation process in this undated photo. Embalming was perfected in the U.S. by Dr. Thomas Holmes just prior to the war, and some private practitioners of the process followed the battles, profiting from families who would pay high prices to have fallen relatives preserved and shipped home for burial. Dr. Holmes practiced in Washington and grew wealthy by embalming some 4,000 soldiers at $100 each.

The Struggle to Control Tennessee

In the final turning point of 1863, Union troops weather defeat and besiegement to open a gateway into the heart of the South

AMERICANS RECALL THE UNION'S ONE-two punch on July 3-4, 1863—victory at Gettysburg and the capture of Vicksburg—as the turning points that would eventually doom the Confederate States of America. But in addition to those events, a series of engagements in a third region created another smashing, pivotal advance for the Union that year. This was the Tennessee theater, where in the fall of 1863 the North weathered a major defeat in the Battle of Chickamauga and the entrapment and potential surrender of an entire Union army inside Chattanooga, until the arrival of General Ulysses S. Grant and several reinforcing Union armies on the scene reversed the momentum of the conflict. By the end of the year, Union armies had won control of the state, and a passage into the Deep South had been opened, through which General William T. Sherman would pass in 1864 as he marched into Georgia and on to the Atlantic Ocean, leaving ruin and destruction in his path.

Grant had established Union control of western Tennessee when he captured Forts Henry and Donelson early in 1862. Vicksburg was the next prize in the Union strategy for this theater, and once it was taken, a long-sought objective beckoned again: Chattanooga in eastern Tennessee, a railroad hub and supply center for the entire mid-South, located near the northern borders of both Georgia and Alabama. "If we can hold Chattanooga and east Tennessee," President Abraham Lincoln telegraphed the Union commanding officer, General William Rosecrans, on Oct. 4, 1863, "I think the rebellion must dwindle and die."

Since the horrific Battle of Stones River that ushered in

the year 1863 in this theater, Rosecrans and his Southern counterpart, General Braxton Bragg, had avoided a major engagement. Rosecrans and his Army of the Cumberland hunkered down in Nashville, in central Tennessee; Bragg and his Army of the Tennessee did the same in Chattanooga. The campaign that followed would be largely shaped by the character of these two leaders.

Rosecrans, a devout Catholic from Ohio, had served ably in Union victories early in the war, but he was a poor practitioner of barracks politics and ended up at odds with both General George B. McClellan and Secretary

CHATTANOOGA *Nestled amid the ridges and mountains that offered commanding positions for artillery fire into it, the city was calm and peaceful under Union occupation in this 1864 picture. But when a Union army was trapped inside it in 1863, soldiers tore down many of its wooden buildings. At right is lofty Lookout Mountain, with the Tennessee River below*

of War Edwin Stanton. He ran afoul of General Grant in campaigns in Mississippi in the fall of 1862 but won acclaim when he helped lead the Union victory at the Battle of Corinth, Miss. He was appointed to command the newly formed Army of the Cumberland late in 1862. More popular with his men than with his superiors, he often had to be prodded into action by orders from above.

Rosecrans' great rival, General Bragg, was a close friend of Jefferson Davis' and served as an unofficial military adviser to the Confederate President. The West Point graduate had won distinction in the Mexican War, but since Stones River he had been pushed around by Rosecrans; his own troops derided him as a general who always chose to retreat rather than take a stand. As the campaign for Chattanooga unfolded, it became clear that Bragg had failed at one of a military leader's most important tasks: he did not command the respect of his subordinate officers, and his headquarters became a nest of envy, backbiting and pessimism, flaws that would be magnified in the heat of combat with deadly results.

The Chattanooga campaign would also be shaped by the challenging terrain upon which it was fought: the ridges, valleys and ravines of eastern Tennessee. This Appalachian mountain landscape was glorious to behold but a logistical nightmare for military men. The duel to come would also reflect the nature of the men fighting it: scrappy, fiercely independent mountain folk and Western pioneers who cared little for authority of any kind, be it a faraway executive power or a nearby sergeant. Let the regiments of Ohio, Virginia and New York drill and preen on the Eastern front; the combatants in Tennessee preferred to wage war, every man for himself, in a frantic, uncoordinated series of skirmishes.

A UNION OFFENSIVE Through the spring and early summer of 1863, Rosecrans and Bragg took the opportunity presented by their superiors' focus on Vicksburg to rebuild their armies, with Rosecrans refusing to budge even when Lincoln repeatedly urged him to take the initiative against Bragg. But after the "Gibraltar of the West" was taken, the spotlight firmly shifted to Chattanooga. On Aug. 10, Lincoln again beseeched Rosecrans to attack the Confederates. "I am very anxious for East Tennessee to be occupied by us," he wired the dilatory general.

This time, Rosecrans heeded the call and got his army marching toward the sunrise. The campaign for Chattanooga began on Friday morning, Aug. 21. Residents were stunned as Union artillery unexpectedly opened fire on

> "I have stood your meanness as long as I intend to. You have played the part of a damned scoundrel, and are a coward, and if you were any part of a man I would slap your jaws and force you to resent it."
>
> —GENERAL NATHAN BEDFORD FORREST, TO GENERAL BRAXTON BRAGG, AFTER CHICKAMAUGA

★

The Commanders in Tennessee
Rosecrans and Bragg were among the war's greatest rivals

WILLIAM ROSECRANS

After graduating from West Point, the Ohio-born Rosecrans left the Army for a career in engineering. Brusque and direct, he clashed with Grant and Secretary of War Stanton. But his men loved "Old Rosy," who didn't put on airs and often led from the front.

GEORGE H. THOMAS

A Virginian who stayed loyal to the Union, Thomas was close friends with Generals Sherman and Lee from his West Point days and served with distinction in Mexico. Plodding and careful, he earned the title "The Rock of Chickamauga" in that Union defeat.

BRAXTON BRAGG

A native of North Carolina, Bragg was a close friend and adviser to Jefferson Davis, a relationship that helped him cling to his post in Tennessee, even when his junior officers repeatedly denounced his leadership and sense of strategy.

★

A Tragedy of Errors

The valleys along both sides of the Chickamauga River formed the natural amphitheater in which the battle was fought, with the river helping carve the dividing line between the two sides. The natural features here, including Lookout Mountain and Missionary Ridge, would play important roles in later struggles in the autumn of 1863.

The battle took place over a three-day period, but primarily on Sept. 19-20. While individual soldiers fought fiercely, poor relations and communication among officers on both sides caused major tactical blunders.

On Sept. 19, troops under able Union General George Thomas clashed with rebels led by General Nathan Bedford Forrest on the Confederate right; much blood was shed, but neither side prevailed. Most of General James Longstreet's troops arrived on the scene later in the day, bulking up the number of rebel troops.

Failures to coordinate Southern attacks on the morning of Sept. 20 allowed the Northerners to create entrenched positions that staved off possible annihilation when the charge came. Hours later, it was the Union leaders' turn to err: a mix-up in orders exacerbated by distrust among them helped create a gap in the Northern line at the center of the battle. Rebels under Longstreet drove a wedge into it that sent Rosecrans and his top officers fleeing for their lives from the field.

Only a heroic defensive stand along Horseshoe Ridge led by Thomas stopped the rebels and allowed Union troops to escape further slaughter, as the Northern soldiers frantically retreated back to Chattanooga.

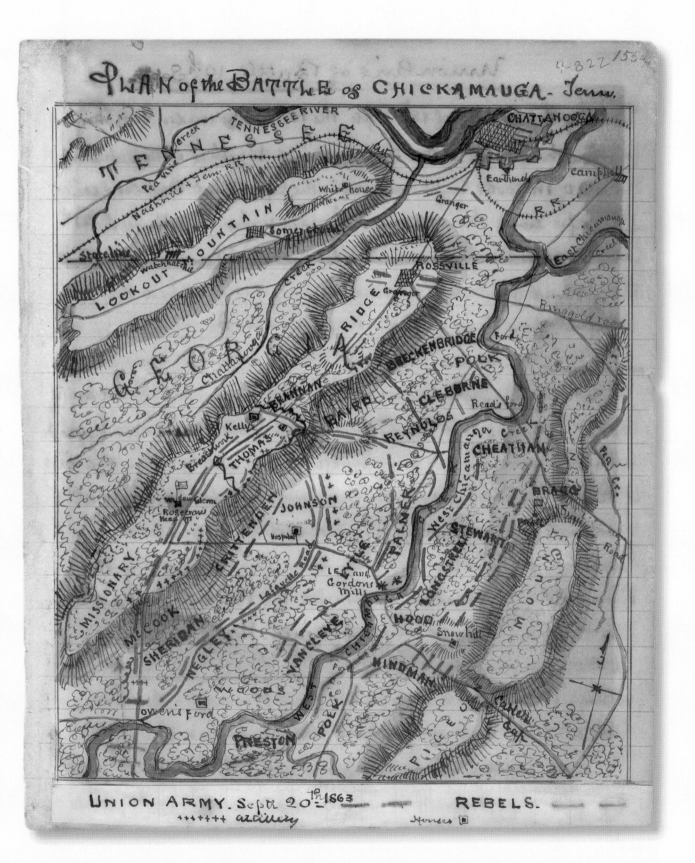

the city from positions on the north side of the Tennessee River. The bombardment spooked Bragg, spooked him so badly that he failed to realize it was a diversion intended to draw attention away from the major Union thrust: Rosecrans had sent most of his army across the river a few miles west of Chattanooga. By month's end, Bragg was outflanked and surrounded by 60,000 Union soldiers. Early in September he evacuated his own force of 60,000 men from the city without offering a fight. With a simple show of force, and with almost no loss of life, Rosecrans seemed to have achieved his goal.

Yet in the aftermath of his triumph, the constitutionally hesitant general seems to have inhaled the oxygen of victory too deeply. Overruling the counsel of his able subordinate, General George H. Thomas, Rosecrans did precisely what Lincoln had been begging his commanding officers to do since 1861: he followed up a success by ordering the immediate pursuit of Bragg's retreating army. But Bragg had an ace up his sleeve: he was withdrawing in order to take a stand, for following Gettysburg, President Davis had ordered General James Longstreet's army, 12,000 strong, to move to Tennessee via rail to support Bragg—and those men were now on the way.

Bragg halted his retreat and dug into a position along the west bank of the Chickamauga River, southeast of Chattanooga, in the shadow of Lookout Mountain, the 2,300-ft. (701 m) peak that overlooks the Tennessee River. Here the armies of Rosecrans and Bragg clashed again on Sept. 18-20, in a battle that was one of the most confused and deadly actions of the war.

On Sept. 18 Bragg moved north and clashed briefly with Union troops. But modern-day readers who attempt to follow historians' laborious attempts to trace the events of the next day can be forgiven if they become just as confused as the leaders and participants seem to have been. Union General Philip Sheridan's troops went thisaway, Confederate General Patrick Cleburne's troops went thataway, while communications on both sides broke down every whichway, and companies and individuals found themselves fighting for their lives in a deadly melee that had little overall direction.

By nightfall, as the generals took stock of the situation, it became clear that the two sides had fought to a standstill, with great loss of life. But Longstreet's troops had begun arriving on the scene late on the 18th, and their

IMPROVISED BARRICADES *Hunkered down inside Chattanooga and encircled by Confederate forces, Union troops tore down houses and used the lumber for firewood and to build fortifications. At left, boards used in a hastily built fence still are still covered in wallpaper from local homes*

growing presence would now tip the balance of the battle. Both commanders planned to take the offensive again the next morning, but when the sun rose on Sept. 20, the battlefield was eerily silent: a planned Southern thrust was delayed as Bragg's querulous subordinates argued about whether the charge should occur before or after a hot breakfast was served to the men.

When the rebel charge was made, the center of the Union line held—until General Thomas J. Wood, fuming after an earlier public rebuke by Rosecrans, followed an outdated order to the letter, allowing Longstreet's just-arrived army to drive a wedge into the center of the Northern lines that quickly became a rout. When Rosecrans' headquarters came under direct attack, the general was forced to flee the scene—and he didn't stop advancing to the rear until he reached Chattanooga, exhausted, and had to be helped off his horse. Only a brave stand by the troops under General Thomas, who refused to follow Rosecrans' order to retreat, saved the day for the Union and prevented the destruction of its armies.

The Battle of Chickamauga claimed some 16,000 casualties on the Union side and more than 18,000 for the Confederates. While clearly a Southern victory, it did not relieve the Northern occupation of Chattanooga, where Rosecrans and his defeated men were now holed up, licking their wounds. Not yet, anyway: against all odds, it was now Bragg who had seized the offensive. He occupied Lookout Mountain and Missionary Ridge above the city and cut off its supply lines. The North had won Chattanooga, but it had become a trap: the town on the river was now a Vicksburg in reverse, with Bragg in Grant's shoes.

ENTER GRANT The rebels had won, yet Bragg's top subordinates now grew even more vociferous in their criticism of their commander, and a group of them made a direct appeal to President Davis to remove him. But when Davis came to Tennessee to assess the situation, he did not do so, even though Longstreet joined the others in denouncing Bragg's leadership, while the despised general sat silent, facing his accusers in the counsel of war.

Lincoln, in contrast, was all too happy to send Rosecrans to the sidelines: he depicted his general as "confused and stunned, like a duck hit on the head." Unlike Davis, the Union President had a master warrior nearby who could be trusted to bring fresh thinking to the crisis. On Oct. 16, he named U. S. Grant the commander of all Union armies in the Western theater and asked him to relieve Rosecrans of his command in Tennessee.

When Grant arrived in besieged Chattanooga to take charge on Oct. 23, he was limping badly; he had taken a fall when his mount was spooked by a locomotive during

Scenes from East Tennessee
The rugged mountain landscape shapes the battles for Chattanooga

RIDING THE RAILS *A railroad yard in Johnsonville, Tenn., is guarded by a company of African-American troops in this 1864 photo. The arrival by rail of Hooker's army from the Eastern front during the battle for Chattanooga, like the earlier movement of Longstreet's army on Southern trains to turn the tide at Chickamauga, illustrated the extent to which railroads transformed and accelerated military logistics in the war*

HIGH GROUND *Gun emplacements on Missionary Ridge, like this cannon that fired 200-lb. (90 kg) shells, played a key role in both the Confederate siege of Union-occupied Chattanooga and the battle to break out that followed*

RIVERSIDE ROOST *Union soldiers are shown in a camp along the Tennessee River outside Chattanooga in 1864, after Federals took control of the key railway hub and used it as the primary supply line through which men, food and armaments were shipped south to support Sherman's troops in Georgia*

TRIAL RUN *Union soldiers of General Gordon Granger's IV Corps, Army of the Cumberland, practice forming for an uphill assault in Blue Springs, Tenn., east of Chattanooga. These men helped save Union lives at Chickamauga as they helped General George Thomas hold the North's line late in the battle. Later, during the conflict at Missionary Ridge, they were among the Union troops who stormed the center of the Confederate lines below the plateau, then, without being commanded to do so, drove the rebels back up the hillside until it was under Union control*

TENNESSEE STATE LIBRARY AND ARCHIVES

a visit to New Orleans. And what he found was a similarly limping army, one that had been severely roughed up at Chickamauga and was now losing morale as the Southern grip around Chattanooga tightened. The soldiers were on quarter-rations and were tearing down houses, using the lumber for fortifications and firewood.

Never did Grant seem more a superman than in the urgent days that followed. Quickly taking in the Union plight, he consulted with General Thomas and another able general, William F. ("Baldy") Smith, and learned that they had already hatched a plan to open a supply line into the city. Grant endorsed their scheme, and on Oct. 27, five weeks into the siege, Union pontoon boats from Chattanooga silently floated down the Tennessee River, carrying some 3,500 troops who surprised an undermanned

rebel outpost at Brown's Ferry and took charge of this key river crossing. When Longstreet's soldiers contested the Union advance the next day at the hamlet of Wauhatchie, they were driven back. The Union now was in control of a supply line, soon dubbed the "Cracker Line," that relieved the siege of Chattanooga—within five days' of Grant's arrival on the scene.

At this critical moment, President Davis directed Bragg to reduce the number of Confederate troops surrounding Chattanooga. He dispatched Longstreet's army 112 miles (80 km) north to Knoxville, Tenn., where another Union army, under General Ambrose Burnside, the disgraced butcher of Fredericksburg, was vying to take control of northeastern Tennessee. Davis and Bragg believed that Union General Sherman's army, on the

LAY OF THE LAND *General Ulysses S. Grant, on left, confers with fellow Union officers on Lookout Mountain after the Union victory. The Chattanooga campaign found Grant no longer challenged by rivers, bayous and swamps but by mountains, hills and valleys*

march from Vicksburg, was heading to relieve Burnside. Yet even as Longstreet's troops were pulling out, a massive number of Northern troops were moving in: General Sherman's divisions, some 17,000 strong, were coming to aid Grant, rather than Burnside, while Lincoln had also dispatched General Joseph Hooker's force of 20,000 men from the Eastern front to Chattanooga.

BATTLE OF CHATTANOOGA With the "Cracker Line" in place and the Union forces growing, Grant began planning to escape from his tight spot. Around Chattanooga, the Confederates occupied the high ground along Missionary Ridge, a 6-mile (9.6 km) -long, 300-ft. (91 m) -high plateau east of the town, and also commanded Lookout Mountain to the south. The Union troops had no choice but to attempt to break the Confederate lines.

Within days of Sherman's arrival on the scene in mid-November, Grant went on the offensive. Preparing for the battle to come—almost all of which would be conducted uphill against entrenched Confederate fortifications—he assigned Hooker to hold down the Confederate left at Lookout Mountain, while Sherman's troops were tasked with turning the rebels' right flank at the northern end of Missionary Ridge. Aware that Rosecrans' former soldiers in the Army of the Cumberland, now under General Thomas, had taken a heroic stand at Chickamauga, he awarded them the easiest assignment, facing Bragg's center line across the middle of Missionary Ridge.

But first Grant decided to test Bragg and see if he was indeed prepared to stand and fight. On Nov. 23, he ordered the Army of the Cumberland to stage a demonstration in the valley below Missionary Ridge to gauge the Confederates response. As Thomas' charges, joined by some of Hooker's divisions, paraded through the valley, it presented a spectacle of war as seldom witnessed in the Western theater, complete with banners and bugles, drums and cadence calls. This may have been the first time during the war that Grant himself had seen such a display of martial pomp, so familiar to generals on the Eastern front.

But this "peaceful pageant," as one Northern officer termed it, was suddenly transformed into a real fight when Thomas' troops, proud of their new commander and perhaps eager to demonstrate their valor to Grant, quickly turned and went on the attack. Southern sharpshooters at the base of Missionary Ridge opened fire on them, but the Federals kept racing uphill, driving the rebels from the outcropping of the Ridge known as Orchard Knob—and sending a galvanizing jolt of electricity through all the Union troops on the scene.

That night, realizing he was in for a fight, Bragg ordered the divisions serving under General Cleburne, whom he had dispatched to Knoxville, to turn back and join the coming fray. The next day Cleburne's men arrayed themselves on the Confederate right flank against Sherman's divisions and stopped the Union general's attack cold, spoiling Grant's grand strategy for the battle.

This setback proved minor, for on the Confederate left flank, where Hooker's troops had been given the seemingly impossible task of attacking rebel positions on Lookout Mountain, the Northerners managed to establish a foothold on the hillside during the course of a fog-shrouded morning. In the Battle Above the Clouds that followed in the afternoon, Hooker's fresh Union troops drove the weary Confederates from the mountaintop. The next morning the U.S. flag fluttered above Lookout.

That afternoon, it was again the Army of the Cumberland's turn to shine. As Sherman's troops continued to struggle against the tough rebels under Cleburne on the Union left, Grant asked Thomas' troops to test the mettle of the rebels entrenched at the Confederate center at Missionary Ridge. The Northern troops not only overran those positions in the valley but also continued their charge uphill, howling a new battle cry: "Chickamauga!" And they just kept climbing, amazing not only the rebels, many of whom turned and fled, but also some other astonished observers. "Who ordered those men up the ridge?" Grant demanded of Thomas. The "Rock of Chickamauga" declared he was innocent of issuing such a command, but he was only too happy to join Grant and the triumphant Union soldiers in celebrating it.

By day's end the Union held both Lookout Mountain and Missionary Ridge, and Bragg's beaten forces were retreating south. They had suffered 6,500 casualties at Chattanooga; the Union, 6,000. The defeat was Bragg's last hurrah: he tendered his resignation at the end of November, and Davis accepted it. When the conflict in Knoxville ended with a Confederate withdrawal, the U.S. flag flew over almost all of Tennessee.

On Sept. 21, Rosecrans' forces, whipped at Chickamauga, had taken refuge in Chattanooga, surrounded by Confederate armies and artillery perched on seemingly impregnable mountain positions. Only nine weeks later, Grant, Thomas and Sherman had completely reversed the course of the conflict; they had driven the rebels from eastern Tennessee and created an east-west wedge across the heart of the Confederacy. At the end of 1863, the Confederate States of America constituted a patchwork of besieged territories whose size was shrinking by the month. More and more, it was coming to resemble what Lincoln had always maintained it was: a failed rebellious faction rather than a great new nation on the world stage. ■

The First Modern Conflict

Steam-powered trains, ironclad ships and observation balloons alter warfare

Underground Mines

The tactic of digging tunnels to surprise an enemy can be traced to antiquity. But the Civil War was the first conflict to see the use of modern mining techniques adapted for warfare. The most famous example is the Battle of the Crater on July 30, 1864, during the Union siege of Petersburg, Va. With progress stymied, mining engineer Lieutenant Colonel Henry Pleasants proposed digging a tunnel and exploding a massive charge behind Confederate lines. The plan was approved, and the resulting linear mine was T-shaped, with a 511-ft. (156 m) primary shaft branching off into two avenues of about 37 ft. (11 m) each. Ventilation was provided by burning a fire near the entrance, heating and forcing stale air out of the tunnel and creating a vacuum that drew in fresh air along a wooden duct running its full length. The tunnel escaped Confederate detection, and when the Union exploded 320 kegs of gunpowder, the horrific Battle of the Crater began. The explosion was drawn by illustrator Alfred Waud, above. At right is a rudimentary Union hand grenade, a gunpowder-filled metal canister bound with hand-tied cord.

The Telegraph

Perfected in the 1840s, the telegraph was a major accelerating factor in the practice of war, abolishing old limitations of distance and allowing participants to communicate in real time. During battle, dispatches were still sent on horseback, but the advent of telegraphy meant that civilian commanders could learn of events hundreds of miles away on the day they occurred. Abraham Lincoln spent many of his nights in the telegraph office of the War Department, awaiting news from the front.

At left, workers string telegraph line for the Union's Army of the Potomac in April 1864.

Railroads

The Civil War was the first major conflict in which railroads played a dominant role. The North profited the most, since it had 20,000 miles of standard-gauge track to the South's 9,000 miles of nonstandard track. Many of the war's great battles were fought to secure railroad corridors.

Trains accelerated the assembly and movement of armies; Stonewall Jackson was only one of the generals who used them to surprise the enemy with unexpected troop deployments.

At right, workers lower a drawbridge that holds tracks, allowing the train to be loaded onto a Union barge on the Potomac.

Observation Balloons

When the war broke out, pioneering aeronaut Thaddeus S.C. Lowe cut short his experiments with hydrogen-filled balloons, which included meteorological exploration and a proposed transatlantic voyage, and volunteered his services to the Union. Eventually, he commanded a unit consisting of seven balloons inflated by hydrogen gas generators.

At left, the balloon *Intrepid* is being inflated in order to make observations at the Battle of Fair Oaks during the Seven Days Battles in 1862. The balloons did not play a major strategic role in the war but helped usher in the age of aerial warfare.

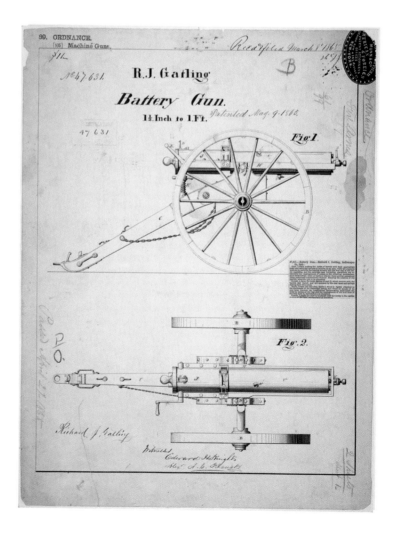

Artillery Innovations

The Gatling gun, right, patented in 1862 by Richard J. Gatling, saw limited use by the Union late in the war; it is considered the forerunner of all later machine guns. The hand-cranked weapon had multiple rotating barrels, not clearly shown in the schematic, that allowed it to fire several rounds in rapid succession.

Above is a Big Wheels, Civil War–style: an animal-drawn caisson called a sling cart and used to transport giant cannon and mortars.

Submarines

The *Intelligent Whale,* above, was a prototype Union submarine that was laid down in 1864. But the proposed submersible, propelled by hand-cranking, was not fully tested until the war ended and proved a dead end.

Far more advanced than the *Whale* was the Confederate submersible C.S.S. *Hunley,* left, designed by Tennessee-born engineer Horace L. Hunley. The 40-ft. (12 m) -long ship was swamped on its first run, killing five of its nine crewmen. Hunley was among the eight men who died when the ship sank on a subsequent training exercise on Oct. 15, 1863; the sub was later raised. On Feb. 17, 1864, in Charleston Harbor, the *Hunley* became the first submersible to sink a warship, when it attached a torpedo to the hull of the U.S.S. *Housatonic,* then detonated it. But the *Hunley* itself sank during the attack; it was eventually located under seafloor silt and was raised in 2000.

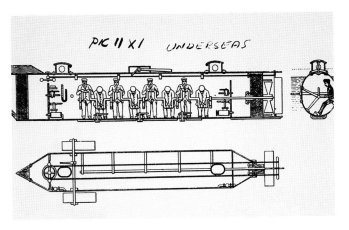

Ironclad Warships

The clash between the two prototype ironclad ships U.S.S. *Monitor* and C.S.S. *Virginia* on March 9, 1862, is a celebrated moment in the history of marine warfare. But that showdown took place early in the war, and experiments with steam-powered ironclads continued for the next several years. More than the Confederacy, the Union continued to refine and develop ironclad technology, and several generations of *Monitor*-class ships saw duty in the Western theater, where the rivers were not subject to the rough sea waves that helped sink the original craft.

At right, Union soldiers man a rowboat on the James River in Virginia with the U.S.S. *Onondaga,* a later *Monitor*-type vessel, behind them. It boasted two circular turrets separated by a tall smokestack and had a flat deck like the *Monitor's.*

1864

———❧———

"When I assumed command of all the armies, the situation was about this: the Mississippi River was guarded from St. Louis to its mouth … East of the Mississippi we held substantially all north of the Memphis and Charleston Railroad as far east as Chattanooga … taking in nearly all of the State of Tennessee. West Virginia was in our hands; and that part of old Virginia north of the Rapidan and east of the Blue Ridge we also held."

—ULYSSES S. GRANT, *PERSONAL MEMOIRS*

MOVING ON *Confederate prisoners await transport at a railroad depot in Chattanooga in 1864. After the Union conquered the city in eastern Tennessee, it became a major hub for shipping supplies to General Sherman's troops in the Deep South—and for shipping captured troops to Northern prisons*

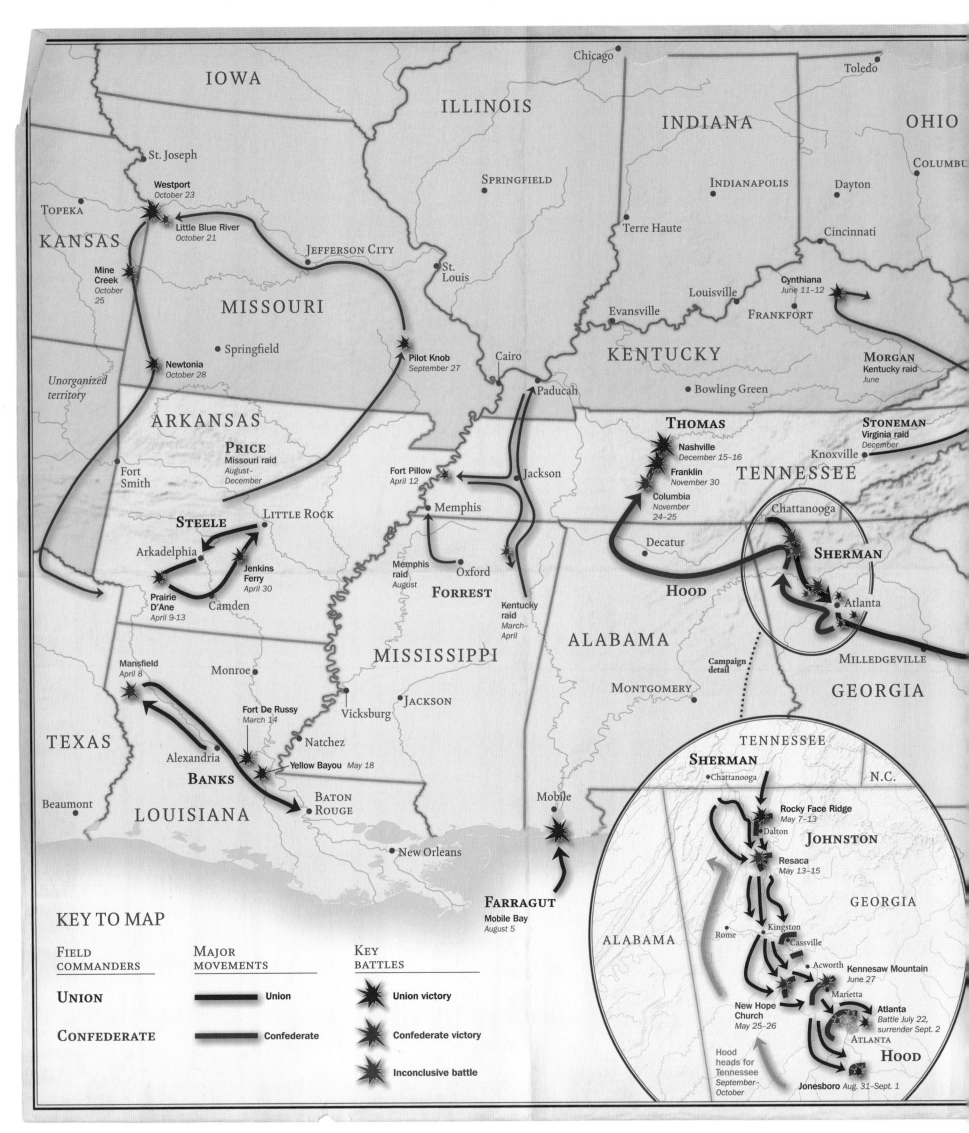

IOWA

ILLINOIS

INDIANA

OHIO

Chicago

Toledo

COLUMBU

St. Joseph

SPRINGFIELD

INDIANAPOLIS

Dayton

Westport
October 23

Topeka

Terre Haute

Cincinnati

KANSAS

Little Blue River
October 21

JEFFERSON CITY

Louisville

Cynthiana
June 11–12

Mine
Creek
*October
25*

St.
Louis

Evansville

FRANKFORT

MORGAN
Kentucky raid
June

MISSOURI

KENTUCKY

Springfield

Pilot Knob
September 27

Cairo

Bowling Green

*Unorganized
territory*

Newtonia
October 28

Paducah

THOMAS

STONEMAN
Virginia raid
December

ARKANSAS

Nashville
December 15–16

Knoxville

PRICE
Missouri raid
*August–
December*

Fort Pillow
April 12

Jackson

Franklin
November 30

TENNESSEE

Fort
Smith

Columbia
*November
24–25*

Chattanooga

STEELE

LITTLE ROCK

Memphis

Decatur

SHERMAN

Arkadelphia

Jenkins
Ferry
April 30

Memphis
raid
August

Oxford

HOOD

Atlanta

Prairie
D'Ane
April 9–13

Camden

Kentucky
raid
*March–
April*

FORREST

ALABAMA

MILLEDGEVILLE

Mansfield
April 8

Monroe

MISSISSIPPI

Campaign
detail

GEORGIA

Fort De Russy
March 14

Vicksburg

JACKSON

MONTGOMERY

TEXAS

Alexandria

Natchez

BANKS

Yellow Bayou *May 18*

Beaumont

BATON
ROUGE

Mobile

LOUISIANA

New Orleans

TENNESSEE

SHERMAN

N.C.

FARRAGUT

Chattanooga

Rocky Face Ridge
May 7–13

Mobile Bay
August 5

Dalton

JOHNSTON

Resaca
May 13–15

GEORGIA

KEY TO MAP

ALABAMA

Rome

Kingston

Cassville

FIELD
COMMANDERS

MAJOR
MOVEMENTS

KEY
BATTLES

Acworth

Kennesaw Mountain
June 27

UNION

Union

Union victory

New Hope
Church
May 25–26

Marietta

Atlanta
*Battle July 22,
surrender Sept. 2*

CONFEDERATE

Confederate

Confederate victory

ATLANTA

Hood
heads for
Tennessee
*September–
October*

HOOD

Inconclusive battle

Jonesboro
Aug. 31–Sept. 1

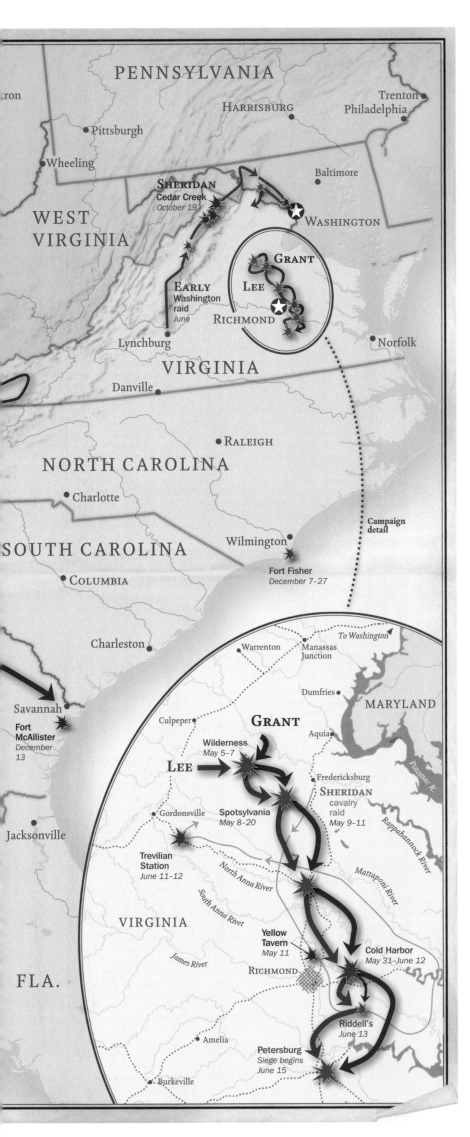

1864
Situation Report

The year starts slowly on the battlefield, but the Union begins a unified campaign in May, as General Ulysses S. Grant drives into Virginia and General William T. Sherman moves south to capture Atlanta

March 9 President Lincoln appoints General Grant to lead all Union armies. General Sherman, a close colleague, replaces Grant as leader of Union troops in the West.

May 5-6 Grant invades Virginia with a large Union force in the Overland Campaign. Lee's troops beat him badly in the Battle of the Wilderness, but Grant presses on.

May 7 Acting in coordination with Grant, General Sherman leads 100,000 men on an advance south from Chattanooga to Atlanta, a major producer of munitions.

May 8-20 The Confederates defeat Union troops in the Battle of Spotsylvania, but Grant continues his advance.

May 31-June 12 In the Battle of Cold Harbor, Grant suffers major losses, and some Northern papers call him a "butcher."

June 15 Grant lays siege to Petersburg, the vital link connecting Richmond to the outside world, beginning a long period of trench warfare that will extend into 1865.

July 20-22 After weeks of skirmishes and battles with Confederates, Sherman draws near Atlanta, where he defeats rebels under new leader General John Bell Hood in the Battles of Peachtree Creek and Atlanta.

Aug. 5 Union Admiral David Farragut captures Mobile Bay in Alabama, further restricting Southern commerce.

Sept. 2 Sherman takes Atlanta, much of which is burned.

Sept. 19 General Philip Sheridan's Union troops beat rebels under General Jubal E. Early, taking control of Virginia's Shenandoah Valley and laying waste to crops and barns.

Nov. 8 Abraham Lincoln is re-elected President.

Dec. 15-16 Union forces win a major victory over the Confederates under Hood in the Battle of Nashville.

Dec. 21 After his devastating March to the Sea, Sherman captures Savannah, Georgia's seaport on the Atlantic.

The Union's Overland Campaign

General Ulysses S. Grant takes charge in the East and invades Virginia, but his forward motion ends outside Richmond

THE FASCINATING PICTURE ON THE LEFT brings us about as close as we may ever come to the men who fought the Civil War. Taken by Timothy O'Sullivan, it shows General Ulysses S. Grant conferring with General George Meade and Under Secretary of War Charles Dana as they consult a map. The photo, which O'Sullivan titled "Council of War," was taken on May 21, 1864, at Massaponax, Va., 17 days after Union troops crossed the Rapidan River, launching the Overland Campaign, the final Union assault on Virginia of the war. In that brief period, Grant's Army of the Potomac had already clashed with Robert E. Lee's Army of Northern Virginia, suffering major losses, in the Battle of the Wilderness. Yet the Northern advance had continued, and a costly second battle around the Spotsylvania Court House was winding down when this picture was taken.

The story behind the strategy session at left begins with another council of war, held in Washington on March 9, 1864, when Grant and other top Union military leaders met with President Abraham Lincoln and Secretary of War Edwin Stanton to discuss Northern strategy for the year to come. After his successes at Vicksburg and Chattanooga the year before, Grant was now the North's indispensable man. Amid his growing renown, he was threatening to become a classic man on horseback, and many voices in the Republican Party were urging him to run to replace Lincoln in the White House in the fall 1864 presidential election.

Grant had other plans: he respected Lincoln, and he knew he still had a job to finish in uniform. Once Lincoln had confirmed Grant's intentions, he named the plain-spoken Ohioan the general-in-chief of all the Northern armies, replacing General Henry W. Halleck, who would now serve as Grant's chief of staff. Grant's first priority would be to do battle with Lee on the Eastern front.

Grant and Lincoln first met on the night of March 8, at a large White House reception. The lanky, awkward President and the stubby general, who resembled a quartermaster more than a lofty commander, must have offered an amusing tableau. Indeed Grant's entrance so galvanized the crowd that the President asked him to stand on a sofa to allow the crush of gawkers to get a good look at him. Perhaps that allowed the two to see eye to eye—just as they did in their war council the next day.

Grant, Lincoln and their colleagues emerged from their meetings with a master plan for the year's campaigns on all the war's major fronts, the first time the North had crafted such a unified strategy. On the Virginia front, Meade, with Grant at his side, would lead the Army of the Potomac against Lee in an invasion of Virginia, assisted by another veteran summoned from the west, General Philip Sheridan, the can-do cavalry commander. On the Southern front, General William T. Sherman would take on the rebels' second major army, led by General Joseph E. Johnston since General Braxton Bragg's resignation. Sherman's goal was to drive south from Chattanooga and capture another major Southern city, Atlanta.

On secondary fronts, General Franz Sigel would take on a task that had consistently foiled Union commanders: winning control of the Shenandoah Valley, the rebels' stronghold and breadbasket in western Virginia. In

PARLEY *Photographer Timothy O'Sullivan made a series of exposures of Union commanders at their meeting on May 21. Their armies had already taken some 36,000 casualties in two battles during the Overland Campaign, then little more than two weeks old. The meeting was held at a Baptist church, whose pews were hauled outside for seating*

159

the South, General Nathaniel Banks and his Army of the Gulf would target the port city of Mobile, Ala. East of Richmond, where a Union army still was encamped on the Virginia Peninsula, General Benjamin Butler would try to cut the vital railroad that connected Richmond with Petersburg, the lifeline of the Confederate capital. He would then mount an attack on Richmond from the south, in tandem with Grant's invasion from the north and west. Richmond itself was not Grant's primary target, however: he hoped to draw Lee away from his fortified positions around Fredericksburg and beat the Army of Northern Virginia in the open field, then take the capital.

IN THE WILDERNESS On May 4, the Army of the Potomac once again crossed the Rapidan River and entered Virginia. The Confederates didn't contest the crossing, for Lee knew that once across the river, Grant would be heading for the Wilderness, that tortuous briar patch where the rebels had hoodwinked Major General Joseph Hooker a year before. Grant had hoped to get past this dismal patch of ground before tangling with Lee, but when Meade slowed his pace to let his supply wagons catch up to his troops, the Union soldiers found themselves camp-

ing on haunted ground, where many of the men reported seeing the unburied bones of their fallen colleagues lying among the weeds and thickets—far from a call to glory.

Lee struck the next day, sending his two main armies, led by Generals A.P. Hill and Richard Ewell, heading east to attack the Union right. The heaviest action was seen at a clearing called Saunders Field, where the rebels butted up against the Federals, quickly erected fortifications and then bore the brunt of a powerful Union thrust that briefly broke through the gray line, only to pull back. Amid the overgrown woods, there was little room for strategy. "It was a mere slugging match," one Confederate said—a description that could be applied to the entire campaign that followed, as Grant and Lee hurled troops against each other in a series of battles whose deadly toll quickly outpaced those of the war's earlier conflicts and left the two sides punchdrunk, exhausted and stalemated.

In this particular bout, however, the South played tag-team: on May 6, General James Longstreet's army arrived in the Wilderness just as the Union troops achieved a breakthrough. As at Second Bull Run and Chickamauga, Longstreet seems to have scripted his arrival to galvanize the rebels, who now drove the Yankees before them. But

ARBOREAL WARFARE
This illustration depicting the Battle of the Wilderness was published in 1887, 23 years after the conflict took place.

The scene is the Orange Plank Road, one of two major arteries cutting through the heavily forested area. The vantage point is from behind the Confederate line, under General A.P. Hill, as Union troops under General W.S. Hancock attacked the rebels on May 5, 1864, and drove them back. The arrival of General James Longstreet's army later in the day handed the initiative back to the Confederates

Spotsylvania Stalemate

Though defeated at the Wilderness, General U.S. Grant kept driving to the east, against the right flank of General Robert E. Lee's army. A race to the next major crossroads at the Spotsylvania (a.k.a. Spottsylvania) Court House ensued, and the South won it. Lee's men then dug a 4-mile (6 km) -long trench in a semicircle, creating a strong defensive position with a salient in the center of the line, the Mule Shoe, a rocky ridge that the rebels heavily fortified.

For three days, May 8, 9 and 10, Grant hurled his troops against the Mule Shoe. The first charge of some 5,000 men, on the 8th, briefly succeeded but was driven back when reinforcements were tardy. A final attack on the 12th was even more deadly, as 15-20,000 bluecoats charged the ridge but were driven back. Some of the most frenzied combat seen in the war raged for some 18 hours around the Mule Shoe, particularly at a hotspot called the Bloody Angle, center, but the day ended in a draw, even though the Union took far more losses.

The battle, which in full lasted from May 8 to 21, ended with 31,000 casualties in blue and gray. Numbered among them were two men who would be sorely missed. Confederate cavalry commander General J.E.B. Stuart died after a May 11 battle at Yellow Tavern, in which his men were badly outnumbered by Union cavalrymen under General Philip Sheridan. The rebels' colorful knight-errant had left his unit briefly to visit his wife and children before the fray. With his passing, at only 31, Lee had lost another leader, like Stonewall Jackson, who could not be replaced. The North lost the beloved Major General John ("Uncle John") Sedgwick, the highest-ranking Union leader to fall in the war.

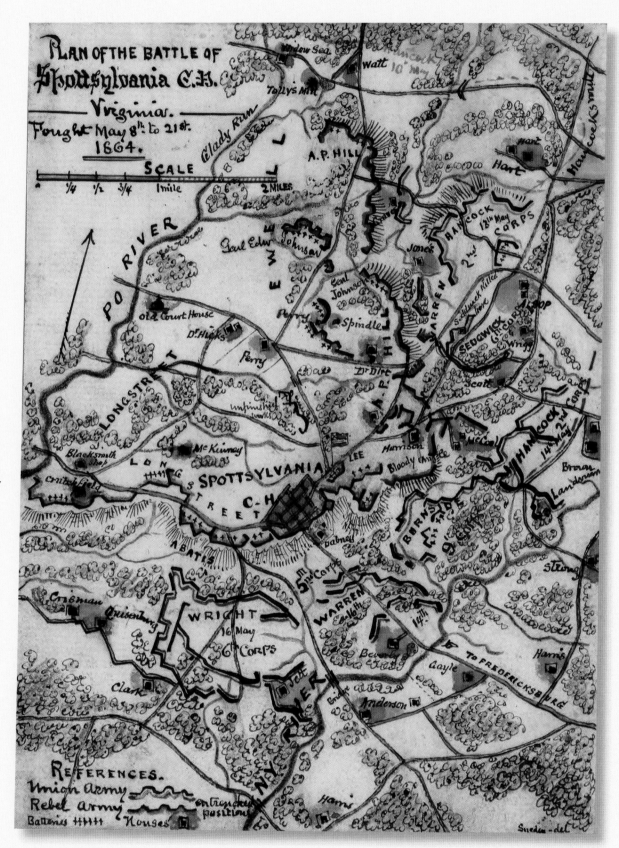

WE HAPPY FEW *After crossing the Rapidan River into Virginia, these soldiers of Company 1 of the 57th Massachusetts Infantry Regiment were immediately caught up in the Battle of the Wilderness. Company 1 numbered 86 men when the Overland Campaign began; when this photograph was taken several weeks later, these nine men were the only survivors*

CORBIS

then came a moment of heart-stopping déjà vu: like Jackson at Chancellorsville, on the same ground and at the same moment of triumph, Longstreet was hit by friendly fire. But unlike Jackson, he lived to fight another day.

NO TURNING BACK Grant also vowed to fight another day—and that is what distinguishes him from every previous Union commander on this front. He had suffered some 17,500 casualties on May 5-6, while Lee had taken some 10,500. Yet Grant didn't consider returning across the Rapidan to regroup. "If you see the President, tell him from me that whatever happens, there will be no turning back," he told a newspaper reporter. Indeed, if Grant didn't quite burn his bridges behind him, he had already demonstrated his resolution. "I had, on the 5th, ordered all the bridges over the Rapidan to be taken up except one at Germania Ford," he dryly notes in his memoirs.

The next day, May 7, Grant's men and supply wagons began moving to the rear, as if to retreat. But late in the afternoon, the formation turned south, not north, once again pushing toward Richmond—and the Union soldiers began to cheer. "For the first time in a Virginia campaign the Army of the Potomac stayed on the offensive after its initial battle," notes historian James McPherson in *Battle Cry of Freedom* (Oxford University Press; 1988), his compelling one-volume account of the war.

Almost immediately, the struggle was rejoined around Spotsylvania Court House, east of the Wilderness, where the enemies fought a bloody, running series of battles from May 8 to 21. As at the Wilderness, Spotsylvania concluded with a staggering casualty count—18,000 on the Union side, 13,000 on the Confederate—and with victory for neither. Yet Grant made clear that he still had no intention of halting his campaign. "I propose to fight it out on this line if it takes all summer," he declared in a dispatch to General Halleck. The phrase electrified the North, just as the general's demand for "unconditional surrender" had done more than two years before.

The campaign would indeed take all summer—and longer. Grant pulled his troops out of Spotsylvania and just kept pushing, moving south and east along Lee's right, keeping his lines open to the Union-controlled ports and storehouses on the peninsula, where Butler's Army of the James was camped. But that general failed in his assign-

THE FALLEN *Workers collect the remains of soldiers killed during the Battle of Cold Harbor. General Grant later said his decision to attack against impossible odds would haunt him until his death. "It was not war, it was murder," said Confederate General Evander Law of Cold Harbor after the war*

ment to keep General P.G.T. Beauregard's forces protecting Richmond busy with an attack from the south. The Confederate attacked Butler at Drewry's Bluff and beat him. After Butler withdrew, both he and Beauregard sent additional troops to the armies fighting to their west.

Foiled at Spotsylvania, Grant next made a dash for a railroad junction just beyond the North Anna River some 25 miles (40 km) to the south, but Lee sniffed out the move and managed to keep his army between Grant and Richmond. The two forces next collided at Cold Harbor, 10 miles (16 km) northeast of Richmond, which, despite its name, is not a port town. After Sheridan's cavalry captured the key railroad junction on May 31, Confederate troops poured in, and both sides began digging trenches and erecting some of the strongest entrenchments of the war along a line that stretched for some 7 miles (11 km).

The battle that followed lasted a full two weeks; it was a grinding, slow slaughter that offered a chilling preview of World War I, as Grant's officers again and again roused Union troops from their deeply entrenched positions and sent them charging across blasted, open wastelands directly into the guns of similarly dug-in rebels.

This sort of combat offered all gore and no glory, and as the casualties mounted, Northern newspapers that had hailed Grant for his determination only weeks earlier now branded him a butcher. The killing reached an apogee on June 3, when Grant ordered the largest assault of the battle—and when many Union soldiers were seen preparing for execution by pinning papers with their names and addresses on their uniforms, to aid the Sanitary Commission workers in shipping their bodies home. Meade's officers succeeded in getting some 20,000 men onto the field of battle: within hours some 5,000 to 7,000 of them were dead, and Grant finally called a halt to the madness.

Years later, Grant continued to regret this needless loss of life and accepted the blame, writing in his memoirs:"I have always regretted that the last assault at Cold Harbor was ever made … No advantage whatever was gained to compensate for the heavy loss we sustained." The Overland Campaign was less than five weeks old, and the two sides had lost almost 70,000 men between them. Lee had outwitted Grant's plans of beating the South on the open field, but even so, the Union armies were now camped only 25 miles outside Richmond, hunkered down around the town of Petersburg, site of the only rail lines still open to the Southern capital. And they weren't leaving. As Confederate fortifications inside the city grew taller, Union trenches outside it grew deeper. Grant's invasion had failed to win the major victory he had desperately sought. It had now devolved into Vicksburg redux: a long battle of attrition around a besieged city. ■

The Siege of Petersburg
The Army of the Potomac digs in for the winter

Frustrated in his attempt to force Robert E. Lee into a battle in the open during the Overland Campaign, General Grant changed his strategy following the Battle of Cold Harbor: he would now focus his forces on assaulting the strong Confederate position at Petersburg, a large town of 18,000 residents some 25 miles (40 km) south of Richmond. Five railroad lines converged on this port city; it was the transit hub that kept Richmond ticking. On June 14, Grant surprised Lee by crossing his army over the James River on a hastily-built pontoon bridge some 2,100 ft. (640 m) long—the largest such military bridge yet created—bound for Petersburg.

Five days before, General Benjamin Butler's Army of the James had attacked Petersburg, but rebels under General P.G.T. Beauregard drove them back. On June 15, another Union assault achieved an early breakthrough, but its leaders failed to follow up on a chance to take the city. Confederate reinforcements began pouring into the city from the west, as Union troops arrived outside it from the east. The Siege of Petersburg had begun: it would last for 292 days. Lee had foiled Grant's attempt to beat him in the open and had forced the North into a battle of attrition. But this was no victory; both men knew which side must prevail in such a contest.

Many skirmishes and operations followed along a trench line that finally grew to be more than 30 miles (48 km) long. They were inconclusive, deadly and, in contrast to the war's earlier battles, humdrum—except for the Battle of the Crater on July 30, in which a Union attempt to create a breakthrough by detonating explosives from a mine dug beneath the rebel lines ended in a scene of chaos and slaughter. For the next eight months, the war on the Eastern front consisted of boredom punctuated by sudden bursts of violence and death, and then a return to stalemate.

HOME SWEET DOME *This barracks bunker at Fort Sedgwick outside Petersburg, named in honor of the Union general killed at Spotsylvania, gives a sense of the war's last 10 months as experienced by the Army of the Potomac. The men's less formal name for the camp: Fort Hell*

Women in the War

Refusing subordinate roles, some U.S. women made history in the conflict

Clara Barton

An authentic American hero, Clarissa (Clara) Harlowe Barton served as a pathfinder and inspiration for generations of U.S. women and left an enduring legacy as the founder of the American Red Cross. Born in Oxford, Mass., in 1821, she learned the practice of nursing by tending to a brother injured in a farm accident, and she took up teaching as a means of overcoming her intense shyness. In Bordentown, N.J., she established a free public school—the first in the town—but resigned when a man was named principal, saying "I may sometimes be willing to teach for nothing, but if paid at all, I shall never do a man's work for less than a man's pay."

Leaving to work at the U.S. Patent Office in Washington, she became the first permanent woman employee of the U.S. Government. She helped gather medical supplies after the First Battle of Bull Run, and in 1862 she began taking her privately funded nursing operation to the battlefields. Barton cared for the wounded at many major battles, including Antietam, where a bullet passed through her sleeve, killing a soldier she was tending. She founded the American Red Cross in 1881.

Frances Clayton

She might have stepped out of the lyrics of scores of old ballads that tell of a woman who dons man's attire and fights on the battlefield or runs off to live as a sailor. But the details of Frances Clayton's service, as reported in a number of newspapers after the war, are so confusing and even contradictory that historians are still trying to track them down. Before the war, Clayton was a Minnesota housewife, but when her husband John enlisted in a cavalry regiment, she pulled on a pair of trousers and enlisted alongside him. It is believed the two were later transferred to a light artillery unit, and Clayton is believed to have fought in a number of battles, likely including the Union capture of Fort Donelson in February 1862 and the Battle of Stone's River at that year's end.

However, the majority of the accounts of Clayton's time in arms agree on the points that would have titillated Victorian readers: she learned "all the vices of men," including drinking, swearing, chewing tobacco and gambling, and she was said to have enjoyed a good cigar. She rode well, shot well and was considered a superior soldier. After husband John's death at Stone's River, legend has it that she continued to serve, stepping over his fallen body to keep fighting. Some accounts say she was discharged shortly after her husband's death; others claim she was wounded in the hip at Fort Donelson, where a doctor discovered her gender. She enjoyed a moment of fame, but following the war she vanished from history.

Mary Tebe

The armies of the Civil War were far different from those of the 20th century. In many ways, they were vast, slow-moving communities, in which the soldiers were supported by a host of behind-the-lines personnel. Typical camp followers included sutlers, traveling vendors who sold the essentials of daily life; doctors and nurses; farriers and blacksmiths to service horses; liquor sellers; prostitutes; and in some cases, soldiers' wives and children.

French immigrant Mary Tebe, widely known as "French Mary," was a vivandière with the 114th Pennsylvania Volunteer Infantry Regiment. Vivandières had a long history in European armies, where soldiers' wives acted as sutlers, carried canteens and tended the wounded. They wore short skirts over trousers and boots and were active on the battlefield; above, Tebe carries a canteen and a holstered pistol.

Tebe was paid the wages of an enlisted Union soldier, plus 25 cents per day for extra nursing duties; the total was probably about $21.45 a week. She was in the midst of the action at Fredericksburg (where she was hit in the ankle by a bullet), at Gettysburg and at some 11 other battles. In the photo above, she is wearing the Kearny Cross, awarded in honor of Union General Philip Kearny, who was killed in action.

Rose O'Neal Greenhow

The most renowned female spy of the Civil War seemed destined for fame: as a girl she was known as "Wild Rose." Born in Maryland in 1817, she moved to Washington to help an aunt run an inn at the Old Capitol building, and after marrying diplomat Robert Greenhow in 1835, she became one of the pre-eminent hostesses of the capital. "I am a Southern woman," she wrote in her memoirs, "born with revolutionary blood in my veins." She also claimed to have learned much from her close friendship with the pro-South, pro-slavery Senator John C. Calhoun of South Carolina. Early in the war, now widowed, and adept at wheedling information from powerful men, she ran a ring that gathered details on Union troop movements and sent them to General P.G.T. Beauregard, helping the rebels win the First Battle of Bull Run.

When Union spy chief Allan Pinkerton uncovered Greenhow's deeds, he placed her under house arrest in what became the Old Capitol Prison, and he soon sent more female Confederate spies to join her at "Fort Greenhow." The glamorous widow eventually became such a heroic martyr figure in the South that the Union released her, exiling her to the South. Upon her return, she was dispatched by Jefferson Davis to Europe to plead the rebel cause in England and France, where she wrote a popular account of her life. Her death in 1864 enhanced her legend: returning to the U.S., her ship ran aground off Wilmington, N.C., while being pursued by a Northern gunboat. Bearing Confederate dispatches, she set out for shore in a small rowboat; when it capsized, she was carried under the waves by the weight of $2,000 in gold, earned from the sale of her memoirs in Europe, that she was carrying to the rebel treasury. Below, Greenhow and daughter "Little Rose," 8, are photographed at the Old Capitol Prison.

Sherman Captures Atlanta

Union armies march through Georgia in a slow, grinding advance on a key Southern city

NO ONE ARGUED THE CASE FOR THE Union's 1864 campaign against Atlanta more eloquently than the President. The fall of Atlanta would "open the way for the Federal Army to the Gulf on the one hand, and to Charleston on the other, and close up those rich granaries from which Lee's armies are supplied. It would give them control of our network of railroads and thus paralyze our efforts," Jefferson Davis declared. Over the course of the war, Atlanta had grown from a medium-sized city to a major manufacturing center of some 20,000 people whose industries helped power the rebel war machine. Nestled deep in the heartland of the South, it was also a symbol of rebel pride whose capture and violation would constitute an agonizing blow for the Confederacy.

Among those who agreed with Davis were President Abraham Lincoln and Lieutenant General U.S. Grant. And they had just the man to take Atlanta: the capable and relentless general named after a famed Shawnee Indian warrior, William Tecumseh Sherman. In the previous two years, Sherman, 44, had been Grant's right-hand

PHOTO-OP *If only war were as clean and tidy as it is portrayed in this Union propaganda photograph, shot in the same captured rebel fort near Atlanta as the portrait of General Sherman shown later in this story. Sherman knew the truth: "War is hell"*

man in the successful campaigns at Vicksburg and Chattanooga. Now he and Grant would work in tandem as they attempted to drive a stake into the heart of the Confederacy. Grant would tackle General Robert E. Lee in Virginia, while Sherman would use Chattanooga as his base camp for a drive south and east to Atlanta.

Opposing Sherman would be a familiar figure, General Joseph Johnston, a specialist in defensive maneuvers who had failed to halt the capture of Vicksburg by Grant. His top lieutenant was General John Bell Hood, an impulsive officer who, unlike his boss, woke up every morning eager to take the fight to the Yankees. The campaign to come would center on logistics and terrain, since the Union troops would be fighting deep inside enemy territory. As Sherman later wrote in his memoirs, "The great question of the campaign was one of supplies." Northern troops would have to forage for food. And as Sherman moved south, he would have to leave troops behind him to hold the railroad line, his crucial link with Chattanooga and Nashville. He would also be battling Georgia itself,

all mountains and ridges and steep valleys bisected by rivers: a landscape shaped for defense rather than offense.

INTO GEORGIA On May 7, three days after Grant traversed the Rapidan River to invade Virginia, Sherman crossed the Georgia border just outside Chattanooga, also southbound. He led a force of almost 100,000 men: its main unit, 60,000 strong, was the proud, battle-hardened Army of the Cumberland, under General George Thomas. Major General James McPherson led Grant's old command, the Army of the Tennessee, with 25,000 men; Major General John Schofield's Army of the Ohio was 13,000 strong.

Johnston's force numbered some 50,000 men—but his ranks were growing every day, thanks to the failure of a key element of the Union's grand strategy for 1864. General Nathaniel Banks did not launch a campaign against Mobile, Ala., that would have pinned down Confederate troops in that state. This allowed General Leonidas Polk to lead his 15,000 troops north to assist Johnston.

Sherman's campaign against Johnston bore an uncan-

OVERPASS *Union engineers built this magnificent railroad trestle at Whiteside, Tenn., to keep the line open from Sherman's advancing troops back to Chattanooga and Nashville. Soldiers are camped nearby to protect the invaluable span, 780 ft. (238 m) long, with four tiers of timber supports at its midpoint. The photograph illustrates the difficult terrain over which the Atlanta campaign was fought*

STRIPPED DOWN *It appears that Confederates may have removed the exterior lumber from the outbuildings in the foreground of the Potter House outside Atlanta to construct defensive-perimeter lines. The crisscross barriers are chevaux-de-frise, logs sharpened into spikes to stop an infantry charge*

ny similarity to the conflict then raging more than 550 hundred miles to the north, where Grant was pressing Lee. Facing Sherman, the master of the attack, Johnston, the master of defense, refused to commit his army to a battle in the open but instead created strong defensive fortifications to stem the Union advance. Sherman's men would assault those positions, suffering losses that often were twice or three times as many as Johnston's—which Sherman knew he could afford. While his main force kept Johnston tied down, Sherman would skillfully deploy his two affiliate armies to probe the flanks of the Confederate position; these gambits, bypassing Johnston, would force him to pull back from his defensive stronghold and seek a new one to the south. Those three words were the key to the campaign: Sherman's armies suffered setbacks and frustrations, but in the end, the needle of the Union compass always kept wheeling, inexorably, to the south.

FIRST BLOOD Johnston's initial line of defense was Rocky Face Ridge, some 25 miles (40 km) south of Chattanoo-

ga. Sherman sent the armies of Thomas and Schofield head on against Johnston, taking light casualties, while McPherson hooked far to the west, around the ridge, to attack the Confederate general's largely unprotected position at Resaca, 15 miles (24 km) to the south. This potentially magnificent stroke failed when McPherson grew timid and passed up a chance to take the lightly defended town—but it still forced the rebels to fall back again.

While Sherman punched directly at Johnston once more at Resaca, McPherson again moved south along Johnston's left flank, forcing him to pull up stakes and fall back another 25 miles to a strong position at Cassville. In 12 days of campaigning, Sherman's forces were halfway to Atlanta at a cost of only several thousand casualties.

Now, Johnston decided, he must make a stand, and the Southern troops cheered when they heard the news. But just as McPherson had wavered at Resaca, Johnston's gung-ho underling, Hood, now became spooked that his flank had been turned, and he called off the attack at the last minute. The Confederates retreated another 10 miles

SHERMAN'S PROGRESS *Wars require heroes, and General Sherman was idolized in the North after he captured Atlanta, when this carefully composed portrait was taken.*

A West Point graduate who did not serve in the Mexican War, Sherman resigned his commission in 1853 and was superintendent of a military academy (now Louisiana State University) when the war began. After distinguishing himself at the First Battle of Bull Run, he suffered a breakdown in the fall of 1861 and was placed on leave for several months.

Sherman credited the return of his equilibrium to his service under General Grant, beginning with the Battle of Shiloh, where he was again wounded and following which he was promoted

(16 km) to a position at the Allatoona Pass fortified earlier, but their more serious retreat was psychological: the troops' morale plummeted, their leaders quarreled, Richmond fumed, and Atlanta newspapers pointed fingers.

BOGGED DOWN Johnston now awaited Sherman at the narrow Allatoona Pass in a prepared position that the rebels considered impregnable. But Sherman paused, rested his troops and resupplied them with 20 days of provisions brought in on the railroad. Then he surprised Johnston with yet another flanking maneuver, swinging west and then south to avoid the pass completely, aiming for Dallas, 20 miles (32 km) to Johnston's rear. Once again Johnston had to pull up stakes. His troops raced to Dallas, where the armies collided at New Hope Church, then clashed again two days later at Pickett's Mill. The rebels technically won both battles, to no avail. As heavy rainfall turned the roads to reddish mud, the armies set-

tled into several weeks of fruitless, frustrating skirmishes.

By late June the rebels had withdrawn to Kennesaw Mountain, where Sherman again hurled Union soldiers at Johnston's strongly entrenched troops head on. The result of this largest battle of the campaign to date was a complete rout of the Union and 3,000 casualties. Yet once again Sherman was using the main battle as an opportunity to develop a flanking avenue, and once again Johnston fell back, this time to the Chattahoochee River. Playing Johnston like a fiddle, Sherman next fooled the Confederate general by flanking him for the first time to the east rather than the west, and the rebels once more performed their familiar two-step: pull out and fall back.

By now President Davis was thoroughly alarmed, and he sent General Braxton Bragg (hardly a disinterested observer) to take Johnston's measure. Swayed by General Hood's arguments that his superior was too timid, Bragg recommended that Johnston be relieved, and on July 17

Marching Through Georgia

General William T. Sherman's campaign to take Atlanta covered more than 100 miles (160 km) and required a full four months, from May to September 1864. The main force, under General George Thomas, most often followed the Western & Atlantic railbed, the vital supply line to the Union base in Chattanooga. Major General John Schofield's Army of the Ohio marched to Thomas' left on the east; Major General James McPherson's Army of the Tennessee was to his right, on the west.

The first test came at Rocky Face Ridge, just north of Dalton, where Thomas' men assailed rebels holding a fortified uphill position, keeping them occupied while McPherson's army bypassed them on the west, bound for Resaca, where they hoped to cut General Joseph Johnston's rail link to Atlanta. But rebel reinforcements arrived just in time to stop them, to Sherman's dismay. On May 14 the Federals attacked the Confederates at Resaca, taking 2,750 casualties in a two-day battle yet still forcing Johnston to fall back.

This pattern—a Union attack stoutly opposed by courageous rebels, ending in more Northern than Southern deaths but failing to halt the Federal advance—would continue through the summer, with the rebels retreating after large battles at New Hope Church, Pickett's Mill and Kennesaw Mountain.

In that last battle, on June 27, as Union troops again charged uphill into Confederate guns, Schofield's flanking movement opened a gateway for a rapid Union drive south, forcing Johnston to again surrender a strong position. For President Jefferson Davis, this was the last straw: he named General John Bell Hood to take Johnston's place and defend Atlanta. Hood proved he had the stomach to sacrifice soldiers, but he could not hold off the Northern tide.

the Confederate President named Hood to replace Johnston, a decision that provoked great controversy then and even today offers armchair generals cud to chew upon. Hood had lost the use of his left arm at Gettysburg and his right leg was amputated after Chickamauga. He had a score to settle with the Union armies, whatever the price.

DESPERATE MEASURES Anxious to make his mark as the anti-Johnston, Hood quickly seized the offensive, challenging Thomas' troops as they crossed Peachtree Creek north of the city's outskirts on July 20. But his attack was tardy and poorly coordinated, and he ended up taking 2,500 casualties to the Union's 1,800, even as Schofield and McPherson continued their advance on Atlanta.

Hood was unfazed. Two days later he launched another bold stroke, sending men under General William Hardee on a 15-mile march through Atlanta in hopes of launching a surprise attack on McPherson's rear. In the Battle of Atlanta that followed, the invaluable McPherson was killed. But the tide of combat turned when Schofield's artillery companies arrived on the scene, and the Confederates took a pounding. The Union had won, and Hood had lost 8,000 men in three days.

Union guns were now close enough to begin shelling Atlanta, whose citizens fled in despair. The military action shifted south and west, bypassing Atlanta, as Sherman attempted to cut the last remaining rail line into the city. Southern troops fought valiantly at Ezra Church on July 28, taking 3,000 casualties to the Union's 600.

Finally, only a single train line, the Macon & Western Railroad, was still running into Atlanta, where Hood's troops hunkered down as some 5,000 shells a day rained upon them. A desperate Hood sent Hardee to attack the Federals, dug in along the railroad line at Jonesborough. When the Union won that battle on Aug. 31, Atlanta's fate was sealed. On Sept. 1, Hood ordered all supplies and arms within it destroyed, and the rebels marched away from the city they had so valiantly defended, leaving a great conflagration behind them, capped off when the explosion of an ordnance train rocked the city.

Those reverberations were felt around the county, as church bells rang in Boston, Chicago, Washington and Philadelphia. Every American, North or South, understood that the Union's capture of Atlanta was a pivotal moment in the war. The victorious Sherman occupied the city until Nov. 15, when he ordered its remnants burnt to the ground as he began his March to the Sea. In his memoirs, he described the scene as he turned to gaze again at his trophy and wasteland: "Behind us lay Atlanta, smouldering and in ruins, the black smoke rising high in air, and hanging like a pall over the ruined city." ■

Scenes from Occupied Atlanta

A stronghold of Southern pride suffers under victorious Northerners

WAGON TRAIN *This splendid panorama shows Union supply wagons loading up with goods brought in by train from Nashville and Chattanooga at the Atlanta railroad depot. Sherman wrote of his great victory in his memoirs, "Of course, the glad tidings flew on the wings of electricity to all parts of the North, where the people had patiently awaited news of their husbands, sons, and brothers, away down in 'Dixie Land'…"*

OUTSIDERS *Union soldiers built shanties on Decatur Street in downtown Atlanta during their occupation, which lasted from Sept. 2 until Nov. 15. Sherman used the time to rest, resupply and regroup as he planned for his next campaign, the march to Savannah and the Atlantic coast*

SHARDS *Only a few battered walls of the main Atlanta roundhouse were left standing after the Union bombardment of the city and its subsequent burning by Confederate troops as they withdrew. For good measure, Sherman burned the remains of the city again when he departed in November.*

At this late stage of the war, most land campaigns, like Sherman's march to Atlanta, were conducted with an eye to controlling railroad lines

HEAVE-HO *Union soldiers, surrounded by debris and rubble, use ropes to tear up railroad lines inside Atlanta. Once out of the ground, steel rails would be heated over bonfires until malleable, then bent around tree trunks to mangle them beyond repair— although a substitute for tree trunks was no doubt required at this particular site*

More Union Advances

Hammering the South from every side, the Union captures a major Southern port and finally controls the Shenandoah Valley

WITH GENERAL ULYSSES S. GRANT advancing closer and closer to Richmond in the late summer of 1864, even as General William T. Sherman was driving ever nearer to Atlanta, most Americans were paying little attention to the naval wars along the coastlines of the South. The Union's ongoing Anaconda Plan may have lacked the drama of the battles waged on land, but this nautical war of logistics and trade blockades played a key role in the tightening Union grip over every aspect of the Southern economy. By the summer of 1864, many of the nation's primary internal waterways, including the vital Mississippi River, were entirely in Northern hands. And thanks to a series of victories along Southern shorelines, as well as Sherman's capture of Savannah in December 1864, the Union

NAUTICAL DINOSAUR
Above is Admiral Farragut's flagship, the U.S.S. Hartford. *The war was the last hurrah for the grand wooden-sided sailing warships, made obsolete by the new ironclads.*

At left, a contemporary Union map shows the Confederate defenses protecting Mobile Bay

had now closed off almost every major port in the South. The two primary arteries that kept the Confederacy's heart beating were Wilmington, N.C., which allowed sea access to Richmond, and Mobile Bay in Alabama, located some 30 miles (48 km) south of the city of Mobile, which provided ocean access for the Deep South.

The Union's greatest naval commander in the war, Admiral David Farragut, set his sights on taking Mobile Bay in the late summer of 1864. Commanding a fleet of 14 wooden ships and four *Monitor*-type ironclads, Farragut challenged Fort Morgan, the most powerful of three fortresses, including Forts Gaines and Powell, that guarded access to the bay. In addition to the 46 big guns placed at Fort Morgan, the 26 at Fort Gaines and the 18 at Fort Powell, the bay was defended by more than 60 torpedoes (as sailors then called naval mines) designed to explode on contact. And the rebels also had a potent naval weapon in the ironclad ship C.S.S. *Tennessee,* designed to ram and sink wooden ships.

On Aug. 5, borne upon a rising tide, Farragut's ships approached Fort Morgan, whose guns opened up on the Union fleet, supported by fire from Southern ships. In order to get a good view of the action, Farragut, a seadog of the old school, had himself lashed to the mast of his flagship, the U.S.S. *Hartford,* by a quartermaster. Perhaps he witnessed a Union setback early in the battle: the ironclad U.S.S. *Tecumseh* collided with a mine and sank, and only 21 men of her crew of 114 survived. Now the entire Union fleet slowed as every captain sought to avoid the *Tecumseh's* fate—but that put their ships dead in the water under the Confederate guns.

What to do? Farragut knew. "Damn the torpedoes! Full speed ahead!" he ordered, giving the U.S. Navy a rallying cry for the ages. The Union ships sailed through, as most of the mines failed to detonate, then engaged the Confederate fleet and pounded the *Tennessee,* commanded by Admiral Franklin Buchanan, until it was a powerless hulk, drifting with the current. The battle was over.

After three more weeks of minor land and sea engagements, the Union took full possession of Mobile Bay. As a result, the closest Confederate port on the Gulf Coast now open to the high seas was in Texas, a long way from the war's key theaters: the Anaconda Plan was working. Farragut's August triumph, combined with September and October Union victories in Atlanta and the Shenandoah Valley, were the antidote for Northerners who had been gripped by frustration and defeatism through much of the summer. The triple salvo of Union advances helped buoy the political fortunes of a political candidate now seeking re-election whose naval experience amounted to two flatboat trips on the Mississippi River: Abraham Lincoln. ■

The Shenandoah Valley Falls
General Philip Sheridan subdues a rebel retreat

Since the first days of the war, the Shenandoah Valley of northwest Virginia had served the Confederacy as an all-purpose resource. Its rich farmlands made it the breadbasket of the Army of Northern Virginia. It saw duty as a retreat when Southern armies needed to rest and regroup. Sometimes it was a trapdoor through which rebel cavalry suddenly appeared on the flanks of an unsuspecting Union army. And it had been the scene of one of the most memorable campaigns of the conflict, when Stonewall Jackson's fleet "foot cavalry" made monkeys out of three pursuing Northern armies in the early summer of 1862.

The magic was still in force in 1864, when General U.S. Grant dispatched Major General David Hunter to tackle General Jubal E. Early's army in the Shenandoah as Grant began the Overland Campaign. Early stopped Hunter in his tracks at Lynchburg, then bypassed him and headed straight for Washington, where Grant had removed many of the soldiers guarding the capital to serve in his invasion of Virginia. An embarrassed Grant had to send troops back to defend the capital.

This wouldn't do. When Grant's campaign turned into a trench war around Petersburg, he sent General Philip Sheridan, the hard-driving cavalry leader, to clean up the valley once and for all. At the Battle of Winchester on Sept. 19 (the third fought at this site), Sheridan whipped the outnumbered Confederates, then did it again three days later at the Battle of Fisher's Hill. Now Sheridan began to apply General William T. Sherman's methodical methods of destruction to the lush valley. By October he was reporting to Grant that he had "destroyed over 2,000 barns filled with wheat, hay and farming implements; over 70 mills filled with flour and wheat … and have killed and issued to the troops not less than 3,000 sheep." In the Shenandoah, the rebels' war was over: the scintillating sleight-of-hand of Stonewall Jackson had given way to the relentless depredations of Philip Sheridan.

HAIL TO THE VICTORS *Alfred Waud sketched General Sheridan's troops as they pursued General Early's rebels in the Shenandoah Valley. After two defeats in September, Early regrouped and launched a counterattack on Oct. 19 at Cedar Creek. Sheridan was 10 miles (16 km) away; he rode hard to the scene and arrived in time to rally his troops to a smashing victory*

Lincoln Wins the Election of 1864

When two old foes collide in a political grudge match, President Abraham Lincoln handily defeats General George B. McClellan

AS A MESSAGE TO ONE WHO BELIEVED IN his cause, it was not exactly a compelling call to arms. "I am going to be beaten," President Abraham Lincoln told a U.S. Army officer in the late summer of 1864, as the presidential election was approaching. "And unless some great change takes place, *badly* beaten." Lincoln's forebodings were justified: as he spoke, the Overland Campaign supervised by General Ulysses S. Grant had turned into a quagmire, and Grant was being denounced in Northern newspapers as a butcher: his troops had suffered some 65,000 casualties, only to end up immobilized outside Petersburg, Va. In Georgia, a campaign that had begun with similar high hopes, General William T. Sherman's daring advance on the city of Atlanta, had also bogged down.

Only a year before, the war's end seemed at hand after the twin Union victories at Vicksburg and Gettysburg. But Southern resolve had not wavered, even after the loss of Chattanooga late in 1863. As casualties mounted and there seemed no end in sight to the nation's nightmare, more and more Northern voices called for compromise, for peace talks, for a deal in which the South could go its own way, with slavery restored as the price of peace.

These peace advocates in the North, or Copperheads, included scholars, journalists, clerics and politicians. And they had a leader: Clement Vallandigham, a former Congressman from Ohio. Vallandigham found a receptive audience when he charged Lincoln with tyranny; few scholars today deny that in his conduct of the war, Lincoln came as close as any U.S. President ever has to the status of dictator. Lincoln sometimes suspended the right

of habeas corpus; he allowed trials of civilians by military tribunals; he selectively imposed martial law; and in some cases he suppressed newspapers and interdicted mail. Vallandigham himself was arrested by the U.S. Army in 1863 and sentenced to prison for the remainder of the war; to avoid making him a martyr, Lincoln allowed him to slip away quietly to the South, and he ended up in Canada, remaining a loud voice against the Administration.

Nor did he lack for company. The Democratic candidate commanded the respect of many Americans: he was former General George B. McClellan, sacked by Lincoln late in 1862 and spoiling for revenge ever since. At their convention in Chicago, Democrats nominated McClellan on a platform that denounced the Lincoln Administration's "arbitrary military arrests" and "suppression of freedom of speech and of the press." The party also pledged to preserve the "rights of the States unimpaired," clearing the way for an eventual return to slavery in the South. But most important, the Democratic platform called for immediate peace overtures to the South. Republicans denounced this position, charging it would render all the sacrifices of the war meaningless.

For his part, Lincoln put on his political hat: to ensure his renomination, he named his Secretary of the Treasury, Salmon P. Chase, to the Supreme Court, removing his most ambitious foe within the party. And he strongly backed an effort to ensure that soldiers serving in the U.S. Army, denied the franchise in some states in earlier elections, now be given a chance to vote: he expected to win those ballots. The President easily won renomination at the convention in Baltimore early in June, where the Republicans endorsed a platform calling for a constitu-

REBRANDED *In an attempt to win votes from as many quarters as possible, Republican leaders decided to forgo the party's familiar name during the 1864 campaign. Abraham Lincoln and running mate Andrew Johnson ran under the banner of the National Union Party.*

General George B. McClellan's running mate was George H. Pendleton of Ohio, a widely respected antiwar Democrat who had served in the U.S. House

tional amendment to outlaw slavery. Senator Andrew Johnson of Tennessee was chosen as Lincoln's running mate, in a gesture of solidarity with Union supporters in the border states.

The 1864 election, as it turned out, would be won as much on the battlefield as at the ballot box. When General William T. Sherman marched into Atlanta in early September, the contest was as good as over. The impact of this smashing victory in the very heart of the Deep South sent Union hearts soaring. The road to Lincoln's victory was further paved three weeks later, when General Philip Sheridan defeated a Confederate army led by General Jubal E. Early at Winchester, Va., in the Shenandoah Valley.

On Nov. 8, Lincoln won a massive victory, taking the popular vote 55% to 45%, carrying all but three states—Kentucky, Delaware and New Jersey—and garnering 212 electoral votes to McClellan's 21. Perhaps most gratifying were the results from the Union soldiers: in the 12 states that allowed them to vote as absentees, they had preferred the President over the former general by 78% to 22%. A second term—and the long-awaited opportunity to end the war and welcome the rebellious states back into the Union in a spirit of charity and forgiveness—now awaited Lincoln. ■

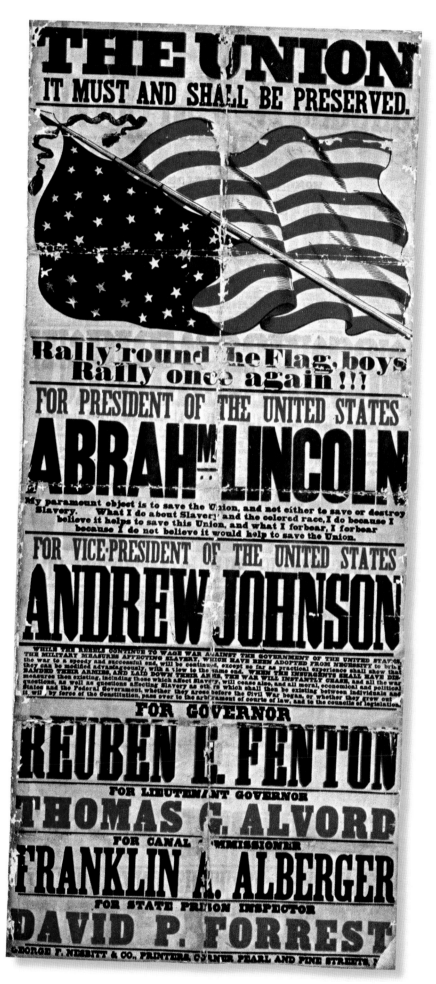

Sherman Marches Through Georgia

After capturing Atlanta, General William T. Sherman moves south and east, scorching the earth to reduce the Confederates' will to fight

ONCE GENERAL WILLIAM T. SHERMAN had captured Atlanta and driven Confederate General John Bell Hood into a camp south of the city, the energetic Union officer was eager to continue his drive into the heart of the Deep South. The next prize in his sights was Georgia's stately port city on the Atlantic Ocean, Savannah. Hood, desperate to derail Sherman's plans, set out to divert his attention back north. In October 1864 Hood led his army, some 40,000 strong, back up Georgia's mountains and ravines, bound for Tennessee and Kentucky.

Hood was betting that Sherman would follow, and U.S. Grant, now in command of all Union armies, urged his close colleague to pursue and defeat Hood before heading further south. But Sherman argued, "If we can march a well-appointed army right through [Jefferson Davis'] territory, it is a demonstration to the world, foreign and domestic, that we have a power which Davis cannot resist." When Grant agreed, as well as a dubious Lincoln, Sherman dispatched Generals George H. Thomas and John Schofield to pursue Hood into Tennessee.

Hood was a gambler of a general, tightly wound and impulsive. When Schofield's troops slipped by two traps Hood had set for them, the enraged general ordered a full-on attack against the well-entrenched Federals at Franklin, some 18 miles (28 km) south of Nashville. The result was a bloodbath that yielded some 6,000 rebel casualties to the North's 2,000 or so. Two weeks later, on Dec. 15-16, General Thomas caught up with Hood's Army of Tennessee closer to Nashville and gave its soldiers a thorough beating. Hood suffered 4,400 more casualties, and the Union half again as many. Tennessee and Kentucky would no longer be major battlegrounds in the war.

Sherman spent the weeks following his Nov. 15 evacuation of Atlanta on his controversial March to the Sea.

This momentous campaign, though it lasted only 36 days, carved a deep place in the soul of Americans: more than defeat on the battlefield, it left many Southerners with a grudge against the North that has yet to fully heal.

As Sherman's 62,000 soldiers traveled the countryside, with an estimated 10,000 liberated slaves forming an unusual band of camp followers as a rear guard, they left a wasteland behind them. The Union's new military leaders, as well as the Lincoln Administration, had determined that to hasten the war's end, the Confederates must be beaten not only on the battlefield: the region's very ability to make war must be eradicated. Railroad tracks must be torn up, and the steel rails bent into "Sherman's neckties." Food stores must be eliminated, lest they feed rebel troops. Civilians, not just soldiers, must be made to feel the full extent of war's privations, the louder to make their appeals for peace to their leaders in Richmond.

"We are not only fighting hostile armies, but a hostile people, and must make old and young, rich and poor, feel the hard hand of war," Sherman wrote to General Henry W. Halleck. To the North, this policy was a harsh but just goad to surrender. But in Southern hearts, Sherman's march was no more than the one-sided act of a bully, a pointless exercise in military cruelty and braggadocio.

On Dec. 13 Sherman faced the first serious opposition to his advance, but Union troops easily overwhelmed outnumbered Confederates at Fort McAllister, the sentinel guarding Savannah's southern approach. When Sherman demanded that the rebel commander inside Savannah, General William Hardee, surrender, Hardee refused to do so: he withdrew his troops across a pontoon bridge north to South Carolina. On Dec. 22 Sherman wired to Lincoln, "I beg to present you, as a Christmas gift, the city of Savannah, with 150 heavy guns and plenty of ammunition, and also about 25,000 bales of cotton." ■

VANQUISHED *Ruined buildings in Savannah were photographed in 1865 by Samuel A. Cooley. Although the Confederates under General William Hardee evacuated the city without a fight, it still suffered through the Northern occupation*

1865

"It is not possible in the moment of jubilee to comprehend the scope of this event. The victory that has been won is not selfish or limited. It is not an American victory only. It is the vindication of the equal rights of men everywhere."

—*HARPER'S WEEKLY*, APRIL 22, 1865

AFTER THE FALL *Alexander Gardner took this photograph of the ruins of Richmond in April 1865, following the Confederate capital's bombardment by Union artillery and its subsequent burning by fleeing rebels*

IOWA

Chicago

OHIO

MISSOURI

St. Joseph

COLUMB...

TOPEKA

KANSAS

JEFFERSON CITY

Torched: After General Sherman's troops occupied Columbia, S.C., in February, the capital city was burned. Reponsibility for the deed has never been satisfactorily resolved

Springfield

Unorganized territory

KENTUCKY

ARKANSAS

NASHVILLE

TENNESSEE

STONEMAN
Virginia-Carolina raid
March–April
Knoxville

Fort Smith

Memphis

HOOD
Retreat from Nashville
December 1864-January1865

Chattanooga

Last Confederate surrender
June 23

Decatur

MISS.

Last Raid: Under General James H. Wilson, some 13,500 Union cavalry troops defeated the remnants of Confederate General Nathan Bedford Forrest's cavalry, capturing Selma on April 2; Montgomery on April 12; and Columbus on April 16

Tupelo

WILSON
Cavalry raid to Alabama–Georgia
March–April

Atlanta

Doaksville, Indian Territory

Talladega

MILLEDGEVILLE

Macon

TEXAS

Alexandria

Columbus
April 16

Selma
April 2

MONTGOMERY

Jefferson Davis captured
May 10

Beaumont

LOUISIANA

BATON ROUGE

Biloxi

Mobile

ALABAMA

Irwinville

GEORGIA

FLORIDA

New Orleans

Pensacola

Appalachicola

Gulf of Mexico

KEY TO MAP

FIELD COMMANDERS	MAJOR MOVEMENTS	KEY BATTLES
UNION	▬▬▬ Union	✸ Union victory
CONFEDERATE	▬▬▬ Confederate	✸ Confederate victory
		✸ Inconclusive battle

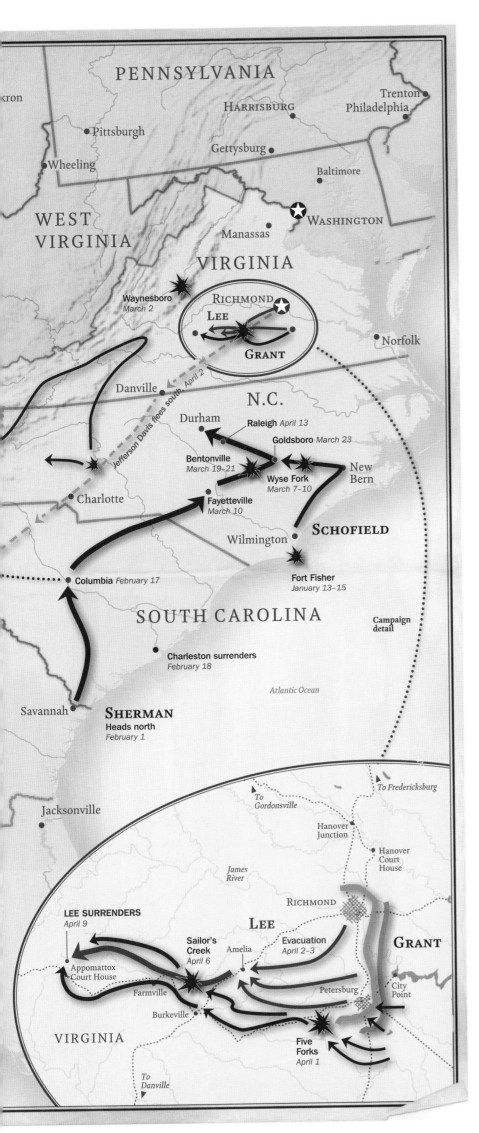

1865
Situation Report

As General U.S. Grant tightens his grip on General Robert E. Lee in Virginia, Sherman continues his advances. Out of resources, the South surrenders, but within days President Lincoln is assassinated

Jan. 31 Congress approves the 13th Amendment, forbidding slavery in the U.S., and the measure is sent to the states for ratification, achieved in December 1865.

Feb. 1 Sherman marches out of Savannah, bound for Columbia, S.C., the state capital. He occupies the city on Feb. 17, and much of the capital is burned to the ground. Rebels also evacuate the port city of Charleston.

March 4 Lincoln is inaugurated for a second term.

March 22 Union cavalry General James H. Wilson begins a devastating raid that will take him through northern Alabama and Georgia in the war's final weeks.

March 25 After being trapped inside Petersburg, Va., by a Union siege for 10 months, Lee attempts to break out of Grant's grip, but his troops are rebuffed and withdraw.

April 2 Union troops break through rebel lines defending Petersburg. Lee abandons his position and advises Confederate President Jefferson Davis to flee Richmond. Withdrawing rebel troops put the capital city to the torch.

April 9 Lee surrenders to Grant at Appomattox Court House, Va. Northern peace terms are lenient, allowing rebel troops to keep their horses and officers to keep their weapons. Union troops salute surrendering rebel soldiers.

April 14 Southern sympathizer John Wilkes Booth shoots Lincoln at a Washington theater. The President dies early the next morning, and most Americans go into mourning.

April 26 Booth is killed by Union troops while hiding in a barn in Virginia. Lincoln is buried in Illinois on May 4.

May 10 Jefferson Davis is captured in Georgia. He would be imprisoned for two years, then set free in 1867. Charges of treason against him were dropped in 1868.

May 23-24 The Union victory is celebrated with an expansive military parade in Washington intended to boost national morale in the wake of Lincoln's assassination.

★

Richmond Falls, and The South Surrenders

The war finally ends as Lee's Army of Northern Virginia gives up its arms, and the Union's lenient terms offer hope of reconciliation

A S THE YEAR 1865 BEGAN, THE END OF the war, so frequently and fervidly anticipated and so long delayed, finally seemed at hand. President Lincoln's annual message to Congress on Dec. 6, 1864, the 19th century equivalent of today's State of the Union Address, was brimming with optimism for the Union cause. Lincoln's re-election the month before had ensured that his experienced Administration would continue to prosecute the war. And the President ticked off other reasons to entertain hope: the U.S. Navy now possessed the world's largest fleet, with 671 ships. With more than 1 million soldiers in uniform—more than 100,000 of whom were African Americans—the U.S. Army was stronger than ever before. The Union, noted Lincoln, had "more men now than when the war began ... We are gaining strength, and may, if need be, maintain the contest indefinitely."

But all hearts in the North, and an increasing number in the South, were now longing for a definite conclusion of hostilities. A tour of the fronts as of Jan. 1, 1865, reveals the extent to which events in 1864 had forced the South closer to surrender. The new hero of Union arms was General William T. Sherman, whose campaigns in the South had brought Atlanta under Union control, devastated the landscape of Georgia and concluded with the triumphant Dec. 21 capture of Savannah.

As Sherman had predicted, his almost unopposed march revealed the full extent of Confederate powerless-

THE VANQUISHED *Shrouded Confederate women walk through the ruins of Richmond in April 1865*

ness: President Jefferson Davis and the rebel military were unable to stop Sherman's men as they laid waste to the heart of Dixie. And now, as 1865 began, Sherman was planning to turn his march to the north, intending to deal the same blows to the Carolinas as he had delivered to Georgia, before entering Virginia from the south and joining his longtime colleague General U.S. Grant in a final envelopment of the forces of General Robert E. Lee.

Everywhere the South was in retreat. The bizarre follow-up to Sherman's successful Atlanta campaign, General John Bell Hood's desperate foray into Tennessee, had been stopped at the Battle of Franklin on Nov. 31, and Union control of Kentucky and Tennessee was firm. Even the Shenandoah Valley, scene of so many humiliations of the North by the South, was now completely subdued. General Philip Sheridan's cavalry had applied Sherman's "total war" methods to the granary and storehouse of rebel armies, ensuring that Lee could no longer look for arms, food or reinforcements from the valley.

The Union's grip on Southern seaports, the much ridiculed Anaconda Plan advanced early in the war by General Winfield Scott, was also prospering. Thanks to Admiral David Farragut, Mobile Bay was now in Union hands; thanks to Sherman's march to the Atlantic Coast, an increasing number of those valuable rebel lifelines were coming under Union control. One of the last major strongholds of Southern naval power was Fort Fisher, which controlled access to Wilmington, N.C. A Union attempt to take control of the fort late in December had failed, but the campaign against this important bulwark, which secured an artery into Richmond, would continue.

NO WAY OUT *The Richmond & Petersburg train depot had been one of the last links between the Confederate capital and the nearby city besieged by Grant for months. By the time the Union troops arrived in Richmond, the depot had been put out of service by artillery shells and the burning of the city*

Confederates took hope from a single source: Lee's Army of Northern Virginia remained intact. But the army was a shadow of its former self. Since Grant's Overland Campaign had bogged down in the Siege of Petersburg in the summer of 1864, Lee's forces, now some 55,000 strong, had been hunkered down inside Petersburg, surrounded by Grant's 120,000 troops. Morale among its once proud soldiers was so low that, by February 1865, Lee was reporting that "hundreds of men are deserting nightly."

At the same time, Grant was pouring additional men and artillery into the entrenchments around the besieged city, stretching the Confederates' defensive perimeter until it was some 35 miles (56 km) long. And as the line got longer, it got thinner. As for Lee's wily stratagems, which had for so long confounded Union leaders—the unexpected divisions of his forces, the breathtakingly fast flanking marches, the sudden appearances of Southern cavalry-

men at the height of a battle—they were now the stuff of memory. Lee was a tethered eagle, and his deteriorating situation at Petersburg was the hinge upon which the final door of the war would close.

MORE UNION ADVANCES The year 1865 began just as the year 1864 had ended: with further victories by Union arms. After the attempt to seize Fort Fisher in North Carolina failed in December, Grant assigned the energetic young General Alfred Terry to lead another invasion. On Jan. 15, Terry's force of some 4,500 infantrymen, supported by 2,000 sailors and Marines, succeeded in capturing it, cutting off sea access to Richmond. This victory is largely forgotten today, but its import at the time was immense. For many in the Confederate Congress, there was no longer any doubt that their side had lost the war. Confidence in President Davis plunged: the rebel endgame had begun.

Two other Union thrusts in early 1865 again brought home the rebels' plight. A Union army landed at Mobile Bay, now under Northern control, and applied Sherman's destructive techniques to southern Alabama. Meanwhile, Union cavalrymen under General James H. Wilson, only 27, drove deep into Alabama from the North, enjoying even greater success—and easily vanquishing a force long feared by Northern armies, General Nathan Bedford Forrest's cavalry. Now an old gray mare of a fighting force, it had too often been rode hard and put up wet.

And then there was Sherman: through January he and his 60,000 troops traveled north from Savannah and through South Carolina—determined to spread havoc and woe in the state that had been first to secede from the Union. Sherman made no bones about his intentions: "My aim then was to whip the rebels, to humble their pride, to follow them to their inmost recesses, and make them

fear and dread us." He succeeded on each count, moving north as his engineers built roads and bridges across the swampy coastal tidelands, until Charleston surrendered on Feb. 18. Columbia, the capital, had fallen the day before, and after Southern troops withdrew, the city was burned. History may never know how that conflagration began, but South Carolinians then and now know where to point the finger of blame: at Sherman and his troops.

SECESSION'S PRICE By March, the South was everywhere outmanned, outgunned, outnumbered. And now it was out of time. More than the government in Richmond, the Army of Northern Virginia was now the repository of any power the Confederate States of America possessed. Lee was prepared to abandon Richmond to its fate, in hopes of keeping his force intact. But first, a final gamble. Late on the night of March 24, he attempted to break out of

PAYING HOMAGE *On his day-trip to Richmond on April 4, Lincoln was greeted by a crush of African Americans who hailed him as "The great Messiah" and "Father Abraham." The tributes disturbed the President, who was accompanied by his son Tad and a few Union soldiers as escorts. Lincoln visited the Confederate White House and sat in the chair occupied only some 40 hours previously by Jefferson Davis*

the Union grip, sending false deserters to surprise and overwhelm Union pickets at Fort Stedman, east of Petersburg. The ploy succeeded, briefly, but a Union counterattack overwhelmed the rebels, and many surrendered. Lee had lost 2,900 men to Grant's 900.

The spell had been broken: now Grant sent General Sheridan's cavalry, back from the Shenandoah Valley, with an additional infantry company, against the Confederate right flank 10 miles (16 km) southwest of Petersburg. There, in hard fighting on March 31 and April 1, Sheridan led the Union to a convincing victory. The next day the Union forces attacked all along the Southern lines in this sector, finally achieving the long-awaited breakthrough. Sheridan had captured the last railroad line into Petersburg—and for Lee, the end had come.

A VISITOR IN THE RUINS That same Sunday morning, April 2, as Jefferson Davis sat in a pew in St. Paul's Church in Richmond, a messenger handed him a note. The President studied it, blanched and left the sanctuary. The rest of the congregation soon followed: everyone sensed that the capital city's guardians at Petersburg were pulling out. Like so many Southerners in so many cities before them, they now fled, carrying gold and goods with them. Mob

rule engulfed the city, as looting and violence spread—and civilians and soldiers put the city to the torch in their wake. As historian James McPherson reminds us of the night they drove old Dixie down: "Southerners burned more of their own capital than the enemy had burned of Atlanta or Columbia. When the Yankees arrived next morning, their first tasks were to restore order and put out the flames."

One early Yankee visitor to the city was certainly unexpected: on April 4, President Abraham Lincoln accompanied Lieutenant General Grant into the fallen city, only 40 hours after Davis had departed. Lincoln had been in the area, visiting Grant to talk strategy; now, as he and his son Tad walked the streets of the shattered capital, they were hailed by Union soldiers. As black Virginians learned that the President was in town, they surrounded him on the streets, cheering him as their emancipator. One knelt at his feet to bless him, but the deeply embarrassed Lincoln helped him to his feet, saying, "Don't kneel to me. You must kneel to God only, and thank him for the liberty you will enjoy hereafter." Soon the President took his leave. The entire incident remains surprising, for Lincoln was not one to gloat; his visit seems to have been prompted more by curiosity than vengeance.

The final days of Lee's army are a study in sorrow. The soldiers had retreated west of Richmond, but every day their numbers were reduced. On April 6 a Union attack near Sailor's Creek netted some 6,000 Confederate prisoners. On April 9, an attempted breakout near Appomattox Court House failed. Grant had been sending couriers to Lee, inviting him to discuss surrender terms. Now, at last, Lee indicated he was ready to do so.

That afternoon, the two men met in the farmhouse of Wilmer McLean. The two generals played their usual, deeply contrasting roles: Major General Joshua Chamberlain, the hero of Little Round Top at Gettysburg, was among those accompanying Grant, and he recorded his impressions: "That sturdy Rebel leader ... was dressed in the brilliant trappings of a Confederate army officer, and looked every inch the soldier that he was ... [General Grant was] wearing an open blouse, a slouch hat, trousers tucked into heavy, mud-stained boots and with only the four tarnished golden stars to indicate his office!"

The Union terms of surrender, as laid out by Grant, were very generous, reflecting President Lincoln's vow that the South must be welcomed back into the Union with malice toward none. Lee's officers could keep their weapons, and all rebel soldiers would be paroled—meaning they would never be prosecuted for treason. In a more practical show of leniency, all soldiers would be allowed to keep their horses, in order to return home and plow their fields and plant crops. Said Lee to Grant, in thanks: "It will ... do much toward conciliating our people."

As when Grant's troops entered Vicksburg in 1863, there was no show of Union gloating at this moment of great solemnity. For there was no Union soldier alive who did not respect Lee and his valiant soldiers—and it was this respect for the martial prowess of Southern arms, shared by both sides, that in future decades would help knit together the former enemies.

Chamberlain tells the rest of the story best, as the entire Army of Northern Virginia, some 28,000 strong, laid down their arms: "I thought it eminently fitting to show some token of our feeling, and I therefore instructed my subordinate officers to come to the position of 'salute' in the manual of arms as each body of the Confederates passed before us ... At a distance of possibly 12 feet from our line, the Confederates halted and turned face towards us ... Bayonets were affixed to muskets, arms stacked, and cartridge boxes unslung and hung upon the stacks. Then, slowly and with a reluctance ... the torn and tattered battleflags were either leaned against the stacks or laid upon the ground ... Some of the men who had carried and followed those ragged standards through the four long years of strife, rushed, regardless of all discipline, from the ranks, bent about their old flags, and pressed them to their lips with burning tears." Their war—America's war—was over. ■

STARTING OVER *The McLean Farm at Appomattox Court House—which is the name of a town rather than of a building—was the scene of the Confederate surrender on April 9, 1865. Inside the room, witnesses recorded a memorable moment as Grant introduced Lee to one of his aides, Lieutenant Colonel Ely Parker, a full-blooded Seneca Indian. "It is good to see one real American here," observed Lee. Parker replied, "We are all Americans"*

Robert E. Lee

The South's great general kept his cause alive in wartime, then accepted defeat with a grace that earned a nation's respect

FLAWLESSLY DRESSED AND MOUNTED ON his famed steed Traveller, General Robert E. Lee rode back alone from Appomattox Court House on April 9, 1865, after surrendering his Army of Northern Virginia to Union General Ulysses S. Grant. A cheer began among the troops, but it was stifled, as "Marse Robert" came through the long lines of exhausted Confederate soldiers. They blanched when they saw him, or stopped suddenly as if in response to a command. Dignity and loftiness remained on Lee's features, but he battled with his tears, and anguish was cut deep in the angles of his mouth. He made disjointed answers to the men. They followed him, thronged around him, tried to touch him. "At his tent in the woods, all who could do so grasped his hand and made their soldierly avowals and then slowly went away to rage, to ponder, to weep or to lie feebly down and to pray for food and rest," historian Douglas Southall Freeman tells us. A Lee aide wrote, "And was this to be the end of all our marching and fighting for the past four years? I could not keep back the tears that came to my eyes." Neither, at last, could Lee.

So ended the war for the South's great commander. His upstart, would-be nation—whose existence the North and President Abraham Lincoln simply refused to recognize—was thoroughly and utterly beaten. Its capital, Richmond, Va., was in ruins. Its infrastructure of railroads and telegraph lines, plantations, farms and cotton mills was destroyed. Its greatest city, Atlanta, had been occupied by a Union army and set to the torch. General William T. Sherman 's March to the Sea that followed laid waste to an enormous swath of the South; it was a preview of the great wars of the 20th century, in which armies conducted "total war" against both a foe's economy and its citizens.

Yet even as he faced the utter defeat of his cause, his troops and his people, Lee's greatest moment was yet to come. Though the war had torn the Union apart, the sheer horror of the conflict seemed to have cleansed some of the bitterness from the American bloodstream, and a spirit of reconciliation was in the air. At Appomattox, Grant had refused to impose the usual terms of surrender, insisting instead that Lee's men keep their horses and guns, so that they could return to their homes and farms and rebuild them as the rebel states rejoined the Union.

Everyone understood that President Lincoln would not tolerate revenge against the rebels. Only five weeks earlier, he had declared in his remarkable Second Inaugural Address that the Union could be made whole again only through mutual forgiveness. "With malice toward none, with charity for all, with firmness in the right as God gives us to see the right, let us strive on to finish the work we are in, to bind up the nation's wounds ..."

Lincoln's magnificent words sounded a reveille for the healing and rebuilding of the Union. But only five days after Lee's surrender, Lincoln was removed from the scene, assassinated by a Southern sympathizer, John Wilkes Booth. Now the burden of advocating charity and forgiveness fell upon Lee, among others, and with fortitude and grace, he took up this unexpected new role.

In the few years of life remaining to him—Lee died in 1870 at 63—the former general accepted an offer to serve as president of Washington College in Lexington, Va. (it is now named Washington and Lee University, in his honor). He took every opportunity to express his belief that the war's wounds must be stitched up, and he supported President Andrew Johnson's plan for Reconstruction while opposing the harsh strictures on the South proposed by the radical Republicans.

Lee had opposed the idea of secession until his home state of Virginia left the Union, and he said of emancipation: "Every one with whom I associate expresses kind

> "It should be the object of all to avoid controversy, to allay passion, give full scope to reason and to every kindly feeling."
>
> —LEE, AFTER THE WAR, IN A LETTER TO A MAGAZINE EDITOR

AFTER THE CONFLICT

Beaten but unbowed, Lee poses for a portrait at the war's conclusion, when his grace in defeat earned the respect of Americans on both sides of the conflict. His formal Oath of Allegiance to the Union in 1865 was apparently pigeonholed by a Northern sympathizer and he was never pardoned. More than a century later, in 1975, Congress passed a bill posthumously restoring his full rights as a U.S. citizen; it was endorsed and signed by President Gerald R. Ford

feelings towards the freedmen. They wish to see them get on in the world ..." But he opposed the awarding of the franchise to the newly freed slaves, believing most lacked the education needed to vote responsibly.

Lee's own life echoed in some respects the experience of the South in the war: the exile from a state of grace into a harsh new reality where survival was not guaranteed but earned. His father, Major General Henry Lee III, was the scion of a noted Virginia family and a nimble horseman who earned the nickname "Light Horse Harry" for his courageous service as a cavalry officer in the Revolutionary War. The elder Lee served as governor of Virginia then in Congress as a Representative of Virginia. He also served alongside President George Washington in quelling the Whiskey Rebellion, the populist revolt against the Federal Government of the 1790s. But Lee's poor head for

business, and a national economic crisis, led to his downfall. He declared bankruptcy late in the 1790s and served a year in debtors' prison in 1809. Badly injured in a Baltimore political riot during the run-up to the War of 1812, he abandoned his family and died in 1818 in the Caribbean when Robert, the fifth of six children, was 11.

Robert E. Lee grew up relying on the kindness of family and friends, as he, his mother and his siblings moved from the home of one charitable relative to another. Family connections earned him an appointment to West Point; after graduating in 1829, he served as an engineer and officer in the U.S. Army. He married Mary Anna Randolph Custis, great-granddaughter of Martha Washington, in 1831; they would have seven children.

When the U.S. declared war on Mexico in 1846, Lee served with distinction alongside many of the officers he would later encounter in the Civil War, including U.S. Grant and Union commander General Winfield Scott. In 1852 Lee was named the superintendent of West Point, where he spent three years, then was posted to Texas to fight against the Apache and Comanche tribes. When his wife's father died in 1857, Lee was faced with the difficult task of reconciling his estate, which was badly in debt and whose holdings included hundreds of slaves.

Lee himself shared the paternalistic and prejudiced racial views common to his class. He wrote to his wife Mary in 1856: "Slavery as an institution, is a moral & political evil in any Country." Yet like many others, he seemed to believe that slavery represented God's will. He also supported his wife's continuation of a school her mother founded on the Custis plantation (now Arlington National Cemetery) at which slaves were taught to read, in violation of Virginia law. Like Lincoln, he felt the best way to resolve the issue of slavery was to found a separate nation for African Americans or to return them to Africa.

As the fires of secession burned brighter in the South, Lee opposed them. He wrote his son William Fitzhugh Lee: "I can anticipate no greater calamity for the country than a dissolution of the Union." He accepted a promotion to colonel from President Lincoln on March 28, 1861, but when Virginia seceded from the Union in April, Lee, like many others, chose to support his state rather than the Union, and on April 23, 1861, he assumed the leadership of the Virginia forces, the kernel of the eventual Army of Northern Virginia. The die was cast. ∎

Lincoln Is Assassinated

He had preserved the Union. But his powerful voice, preaching forgiveness, was stilled before he could heal the nation's wounds

FOUR YEARS BEFORE, WHEN ABRAHAM Lincoln had stood on the steps of the U.S. Capitol to take the oath of office as President of the United States, those states were actively disuniting. Now, on March 4, 1865, as Lincoln appeared at the Capitol to be sworn in for his second term in office, all the scorching questions that had hung in the air in 1861 had been answered. Yes, the Southern states, 11 of them in all, had seceded. Yes, the nation had endured a great sectional war. Yes, young men had died by the tens of thousands as they fought to preserve the integrity of their nation, or their state, or simply their way of life. But now it appeared that all these events, dreaded for so long,

would soon be outweighed in the balance of history by an equally long-anticipated outcome: No, the Union would not be destroyed, for the North was winning the war.

Now, as Lincoln addressed thousands of spectators on a rainy afternoon, he took the opportunity to reflect on those perilous days when he had first taken the oath of office. "On the occasion corresponding to this four years ago all thoughts were anxiously directed to an impend-

FINAL WORDS *Lincoln speaks at his second Inauguration, on March 4, 1865, a rainy day in the capital. John Wilkes Booth was present in the crowd. Above is a portrait of Lincoln taken early in 1865; it reveals the extent to which the war years had aged him*

ing civil war," he declared. "All dreaded it, all sought to avert it. While the Inaugural Address was being delivered from this place, devoted altogether to saving the Union without war, urgent agents were in the city seeking to destroy it without war—seeking to dissolve the Union, and divide effects, by negotiation. Both parties deprecated war, but one of them would make war rather than let the nation survive, and the other would accept war rather than let it perish, and the war came."

A deep irony lurked in Lincoln's words, for even as he spoke of the Southern agents who had lurked in Washington four years earlier, hoping to overthrow the Union, another person of the same ilk was listening to his words. John Wilkes Booth, 26, a Southern sympathizer who was the younger brother of the most famous living American actor, Edwin Booth, leaned against a pillar above Lincoln. Distressed by the impending defeat of the South, Booth was already scheming with others to assassinate not only Lincoln but also Secretary of State William Seward, Vice President Andrew Johnson and perhaps others as well.

Lincoln was, of course, unaware of Booth's presence as he continued his remarks, which reached a soaring apogee when the President called on all Americans, in North and South alike, to extend charity to one another, and refuse to harbor malice in their hearts, as they got on with the urgent business of binding up the nation's wounds.

No one who knew Lincoln—and most Americans felt they knew him very well by now—doubted that the President would see to it that his appeal to the better angels of his listeners would be enforced by all the power at his disposal. But he was essential to that process: no other figure in the nation, including the admired military leaders on both sides of the struggle, could stand above the conflict as Lincoln could, speaking for all his countrymen and reining in the extremists in both North and South who were determined to propagate hatred and revenge rather than forgiveness and amity. Booth, an agent of malice, havoc and revenge, stood with this last group.

Booth's complicated skein of proposed murders was destined to fail in every aspect, except for the mission he assigned himself, the assassination of the President. Only five weeks later, on April 14, Booth visited Ford's Theatre in Washington; like his brother, he was an actor, though he lacked Edwin's skill, and he often had his mail sent there. Learning that the President was to attend a performance of the comedy *Our American Cousin* that night, he decided to put his plans into action.

Booth easily gained entrance to the theater and, thanks to some fortunate timing, managed to slip by the President's careless security detail. Familiar with the play, the actor waited for its biggest laugh line, turned the handle

ASSASSIN *John Wilkes Booth was a violent racist and Southern sympathizer. He had been detained earlier in the war in St. Louis while touring as an actor for making treasonous statements against the Union government, but he was not charged and was soon released*

on the door of the President's box as the crowd roared, and fired a .44-cal. bullet from his single-shot derringer diagonally through Lincoln's brain. The President slumped forward, even as Booth made a dramatic leap from the box onto the stage, badly injuring his leg in the process, and uttering a cry that most recalled as *"Sic semper tyrannis"* ("Thus always to tyrants," Virginia's state motto). Others thought they heard "The South is avenged!"

Lincoln was carried out of the theater and across the street to a boarding house, but he never regained consciousness. The 16th President of the United States died at 7:22 a.m. on the morning of April 15—only days after the war had come to an end in the moving ceremony at Appomattox, where Union and Confederate soldiers had joined together in a show of mutual respect that was rich with promise of reconciliation to come.

As the news traveled around the nation at the speed of the telegraph line, most Americans were plunged into deep mourning. Lincoln was the first U.S. President to be assassinated, and the galvanic shock felt by his countrymen rippled around the world. Some voices in the South celebrated, but many others mourned the loss of this apostle of moderation. Church bells rang, cannons boomed. There were incidents of violence, as Northerners exacted revenge upon Southern sympathizers.

Lincoln's casket was borne across the nation on a crepe-shrouded funeral train that followed the same route

"With malice toward none, with charity for all, with firmness in the right as God gives us to see the right, let us strive on to finish the work we are in, to bind up the nation's wounds ..."

—ABRAHAM LINCOLN, SECOND INAUGURAL ADDRESS

CONSPIRACY'S END *Union soldiers look on as four of John Wilkes Booth's accomplices are hanged on July 7, 1865, at today's Fort McNair in Washington. Booth was killed at the time he was tracked down to a barn in northern Virginia*

as the train that had taken him from Illinois to the capital in 1861 as President-elect. The two-week trip covered more than 1,600 miles (2,574 km), and millions of people paid their respects. The train made stops in cities across the north, where it generally was greeted by dignitaries who would escort the casket to a church or state building for public viewing. The train reached Springfield on May 3, where Lincoln was laid to rest.

As for Booth, he fled Washington, aided by accomplices, and became the subject of an enormous manhunt. Heading south, where he hoped to find sympathizers and even admirers, he was finally tracked down on April 26, hiding with accomplice David Herold in a barn near Port Royal in northern Virginia. Pursuing soldiers set the barn on fire and shot Booth dead as he moved around inside. Herold and three other conspirators were tried, found guilty and hanged on July 7, 1865; four other defendants were sentenced to jail terms ranging from six years to life.

Justice was served, but Booth had achieved his goal: he had murdered not only a man but also the promise he embodied. The little-known Illinoisan who had been ridiculed as a backwoods illiterate when he first appeared in Washington, the man whom General George B. McClellan had described as "the original gorilla" in letters to his wife, had become a beloved, admired figure over the course of the horrible war. Lincoln's words had explained—and still explain—why Americans were fighting and dying in the great conflict.

Few scoundrels have altered the course of history so profoundly as did Booth on that April night, for Lincoln could not be replaced. In the years to come, the radical Republicans whom he had kept under check during his Administration would take power in Washington and visit their revenge on the South in the form of a Reconstruction program that ensured the wounds of the war would not be bound up for decades. ∎

The Last Hurrah

The Union Army celebrates its victory in the war, as Americans in both the North and South ponder life after the conflict

O N MAY 23 AND 24, 1865, TROOPS OF THE victorious Union Army crowded the streets of Washington to celebrate their success in the war. The parade brought together the veterans of the two great forces that had finally beaten the South into surrender: the Army of the Potomac, led by Generals Ulysses S. Grant and George G. Meade, and the Army of Georgia, commanded by General William T. Sherman. The jubilant marching throngs had certainly earned their laurels: historian Drew Gilpin Faust notes in her book *This Republic of Suffering* that some 620,000 Americans on both sides died in the war, while an estimated 50,000 civilians perished.

But amid the celebrations, a commanding figure was conspicuously absent at the reviewing stand. Americans were still mourning the loss of President Abraham Lincoln, now in the process of being transformed from a complex political figure into an icon. Lincoln's removal from the scene was in some ways a final spasm of violence, the last act of a national tragedy. But in practical terms it created a political vacuum, as the nation's most eloquent voice for moderation was stilled.

In the years to come, extremists on both sides of the recent war would take power, as radical Republicans in the North used Reconstruction to punish the South, while the Ku Klux Klan and other groups fought for white racial supremacy in the South through violent intimidation of newly free African Americans and their white supporters.

No group of Americans felt Lincoln's loss more than the slaves whom the late President had freed from bondage through the Emancipation Proclamation and the 13th Amendment, which would be ratified late in 1865.

Now politically free, they were still mired in poverty and struggling to compensate for the education previously denied them by law in most Southern states.

In the early 20th century, many Southern blacks migrated to the cities of the North in search of economic freedom, only to discover a truth that Southern whites had always insisted upon: racial prejudice was not a Southern problem; it was an American problem. To the nation's shame, it would take some 100 years for U.S. blacks to win their full political rights, and those rights were won only through years of protest against Jim Crow laws, some approved by the U.S. Supreme Court, that treated African Americans as second-class citizens in public facilities that bore the fictional façade of being "separate but equal."

But however imperfect the peace that followed the war, the great questions that began it had been resolved. Slavery was no longer legal in America. Nor was the U.S. any longer a loose body of states in which some citizens were more equal than others: rather, it was a Union dedicated to the proposition that all men are created equal. In his Gettysburg Address, Lincoln had called on Americans to honor the principles of the Founding Fathers and to bring forth a nation revived through "a new birth of freedom." The Civil War achieved that goal, moving Americans much closer to the ideal of the "more perfect Union" that continues to serve as a beacon: that government of the people, by the people, and for the people—all the people—shall not perish from the earth. ∎

AT LAST, PEACE *Spectators enjoy the Grand Review of the Armies, as troops of the Army of Georgia parade along Pennsylvania Avenue in Washington*